What Christians
Believe about the
Bible

What Christians Believe about the
Bible

A CONCISE
GUIDE
for Students

Don Thorsen
and
Keith H. Reeves

Baker Academic
a division of Baker Publishing Group
Grand Rapids, Michigan

© 2012 by Don Thorsen and Keith H. Reeves

Published by Baker Academic
a division of Baker Publishing Group
P.O. Box 6287, Grand Rapids, MI 49516-6287
www.bakeracademic.com

Printed in the United States of America

Library of Congress Cataloging-in-Publication Data
Thorsen, Donald A. D.
    What Christians believe about the Bible : a concise guide for students / Don Thorsen and Keith H. Reeves.
        p. cm.
    Includes bibliographical references and index.
    ISBN 978-0-8010-4831-9 (pbk.)
    1. Bible—Criticism, interpretation, etc. I. Reeves, Keith Howard, 1957– II. Title.
BS511.3.T46 2012
220.1—dc23   2012008411

The internet addresses, email addresses, and phone numbers in this book are accurate at the time of publication. They are provided as a resource. Baker Publishing Group does not endorse them or vouch for their content or permanence.

In keeping with biblical principles of creation stewardship, Baker Publishing Group advocates the responsible use of our natural resources. As a member of the Green Press Initiative, our company uses recycled paper when possible. The text paper of this book is composed in part of post-consumer waste.

12   13   14   15   16   17   18   7   6   5   4   3   2   1

Don dedicates this book to his daughter
Liesl Thorsen

Keith dedicates this book to his wife
Karen Reeves

Contents

Preface

We are passionate about the Bible, which is why we are writing a book about it. In our experience, people want to know more about the Bible and to study it better, but they are not entirely sure what they think about the Bible itself. Moreover, after people read the Bible, they are not always sure about how they should interpret it. There are so many things to consider that they become overwhelmed. This feeling of being overwhelmed is understandable. It also occurs among those who study the Bible in institutions of higher education, where we have more than fifty years of combined experience in teaching college, university, and seminary students about the Bible.

We want to help people learn more about the Bible in terms of the wealth of what it has to say, how it reveals God to us, and how people have viewed and interpreted the Bible over the centuries. We do not want people to be ignorant of the Bible. On the contrary, we want them to study it and develop a mature understanding and interpretation of the biblical texts, learning to interpret them as historical texts as well as sacred Scripture. Part of the maturing process involves becoming familiar with the variety of views that Christians have about the Bible. We do not think that people should fear learning more about the Bible, its historical and literary contexts, and the ways that people have viewed it at different times and places in church history. Such an investigation helps the maturing process, both intellectually and spiritually. Indeed, we consider such study to be as helpful to the intellectual development of people as to their spiritual and moral development.

In his spare time (somewhat of a misnomer), Keith works as a real estate agent. The slogan often identified with real estate values is "location, location, location." With regard to Christian beliefs and values, we promote the slogan "Bible, Bible, Bible." We do not promote study of the Bible because we think that the sheer quantity of study helps people mature. Indeed, sometimes those who know lots about the Bible have a very immature—if not distorted or immoral—understanding of it. Nor do we think that there is anything "magical" about biblical studies, though we do believe that God's Holy Spirit aids people as they prayerfully study the Bible. In sum, we believe that critical, informed thinking as well as a devotional approach to the Bible aids people in all dimensions of their study of it and in the ways that God works in and through their lives as a result of their study.

Unless otherwise noted, all biblical quotes and references are to the New Revised Standard Version (NRSV). When other Bible translations are used, we will identify them. (A key of abbreviations for different Bible translations is included in the book.)

In this book, we try to present the Bible in all its relevance, intellectually and spiritually. We also present a variety of views about it in ways that are comprehensive and fair, reflective of centuries of Christian understandings about the Bible. In presenting our "concise guide" to "what Christians believe about the Bible," we want to help people, especially students, develop their understanding, interpretation, and application of it. Indeed, it is our hope that people share the passion we have for the Bible and the divinely inspired revelation it represents.

Don Thorsen and Keith H. Reeves

August 2011

Acknowledgments

We want to acknowledge those who have been most helpful in completing this book. We begin by thanking our initial editor, Shirley Decker-Lucke, who encouraged the writing project, and Bob Hosack, who provided primary editorial oversight in publishing the book with Baker Academic.

We also want to thank Azusa Pacific University, the academic institution where we both teach. In our research and writing, Don was aided by the university's library, writers' retreat, and doctoral studies grant for a research assistant. Thanks go to Matthew Sperrazza, who served in the latter capacity. Keith was aided by a sabbatical leave he received from the university. Colleagues who helped and encouraged us throughout the writing project include Paul Gray, John Park, Kay Smith, Roger White, Karen Winslow, Enrique Zone, and especially Steve Wilkens.

Don wants to thank his daughters, Liesl, Heidi, and Dana. They continue to be friends as well as family, encouraging him in writing and in other ways. May the Bible continue to be the divinely inspired compass for their lives, as it has been for them in the past. Special thanks go to his oldest daughter, Liesl, to whom Don dedicates this book. Blessings!

Keith wishes to thank his daughters, Megan, Melanie, and Molly, who have patiently endured and maybe sometimes wondered what their Dad does in his spare time. Thanks go to his parents, Don and Genevieve Reeves. (Thanks, Mom, for reading me those Bible stories when I was a kid.) Special thanks go to his wife, Karen, who has lovingly, wisely, and patiently stuck with him the last thirty-three years.

Abbreviations

ASV	American Standard Version
AV	Authorized Version
BCE	Before the Common Era, or Before the Christian Era; same numbering as BC ("before Christ")
CE	Common Era, or Christian Era; same numbering as AD (Anno Domini, Latin, "in the year of the/our Lord")
KJV	King James Version
NAE	National Association of Evangelicals
NASB	New American Standard Bible
NCC	National Council of Churches
NIV	New International Version
NKJV	New King James Version
NRSV	New Revised Standard Version
RSV	Revised Standard Version
RV	Revised Version
TNIV	Today's New International Version

INTRODUCTION

1

We Are All Students
of the Bible

Christians have long praised the people in the town of Beroea for their study of the Bible. According to the book of Acts, the apostle Paul preached the gospel of Jesus Christ to many in Jewish synagogues throughout the Roman Empire. Some were receptive to Paul's preaching; others were not. However, the Jews in Beroea were distinguished for their receptivity to the gospel and for their eager examination of "the Scriptures"— the sacred writings of the Bible. Acts 17:11 says, "These Jews were more receptive than those in Thessalonica, for they welcomed the message very eagerly and examined the scriptures every day to see whether these things were so." The Beroeans were receptive both spiritually and intellectually to the gospel that Paul proclaimed to them.

The Beroeans were not willing to believe Paul based solely on his authority. They knew that clever, charismatic speakers can be misleading, especially those who are from out of town. The Beroeans also knew the Jewish Scriptures (which became the Hebrew Bible, or Old Testament); they based their knowledge of God and salvation on them. If they were to welcome Paul's gospel, then it needed to be investigated in light of truth that God had already revealed to them. The book of Acts does not specify the particular Scriptures the Beroeans studied. In fact, neither the canon of the Jewish Scriptures nor the Christian Scriptures (New Testament) had yet been established. But Scriptures were widely available to the Jewish synagogues, and the Beroeans faithfully studied them in order to discern the truth of the gospel Paul preached.

Not only did the Beroeans investigate the Scriptures, but they also did it on a daily basis. The Beroeans' determination as much as their spirituality has been praised by Christians. Both the quantity and quality of their investigation of the Scriptures have been a motivation, as well as a role model, for those who seek truth about God, salvation, and other matters pertaining to the Christian life. We begin this book with reference to the Beroeans because we think that they remain exemplars for the kind of Bible study that we encourage people to undertake.

In a sense, we are all students of the Bible who read, reflect, and sometimes meditate on what it says. As students, we should do our best to understand, embody, and apply its teachings. Like the Beroeans, we should focus on both how we study the Bible and our commitment to that task.

■ Challenges to Studying the Bible

There are many ways that people study the Bible, which we would reasonably expect. Some read the Bible devotionally; others read it casually; still others read it to disprove the Bible. How people read the Bible depends a great deal on the expectations they bring to their study of it. When they read the Bible with faith that, in one way or another, it represents divinely inspired revelation from God, their study tends to be more open, agreeable, and desirous of what is contained therein. When people read the Bible in the context of prayer, they expect that God's Holy Spirit will be at work in aiding, illuminating, and empowering their intimacy with God and their application of the Bible. Christians tend to read it with some sense of expectancy of—by God's grace—what they may learn, of how they may become more like Jesus, and of how they may love God and others better for having studied the Bible.

Christians often study the Bible earnestly, and some have dedicated their lives to understanding and applying it to the needs of people. Christian scholars and pastors, for example, have methodically studied the Bible for centuries. Those who followed have benefited from the studiousness of their predecessors. Some have studied the Bible in scholarly ways that have greatly comforted, guided, and encouraged those who read their work; others have studied it in ways that have caused people to question, doubt, and reject the Bible and what it says about God and salvation. The cumulative effect has led people today to realize that the Bible cannot be interpreted in simplistic ways, hoping that a plain and obvious meaning of the biblical texts will jump out at those who read them. We want to help people interpret the Bible better, but in the long run they need to take responsibility for doing the needed work of interpretation.

Some meanings of the biblical texts are plain and obvious. It is a grievous mistake, however, to think that all biblical teaching is instantly recognizable; the more Christians study the Bible, the more they know that interpretation requires intellectual and spiritual discernment. A mature understanding of the Bible requires dedication, methodical study, and thoughtful reflection in order to discern its truth and meaning. Although Christians may appeal to what they describe as the evident truth of the Bible, those who have studied it extensively know that properly interpreting and understanding the biblical texts takes time and effort. They may learn a great deal from pastors and scholars who aid them in the interpretive process. But they ought not to rely on the endeavors of others without doing their own due diligence in "rightly explaining the word of truth" (2 Tim. 2:15).[1]

■ Ways to Study the Bible

There are many ways to become more effective students of the Bible. Individually, people can undertake careful, systematic studies. They can read the Bible more, use study Bibles and other interpretive aids, memorize it, and apply it more and more to their lives. People can also develop the study of the Bible through participation in collective contexts: church services, Christian education classes, midweek fellowships, and other groups that focus on Bible study. Some parachurch organizations are dedicated entirely to in-depth, group-oriented, prolonged biblical studies. All of these methods greatly benefit people committed to understanding and interpreting the Bible.

Another way to become more proficient in biblical studies is taking Bible courses in a college, university, or seminary. Most often, though not always, such courses are taught in Christian higher education. Biblical studies courses provide students with methods and skills to interpret the Bible in ways unimaginable to those who are untutored in its study. In our experience, students are spiritually inspired and intellectually enlightened at discovering depths of meaning in the biblical texts that they may not have found without the tutelage of those who have committed their lives to academic study of the Bible.

Although Christians sometimes view their study of the Bible as an act of worship in interpreting sacred Scriptures, we think that there are advantages— indeed blessings—for those who critically investigate the biblical texts, utilizing formal disciplines for unlocking deeper understanding of them. To be sure, some Christians may feel that such rigor does an injustice to the spiritual and

---

1. In the King James Version, 2 Timothy 2:15 says, "rightly dividing the word of truth"—a common phrase among Christians, emphasizing the need for proper interpretation of the Bible.

ministerial heart of the Bible. But academic studies of it are not afraid of what critical investigations of the Bible may reveal. If all truth is God's truth, then Christians ought not to be afraid of any truth about the Bible. Of course, the Bible ought not to be looked at only as texts to be analyzed and assessed. It remains sacred Scripture, which represents a special means by which God encounters those who prayerfully read and study the Bible. Devotional and critical studies ought to be considered complementary, rather than contradictory, interpretive approaches.

Students may find themselves stumped by questions about the Bible that they never imagined—much less studied—prior to taking courses in a college, university, or seminary. When something is studied in-depth, questions often arise that are uncomfortable and not easily understood or resolved. The same is true with study of the Bible. Church history is filled with progressively difficult questions that people—both Christians and non-Christians—have asked about the Bible, including, for example, questions about its authority, inspiration, and trustworthiness. People have raised such questions since the beginning of Christianity. But the questions seem to be cumulative. Since some questions are not easily resolved, additional questions are added that make the interpretive process increasingly complex and challenging.

Questions and concerns about the nature of the Bible seemed to grow exponentially during the nineteenth century, with the rise of historical and critical methods of biblical interpretation. No longer was it assumed that the Bible is best interpreted from the standpoint of Christian faith and presuppositions of divine inspiration. Instead, people wondered what would happen if the Bible was interpreted as is any other book. If people no longer presumed divine inspiration, or if they interpreted the Bible as a book of human origin, how would their interpretations change? It became increasingly evident that historical and critical methods of interpretation raised many questions about the biblical texts—problems that previous interpreters had largely overlooked or rationalized as unimportant relative to the overall contributions of the Bible.

Once Christians as well as non-Christians became more willing to talk about contested biblical texts, it was unclear what consequences would come about due to increased questioning. Issues of historical accuracy and the internal consistency of biblical texts were raised. Questions also arose over ethical perspectives found in the Bible, which people increasingly found problematic, including slavery, polytheism, polygamy, treatment of women, genocide, and so on. A host of additional challenges were made, based on the presuppositions of scientific method that interpreters brought to the biblical texts. For example, ancient Christian interpreters often overlooked difficult-to-understand passages—that is, passages that were not easily reconciled logically or with extrabiblical information found in history and science. Now, possible errors became visible throughout the Bible, threatening the belief that it was exempt from such historical and scientific investigations.

In addition to interpretive questions, other questions arose about the Bible itself. How did it come into existence? What were the criteria by which the biblical canon was determined? In what sense is the Bible authoritative? In what sense is it inspired? Is the Bible true? In what sense is it true? To what degree should historical and critical methods of biblical interpretation shape our understanding of the Bible? What of other modern and postmodern questions that arise about it? To what degree is the Bible relevant today?

To some people, these questions seem commonplace. However, to people for whom the Bible plays a central role (or those who want it to play such a role), these are life-and-death issues. It could even be said that they are eternal-life-and-death issues. So the stakes are high with regard to how the Bible ought to be understood theologically and how it is best interpreted.

■ A Concise Guide for Students

We wrote this book primarily for students in colleges, universities, and seminaries who take courses in biblical and theological studies. Of course, though we want to help students, we believe that our book will be of help to anyone interested in learning more about the Bible. So long as readers are committed to developing greater depth of understanding in interpreting the Bible and in integrating it theologically into their lives, they will find this book to be insightful and constructive.

The original motivation for this book came from conversations we had about questions and concerns that students raised in our courses. Keith teaches biblical studies courses, and he focuses on the interpretation of the Bible. Thus he discusses issues of genre, historical and literary contexts, and other considerations in biblical interpretation. As Keith teaches principles and methods of Bible study, students invariably ask questions about the nature of the Bible itself and not just about interpreting the particular texts under investigation. From his perspective, the questions are relevant and important for students to consider in the development of their beliefs (or theology) about the Bible. However, such questions are complex and require more time to discuss than can be easily accommodated in every Bible course that he teaches. It would be helpful to Keith if students read a concise introduction to the Bible that talks about theological issues such as biblical authority, divine inspiration, and the trustworthiness of the Bible. Such issues could then be discussed in class without having to distract interminably from the task of biblical interpretation.

Likewise, Don teaches theological studies courses, and he focuses on the kinds of theological or doctrinal investigations that deal with biblical authority, divine inspiration, and the trustworthiness of the Bible. These are "big picture" issues that do not generally require the same rigor of hermeneutics (from Greek *hermēneutikē*, "interpretation" or "rules of interpretation") found in biblical studies courses. Yet Don wants his students to realize that theological conclusions do not arise plainly and obviously from the biblical texts; they take hard work and familiarity with methods of biblical interpretation. A degree of expertise in historical and critical methods of interpretation is required for the affirmations Christians make about the Bible. He does not want students to make affirmations of belief without an awareness, first, of the biblical exegesis (from Greek *exēgēsis*, "interpretation") required to establish them, and second, of diversity in the theological conclusions Christians reach. Too often, students assume that their beliefs and values are the only ones or the only right ones. They may do this because they have never thought through their beliefs or because they have never questioned the beliefs handed down to them by parents, pastors, or churches they attended. Sometimes students are naive about alternative views about the Bible or even intentionally ignore them, which is the root of much ignorance. Even worse, students sometimes judge or condemn alternative views, not because they necessarily reject the arguments of others, but primarily because they are different. Part of Christian maturity and academic discovery includes familiarity with and tolerance of the views of others, even when they differ from one's own views.

We wanted to write a book that would meet the needs of students in both of our classes. The book would help Keith's biblical studies students because they could read about the variety of views that Christians have about the theological nature of the Bible. It would help students establish a baseline of definitions and viewpoints, so that constructive discussion would occur in the development of their biblical beliefs and values. Likewise, the book would help Don's theological studies students because they would read about the variety of views that Christians have about rightly interpreting the Bible. It would help them to become more critical in their understanding of multiple layers of meaning found in the biblical texts, requiring awareness of different genres and their historical and literary contexts. Once students accept that Christians do not always view the Bible and its interpretation the same way, it helps them become more knowledgeable, civil, and, potentially, cooperative in working constructively with other Christians, acknowledging that we do not always think, speak, and act the same way.

■ Differences of Opinion

Christians too often cringe at differences of opinion they have about the Bible and its interpretation, as well as a myriad of other beliefs, values, and practices related to the Bible. One approach to such differences is to ignore them. In this instance, Christians either live in oblivion or they spend their time withdrawing from other Christians (and possibly all of society). Another approach is to attack them. When attacks occur, which may involve an attitude of judgmentalism at best or persecution at worst, it is unfortunate for Christians, churches, and society as a whole. Christians should first try to understand those who differ from them, lest they unnecessarily and unlovingly disregard them.

Some Christians claim that they possess "truth" and not mere "opinions" or "points of view." According to them, truth is verifiable through reason and experience—that is, through logical reasoning and biblical evidence that involves conformity with reality and fact-based beliefs. These claims include propositional statements about the Bible and other theological affirmations. The problem, however, is that the Bible, God, salvation, and other spiritual matters do not easily lend themselves to rational and empirical verification. Opinions, though, are thought to be of lesser quality, relying on argumentation but lacking certainty. But claims to certainty are not always a reliable guide to discerning truth. People sin, commit civil crimes, and deny the existence of God while claiming certainty about the rightness of their actions. So, certainty alone does not guarantee truth, much less certainty about righteousness and justice. Moreover, what happens when multiple Christians claim to speak truth yet differ with one another? Authoritarian claims—even those by Christian leaders and scholars who are greatly respected—may sway some people some of the time, but can they convince all people all the time?

Opinions are what we refer to when people in general, and Christians in particular, have different beliefs, values, and practices, including those about the Bible. Church history is not monolithic in the sense that Christians have been in agreement at all times and in all places about the Bible and its interpretation. That does not mean that there has not been agreement, since there have been significant amounts of agreement about the facts of Christianity, including biblical facts. But Christians have not always interpreted those facts the same way. To be sure, some opinions have been more persuasive and pervasive in church history. Still, Christians have differed, and it is important for students of the Bible to be aware of *why* such differences of opinion occur, especially if they want to become more mature in their own beliefs, values, and practices.

Differences of opinion are not bad in and of themselves. Even the apostle Paul had differences of opinion with other Christian leaders, including his longtime partner Barnabas. In Acts 15, Paul and Barnabas disagreed with each other over whether to bring a onetime colleague, John, called Mark (or John Mark), on their next missionary journey. Because John Mark had abandoned them on a previous ministerial trip, Paul did not want him to come. However, Barnabas wanted to give John Mark another chance. Acts 15:39 says, "The disagreement became so sharp that they parted company." So Paul traveled with Silas, and Barnabas traveled with John Mark. Both had successful ministries according to Acts, yet they did so having differed dramatically in their opinions of what was best for their ministry.

Differing beliefs, values, and practices among Christians are not necessarily wrong, bad, or disadvantageous to God, God's mission, and churches. Paul insists on diversity in unity in his analogy of Christians as the "body of Christ." In talking about the community of believers, Paul says the following:

> Now there are varieties of gifts, but the same Spirit; and there are varieties of services, but the same Lord; and there are varieties of activities, but it is the same God who activates all of them in everyone.
>
> . . . As it is, there are many members, yet one body. The eye cannot say to the hand, "I have no need of you," nor again the head to the feet, "I have no need of you." On the contrary, the members of the body that seem to be weaker are indispensable, and those members of the body that we think less honorable we clothe with greater honor, and our less respectable members are treated with greater respect; whereas our more respectable members do not need this. But God has so arranged the body, giving the greater honor to the inferior member, that there may be no dissension within the body, but the members may have the same care for one another. If one member suffers, all suffer together with it; if one member is honored, all rejoice together with it.
>
> Now you are the body of Christ and individually members of it.
>
> 1 Corinthians 12:4–6, 20–27

Often Christians have interpreted this analogy as describing a local church. God provides churches with believers and other resources to fulfill the various needs of God's mission within a particular church context. No one within the church ought to lord it over others, even when the others are perceived as being weaker, less honorable, or somehow inferior.

However, the analogy of Christians as the body of Jesus Christ can also apply to churches worldwide. Christians in different denominations, national settings, and cultural and linguistic contexts do not necessarily thwart the reign of God. The diversity may, in fact, contribute to the overall strength of mission that Christians and churches perform in the world on behalf of God and God's Holy Spirit working through them. Although they share many of the same beliefs, values, and practices, Christians and churches do not share them all. Yet God's mission works through them.

Certainly, points arise where Christians and churches go too far in straying from biblical and historical boundaries that identify Christianity. There are limits—spiritual and other—to what it means to be faithful followers of God. Moreover, the Bible warns us about false teachers and prophets (see, for example, Jer. 23:16; Matt. 7:15; Rom. 16:17–18). But the mere presence of diversity and differences of opinion does not necessarily signal a boundary Christians may not step over. Part of the process of discerning God's will among various beliefs, values, and practices has to do with, first, becoming aware of the diversity. Judgments ought not to be made without first examining and evaluating the views of others in ways that are fair and not prematurely dismissed due to misunderstanding or lack of information. Second, once people know the diversity of opinions that Christians and churches have, they may be more discerning, effective, and redemptive in evaluating Christian teachings. There is more than one way for Christians to be biblical, faithful, effective followers of God. God uses the particular gifts, talents, skills, temperaments, and even the quirkiness of people. Homogeneity (or sameness) among Christians is not desirable, much less possible, in the richly diverse world God created.

One of the reasons we gave this book the title *What Christians Believe about the Bible* is our desire to teach people about the diversity of Christian beliefs, especially those pertaining to the Bible. Although hearing too much information at once can be confusing, people benefit in the long run if they study views of the Bible different from their own. This is especially true for those who take Bible courses in colleges, universities, and seminaries. Contrary to some fears people have, new learning can be helpful, and it is essential for those who want to develop a more mature understanding and interpretation of the Bible. So, in order for readers of this book to become more convinced of their own beliefs, they need to learn about both historic and contemporary views of the Bible. Being introduced to alternative opinions may help them sharpen their own understanding and application.

New learning can be challenging, even threatening. People do not generally like to be forced out of their comfort zone of long-held beliefs, regardless of how thoroughly such beliefs have been investigated and assessed. But new learning may also bring clarity, insight, or helpful alternatives previously unknown. If Christians want to develop their study of the Bible, then learning about what Christians believe about the Bible provides an opportunity they ought not to ignore. To be sure, there are always risks when people openly and honestly study complex issues. But we consider it worth the risk because the benefits are too great to pass up. So we wrote this book about what Christians believe about the Bible.

■ Induction, Deduction, and the Bible

We do not know many people who immediately warm up to the topic of logic. This tepidness is regrettable, since even an elementary knowledge and use of logical reasoning can greatly enhance both their lives and their study of the Bible. For the sake of this book, we want to talk about the logical use of induction and deduction in relationship to biblical and theological studies.

Those who have studied the Bible in academic settings may have heard the phrase "inductive Bible study" or "inductive Bible study method." Induction has to do with the gathering of facts, investigating them, and formulating conclusions or general concepts that summarize research of the data. In particular, inductive Bible study has to do with looking at all of the relevant data in the biblical texts. For example, if people want to investigate the meaning of "covenant," then they would look at all the verses in the Bible that deal directly or indirectly with covenants. They would find references to covenants in both the Old and New Testaments. After investigating the biblical data, they would make informed conclusions or state general concepts that encapsulate the whole of what the Bible says about covenants. Of course, conclusions are not final, since induction is concerned with thorough research and remains open to new data and insights that may provide greater insight into the nature and implications of covenants in the Bible.

Similar inductive logic is used in day-to-day life decisions. For example, let us imagine a group of friends trying to decide what movie to go to. They begin the decision-making process by talking about what movies are available in local theaters and what the starting times are. The friends may then enter into a discussion of the kinds of movies and actors they want to see or what kinds of movies and actors they have seen before, so that everyone has a greater chance to see the type of movie they enjoy. After having discussed the relevant data, they then make conclusions (or a single conclusion) about the movie they want to see. Of course, if new data arises, for example, the movie they want to see has already sold out, then they need to be willing to alter their decision. But their decision making relied on the inductive gathering of data relevant to their movie selection.

Although Christians tend to emphasize the importance of inductive Bible study, it is incorrect to think that deduction does not also play a role. Deduction explains or proves the conclusions or general concepts determined by inductive reasoning and research. So, with regard to the study of covenants in the Bible, deductive reasoning is used to explain how the conclusion (or conclusions) was determined from the investigation used to reach it. Deductive reasoning may also be called on to prove or give an apologetic (or defense) for why the conclusion was reached. Syllogistic reasoning is a type of argumentation used to convince others—for example, when a proposition (or conclusion) is inferred from two other propositions (or premises). Such logical argumentation is thought to provide necessarily true conclusions based on the rules of logic. Whereas induction is more invested in gathering information for the sake of raising the probability of being right based on repeated observations, deduction is more invested in establishing with certainty that a conclusion is right. With regard to the friends' decision about the movie they watch, deduction has to do with explaining or proving why one movie was chosen, rather than another, to those less convinced about the choice of movie.

An inductive approach to Bible study is advocated because, among other reasons, it emphasizes doing the investigative work by oneself, without relying too much on the research and expertise of others. This is not intended to downplay the importance of such resources but to play up the importance of interpreting the Bible for oneself. Induction also wants the interpreter of the Bible to remain open to new learning and insights that may be different from previous learning and insights, which may have been shaped by the conclusions of others but that do not fit with the facts. In other words, everyone is shaped by their life experiences—who they are and what they have heard, experienced, and read. Their background is invaluable in helping them understand the Bible and the world. However, it is possible that previous learning and life experiences that make up the cultural context they live in may be unhelpful or misleading in gaining greater understanding of biblical texts. So the inductive Bible study method wants students to both learn about the texts for themselves and be open to new learning and insights in their interpretation of the Bible.

Theological and biblical studies use inductive and deductive reasoning. Whereas biblical studies tend to focus more on data from the Bible, theological studies focus on the Bible and on other relevant data that help to develop a more holistic Christian worldview. Theological studies are open to church tradition, critical thinking, and relevant experience. Such investigations help people grow spiritually and discern greater truth about God, themselves, others, and the world.

■ Faith Integration and Apologetics

Although faith integration is not at the forefront of what we are trying to accomplish in this book, the contextualization and application of the Bible is inextricably bound up with what we want to teach students. We do not talk about biblical and theological studies for their own sakes. On the contrary, we undertake such studies so that we might learn more about God, grow spiritually in relationship with God, and then live more Christlike, loving lives toward God and others. Thus the practical application of our biblical and theological studies represents the eventual goal of our efforts.

One of the reasons people sometimes resist the academic study of the Bible is fear—rational or irrational—that such studies lead to a deconstructing of the Bible that in turn leads to the deconstructing or loss of faith. To be sure, people's faith may be challenged by increased learning about the Bible. However, growth, including spiritual growth, often seems to involve some kind of "growing pain." And the disdain of opportunities for greater understanding afforded through academic study of the Bible may be even more dangerous. It is our opinion that people's faith will more likely be threatened if their knowledge of the Bible remains limited, naive, or possibly corrupted by false teaching. How will they know for sure unless they study the Bible more for themselves? We think that people's experiences of God, salvation, and the Christian life are aided when they learn more about the Bible in every dimension of what it has to say.

Faith integration is related to the inductive nature of both biblical and theological studies. Faith integration may occur in many ways. It occurs individually as people develop knowledge of the Bible and other aspects of life in order to be more relevant and effective in their decision making. Faith integration also occurs academically as biblical and theological studies are combined with interdisciplinary studies to discover knowledge that may be integrated, applied, and taught in ways that advance Christian spirituality and academic knowledge. The two are not in conflict; people know and love God with their minds, hearts, souls, and strength (see Mark 12:28–31). They conflict only when truth is distorted by sin, ignorance, or other aspects of finite human life. In practice, Christians are all too happy to apply the sciences, behavioral sciences, humanities, and other academic studies when they offer personal help—for example, in medicine, technology, music, arts, movies, television, and so on. Unfortunately, people may attack the very sciences and arts that they use on a daily basis if they think that such integration conflicts with teachings in the Bible. Discernment and wisdom are needed in order to have integrity with regard to how the various disciplines of knowledge are integrated into a Christian worldview. In our opinion, an emphasis on faith integration is a positive, hopeful way of approaching the Bible. It encourages greater knowledge of the world, the Bible, and our interdependent relationships with one another. Faith integration wants to learn as much about the Bible as possible, seeing its interconnectedness with all aspects of life. Such integration helps people spiritually and in developing a holistic Christian worldview.

Apologetics is another goal of biblical and theological studies. Apologetics has to do with the defense of the truth of Christianity—of the Bible, church, Christians, and their ministries. Such efforts are needed lest Christianity become marginalized, and possibly persecuted, intellectually and in other ways. Because apologetics are self-defense oriented, they are heavily invested in being right and in showing how others are wrong. Deductive arguments are often used to debate with others and to show the truth of Christianity in contrast to alternate worldviews. Despite the legitimacy and necessity of apologetics, this book is more involved in faith integration. We do not write in order to point out who is right and who is wrong; we will let readers decide for themselves. Instead we are concerned with showing a commonsense approach to biblical studies that anyone can easily—yet critically—follow, and showing the variety of theological conclusions that Christians have reached based on their study of the Bible. As such we want to broaden rather than narrow Christians' understanding of the Bible. We think that Christians suffer more from narrow understanding than from a lack of apologetic expertise. To be sure, apologetics have their place in Christianity. But our concern is more with advancing the knowledge and applicability of biblical and theological studies through the integration of faith in all aspects of life.

■ Modernism and Postmodernism

One of the challenges to biblical studies is the growing realization that people bring more than the facts of the Bible to their interpretation of it. They may set aside Bible study aids, commentaries, and other resources that prematurely influence their interpretive process. But is it possible to undertake an entirely objective and unbiased—either consciously or unconsciously—approach to biblical interpretation? The Enlightenment, also known as modernism, emphasized that objectivity was possible and that it was a goal of rational and empirical investigation. Modernists also thought that, in the Christian study of the Bible, it was possible to find explicitly the meaning of every biblical text, which conveyed universal truth applicable to people at all times and in all places. Christians accepted these assumptions about objective truth advocated by modernism even though they rejected modernism's conclusions, especially those critical of religious authority. Incongruously, Christians wanted to do their biblical and theological studies in accordance with modern assumptions and methods, even though the same assumptions and methods were used to debunk Christianity and its truth claims.

The rise of postmodernism has complicated things intellectually for Christians because of its challenge to the legitimacy of making truth claims based on rational and empirical criteria without acknowledging personal, cultural, and other influences that affect people's knowledge. Although postmodernism will be discussed more in later chapters, it is skeptical of propositionally stated truth claims that are thought to be legitimated through rational and empirical evidence. According to postmodernism, truth involves more than argumentation that appeals to rational and empirical evidence; claims to truth are more complex, more influenced by personal, cultural, and other components, than modernists are willing to admit. Given the complexity of making truth claims, postmodernists argue that people may need to become more humble and self-aware with regard to the certainty of propositional truth claims they make, including those having to do with the Bible.

If we think of the group of friends making a decision about where to attend a movie, they did more than look at the facts about the what, when, and where of the movies. They brought to their decision-making process a host of personal and cultural backgrounds that undoubtedly shaped their interpretation of the movie data they gathered. Some friends like drama or romance movies, while others like adventure, science fiction, or horror movies. Although they had to deal with empirical evidence, their reading, evaluation, and application of the data reflected personal background and cultural influences that may have powerfully shaped their interpretation of movie options and their contribution to the group's decision. Likewise, postmodernism questions the personal and cultural intangibles that influence people's interpretation of facts, even those of the Bible. No facts are thought to be so objective, value neutral, or plain and obvious that they preclude the influence of personal and cultural factors on their interpretation, valuation, and application of the Bible. So, as we proceed in our study of what Christians believe about the Bible, we will need to reference both modern and postmodern concerns when discussing how Christians understand and interpret the text.

■ What Christians Believe about the Bible

Although Bible study can become quite complex, we think that a commonsense approach to biblical interpretation coupled with a theological discussion of Christian views of the Bible will be of immense help to those who undertake serious, thoughtful study. Biblical studies students will benefit from a clear introduction to interpretive methods that include consideration of genres, historical contexts, and literary sources. They will also benefit from a discussion of theological issues that invariably arise among students, pertaining to the Bible's authority, inspiration, and trustworthiness. Such issues are not always discussed in biblical studies courses because they can distract from the interpretive process at hand or because such discussions are not immediately relevant to inductive Bible study.

Likewise, theological studies students will benefit from the discussion of interpretive methods because they may not be sufficiently aware of them as they study theology. Regrettably, books in theology often presume awareness of historical and critical methods of biblical interpretation but do not draw connections between theological discussions and their biblical foundations. Sometimes students know the connections but have trouble formally making or remembering them. Not all students of theology have been trained in basic principles of biblical interpretation, and that inexperience leaves them unprepared to make key connections between the Bible and theology.

Biblical and theological studies are inextricably bound up with each other, though sometimes Christians keep them separated. Perhaps they are unwilling to do the due diligence that would prevent the Bible and theological studies from becoming bifurcated, or somehow isolated from one another, in gaining greater insight into Christian beliefs, values, and practices. Certainly it is difficult to keep in mind every possible consideration, since the study of the Bible is complex, and it is difficult to juggle every one of them. However, the lack of such knowledge has led Christians and others into ignorance—intentional or unintentional—of one another's views or opinions. Since ignorance can lead to misunderstanding, and misunderstanding can lead to judgmentalism or worse, students of the Bible ought to avoid such ignorance, lack of understanding of the opinions of others, and missed opportunities for learning, cooperation, and application of the Bible.

We are big fans of faith integration, which contributes to biblical Christianity through the interdisciplinary study and application of ideas that make the proclamation of the gospel of Jesus Christ more effective. We believe that God gives the increase to our labors, as Paul states in 1 Corinthians 3:6. So, like the apostle Paul, we are to plant and water seeds of effective biblical and theological studies; it is God who gives the increase to our faith integration through such studies. Apologetics are important because Christians need to defend their beliefs, values, and practices, but those who promote faith integration have more creative and wide-ranging opportunities to advance God's will in the world.

In talking about what Christians believe about the Bible, we begin by presenting a brief history of the Bible. One of the challenges that people sometimes run into is that they have never thought much about how the Bible came into existence. While most of them would not say that the Bible just "dropped out of heaven," they seem to function as if it did. When people hear of historical and critical questions about the Bible, they are tempted to react negatively, since it seems disrespectful to discuss such historical matters unless it is to praise and promote confirmation of biblical teachings. Yet Christians miss out on a richness and depth of meaning that comes after having learned even a little about the historical development of the Bible. Once a person begins to learn about its archaeological background, interaction with multiple cultures and languages, and literary sources, such a person may never want to cease learning about the history of the Bible.

Next we will talk about a commonsense approach to biblical interpretation. Special emphasis will be given to learning about different genres or types of literature, which is essential to interpreting what the Bible says. It is an over-statement to say that "context is everything," but the historical and literary context of what is said in the Bible is crucial to interpreting it. So an additional chapter will include study of the literary context of the Bible, investigating sources of what it says and the Bible's corresponding influence on others.

We will conclude with a survey of theological issues Christians are perennially concerned with. They include the authority of the Bible, its inspiration, and its trustworthiness. Christians have a variety of views about these issues, and the particular view they have strongly shapes the way they understand God, the church, and the Christian life. We ought not to scoff at such differences of opinion but rather try to understand them. We may learn something; we may not. We should at least learn how to communicate better and possibly cooperate with one another in becoming better students of the Bible and in applying it, by the grace of God.

2

A Brief History
of the Bible

In order to understand the Bible and properly interpret it, we must begin with a brief history of the Bible. The Bible did not simply fall down from heaven in its finished form. It has a long and fascinating history. Indeed, the written history of the Bible is rather complex. For example, even before the written text existed, for both the Old Testament and New Testament, much of the material in the Bible had an oral tradition. The transitions from oral to written traditions may never be fully known. Be that as it may, we must remember these dynamic, developmental characteristics when studying the history of the Bible.

The history of the Bible is probably one of the most complex questions that we have to face because there are multiple issues involved. In the most basic sense, we can ask when the biblical texts were written and by whom. These questions of authorship and provenance are standard fare. Another question we can ask is when these texts became authoritative. Were they seen as authoritative when they were written? Did it take a period of time before they were recognized as authoritative? Even this question can be broken down into several parts because authority can initially be seen as simply providing useful advice. Then, of course, the text can take on a second level of authority when the text is actually seen as the Word of God. So the Bible's history is indeed a very complex issue.

The study of the history of the Bible also has some of the greatest amounts of disagreement among Christians today. For example, who wrote the Torah—the first five books of the Bible? Some folks think Moses wrote it, or a large portion of it. Others think that Moses was influential but that the text was edited by others. Others see this material as largely legendary, composed long after the time of Moses. What can be known with certainty, and what are matters of faith? These are some of the challenges that we face as we discuss the history of the Bible.

■ Preliminary Definitions

When we talk about the history of the Bible, the first question we must ask is, what do we mean by the Bible? The English word for "Bible" is derived from the Greek word *biblion*, which simply means "book." Most older English editions of the Bible will have the title "Holy Bible," because the Bible was not seen as just any book but as a special book—a book divinely inspired, unlike any other. Thus the book is considered "holy" or "set apart."

But which books within the Bible are we discussing? The term "canon" is typically used to designate which books are included. The English word "canon" derives from the Greek word *kanōn*, which was simply a "measuring rod." Thus "canon" came to be used as the measure that designated which books were considered authoritative and which books were not authoritative. Ultimately, if a book made the final biblical list, then it was "canonical." Different church traditions, however, have different canons or authoritative lists of the Bible (see the appendixes). In fact, some argue that the Christian canon should include more than the Bible; it should also include creeds, ancient liturgy, patristic writings, iconography, and sacraments as well as sacred Scripture. Although some Christians indeed argue that more than the Bible should be included in the concept of canon, the focus of this book centers upon the more common understanding of canon, which has to do with the establishment of sacred Scripture.

The Jewish biblical canon includes three parts, reflective of the following Hebrew words: *Torah* ("Law"), *Nevi'im* ("Prophets"), and *Ketubim* ("Writings"). Protestants accept these texts, which they have traditionally called the "Old Testament," which refers to the "testament" or "covenant" God made with Israel. The arrangement of these books in the Christian Old Testament is different from the arrangement in the Jewish canon, but the material is the same. Roman Catholics have a larger canonical collection. These additional books are called "deuterocanonical" (or "second" + "canon") by the Roman Catholic Church. The Deuterocanonical Writings consist of writings included in the Greek Septuagint and Latin Vulgate translations of the Old Testament but not included in the Hebrew Scriptures (or Hebrew Bible). The Septuagint was an ancient Greek translation of the Hebrew Bible, most likely produced during the third to first centuries BCE. The Vulgate was Jerome's Latin translation of the Bible in the fourth century, in which he used Greek manuscripts for both the Old Testament (namely, the Septuagint translation) and New Testament. Both the Septuagint and Vulgate contained writings not part of the protocanonical (or "first" + "canon") books of the Hebrew Bible. After the Protestant Reformation, Roman Catholics determined at the Council of Trent (1545–63) that the Deuterocanonical Writings were equal to the canon of the Bible. Protestants, however, considered them apocryphal (Greek *apokryphos*, "hidden") or pseudepigrapha (Greek "false" + "inscription"). Although they may contain godly teachings, they were of hidden or uncertain origin. Thus Reformers such as Martin Luther referred to the Deuterocanonical Writings as the Apocrypha, rejecting the writings as noncanonical. Today such writings are also referred to as the Apocryphal/Deuterocanonical Books.

Of note, the Old Testament used by Roman Catholics is actually closer to the Scriptures that the first-century Christians used. Since early Christians were predominantly Greek speakers, they read the Septuagint translation of the Hebrew Bible. The Protestant Old Testament, however, is closer to what the first-century Jews used, since they most likely used the Masoretic Hebrew text. Use of the Septuagint helps to explain why some New Testament citations of the Old Testament vary from one another; different Bibles—or Bible translations—were being used. The Orthodox Church's Bible also includes additional writings that neither the Protestant churches nor the Roman Catholic Church include. They are known as the *Anagignōskomena* (Greek "things that are read"). Thus we see that, while the Christian tradition is shaped by its Bible, its Bible is also shaped by its tradition.

■ The Jewish Canon

The Torah—Law

The oldest canon is the Jewish canon. It forms the basis for all of the other canons. So we begin our discussion here. As mentioned earlier, the Jewish canon contains three divisions: *Torah*, the *Nevi'im*, and the *Ketubim*. The Jewish canon is known as the *Tanakh*, based on an acronym of the first Hebrew letters from each division (it is also known as the Masoretic Text). The Torah is the oldest part of the collection. It represents "law" or "teaching." The Torah includes the first five books of the Bible: Genesis, Exodus, Leviticus, Numbers, and Deuteronomy. These books are also known as the Pentateuch (Greek *pente*, "five" + *teuchos*, "books" or "scroll cases"). The exact date and nature of the composition of these books is particularly complex and disputed. A few would argue that Moses wrote the entire fives books himself, though most of these folks would allow that the story of Moses's death (Deut. 34:5–12) was written at a later time. Some historical critics of the Old Testament think that the material was all composed after the exilic period in Jewish history, when the Jews were conquered and exiled to Babylon (ca. 586–538 BCE). For example, scholars have distinguished between at least four possible sources or documents in the Torah: Yahwist source (J); Elohist source (E); Deuteronomic source (D); and Priestly source (P).

This documentary hypothesis, formulated by Julius Wellhausen in the nineteenth century, argues that several noticeably different sources were combined by editors (or redactors) to create the final biblical texts. This hypothesis is based on historical and literary examinations of the Torah.

Most Christian scholars fall somewhere in the middle of the aforementioned debate. They recognize or allow for ancient material from the time of Moses, or even earlier, but see the work of later editors throughout this section of the Bible. Regardless of the date of composition, it is generally agreed that the Torah became authoritative by the time of the reforms under Ezra, shortly after the exilic period (late sixth century BCE).

The Nevi'im—Prophets

The second part of the Jewish canon is known as the *Nevi'im* or the "Prophets." The Prophets are further divided as the "Former Prophets" and the "Latter Prophets." The Former Prophets include Joshua, Judges, 1 and 2 Samuel, and 1 and 2 Kings, and are sometimes called "Historical Books" in the Christian canon. The composition of the Former Prophets, like the Torah, is disputed. The majority of Christian biblical scholars accept early material with various stages of editing.

The Latter Prophets include the large works of Isaiah, Jeremiah, and Ezekiel—the Major Prophets—and "the Twelve"—Hosea, Joel, Amos, Obadiah, Jonah, Micah, Nahum, Habakkuk, Zephaniah, Haggai, Zechariah, and Malachi—sometimes called the Minor Prophets by Christians. They are called Minor Prophets not because they are less important but because the works are shorter in length than the Major Prophets.

Did the prophets these books are named for actually write them? There is no certainty on this. Jeremiah gives us a window into the composition of the work named after him: we read that Jeremiah had a secretary named Baruch. The Lord commands Jeremiah to "take a scroll and write on it all the words that I have spoken to you against Israel and Judah and all the nations, from the day I spoke to you, from the days of Josiah until today" (Jer. 36:2). "Then Jeremiah called Baruch son of Neriah, and Baruch wrote on a scroll at Jeremiah's dictation all the words of the LORD that he had spoken to him" (Jer. 36:4). This is one of the clearest examples of how the actual composition of a work took place.

One of the fascinating things about Jeremiah is that there is more than one "version." The Septuagint version of Jeremiah is significantly shorter than the version in the Hebrew text. The Septuagint, as mentioned earlier, is an early Greek translation. It was the first known translation of the Bible. It was often thought that the Septuagint was the result of bad editing or of the translator(s) taking liberties with the text. The Dead Sea Scrolls version of Jeremiah, however, agrees with the Septuagint. (The Dead Sea Scrolls, which predate the time of Jesus in the first century and were discovered in 1947, are the oldest manuscripts found of the Old Testament writings.) Thus there were apparently two different versions of the book of Jeremiah in existence. How can we account for this?

In Jeremiah 36, we read that King Jehoiakim of Judah had Jeremiah's scroll read to him. After a section was read, the king would take his knife, cut off a piece of the scroll, and throw it into the fire (Jer. 36:23). Jeremiah then wrote another scroll, using Baruch as his scribe. When the scroll was rewritten, "many similar words were added to them" (Jer. 36:32). It is very possible that this action might have been responsible for the multiple versions of Jeremiah.

Were other prophetic books written in the same way? It is likely that many of the prophets had students or schools. At times the prophets might have written down their own words, but it is more likely that the students of the prophets preserved the words of the prophet as they were remembered or as they were dictated to them.

Much of the writings of the prophets are shrouded in mystery, but they apparently had become a collection and were considered authoritative no later than 132 BCE. We know this date from a reference by Ben Sira—a rabbi and scribe, knowledgeable of the Hebrew Bible—where the author refers to "the Law," "the Prophets," and to other books.

The Ketubim—Writings

The final section of the Jewish canon is known as the *Ketubim* or the "writings." This includes collections such as Psalms and Proverbs, but also writings such as Ruth, Daniel, and Esther, which are found in a different order in the Christian Old Testament.

During the time of Jesus, this third collection was still somewhat in flux. Traditionally, it was thought that the writings were closed at the Council of Jamnia (*Jabneh* in Hebrew), located in Israel, around the year 90. Recently, however, this view of the Council of Jamnia as an authoritative council has been doubted or altogether dismissed as apocryphal. The best we can say is that the final form of the writings was set during the first or second century of the Christian era.

■ The Old Testament

How did we get from the Hebrew Bible to the Christian Old Testament? Most of the Hebrew Bible was written in Hebrew at a time when it was the native tongue of the Jewish people. After the exile in approximately the fifth century BCE, however, Aramaic became the common language. Portions of the Bible written in this period were written in Aramaic. Still later, after the conquests of Alexander the Great in the fourth century BCE, Greek became the common language. During the Greek period, the Bible was translated from the original Hebrew and Aramaic into Greek. According to an ancient legend, this translation was done by seventy (or seventy-two) Jewish elders. So this translation became known as the Septuagint, the Greek word for "seventy." It is commonly referred to as the LXX, its Roman numerals. The Septuagint also incorporated additional writings, including writings composed in Greek. These additional Greek writings were what were referred to earlier as deuterocanonical or apocryphal.

The Septuagint was the Bible of the early Christians. It was the Bible of Jesus and of Paul. After the first century, the Septuagint was translated into many languages, including Latin. The Latin translation, known as the Vulgate, became the basis for the Christian Old Testament. During the Protestant Reformation, the Protestant Reformers went back to the Jewish canon, rather than using the Latin Vulgate, thus eliminating those Deuterocanonical Writings that were originally written in Greek. The Roman Catholic Church, however, maintained the larger collection, which continues to be a point of theological divergence between Catholics and Protestants.

■ The New Testament

The shape of the New Testament is much easier to sketch, since we have more complete records and are closer to the events. Nevertheless, we still lack much information.

Let us begin by looking at the writings thought to be the oldest Christian words recorded. Although the chronological sequence of these writings is not an exact science, amazing insights can be gleaned by learning about the history of the New Testament.

The Letters of Paul

The earliest collection would have been the letters of Paul. Paul was a Jewish rabbi who was converted by an encounter with Jesus (Acts 9:3–9; 22:6–11). Paul felt it was his mission to travel throughout the world to share the message of Jesus with whomever would listen. Paul traveled throughout the Mediterranean world and established many churches. He would then write letters back to these churches. These letters were written to particular churches with particular problems. They were useful beyond their original purpose, however, and eventually many of these letters were collected by the various recipients and shared with others. We do not have all of the letters that Paul wrote. We know that Paul wrote at least four letters to the church in Corinth. We possess only two of those letters, though some scholars think that what we call 2 Corinthians might be two letters combined into one.

The letters of Paul were apparently considered a collection by the early second century. The earliest known collection did not include the so-called Pastoral Letters (or Epistles), which constitute 1 and 2 Timothy and Titus, but later lists include them. The book of Hebrews was attached to the letters of Paul by the church in Egypt, but the Western church did not accept this work until the fourth century.

The Gospels and Acts

The formation of the Gospels—the books of Matthew, Mark, Luke, and John—is an interesting question in and of itself. The word "gospel" derives from the Greek word *euangelion* (*eu-*, "good" + *angelion*, "message"), which is commonly stated as the "good news" about the life and ministry of Jesus Christ. Entire books have been written on this question alone, but we will only be able to sketch the formation of the four Gospels with broad outlines. Jesus did not write any books. The only reference to Jesus writing anything is in the Gospel of John. Jesus stooped down and wrote something in the sand (John 8:6). We do not know if Jesus wrote actual words in the sand or what exactly he was doing.

Jesus's native tongue was probably Aramaic, yet all of the Gospels are in Greek. How did this come about? Jesus apparently did not write anything down, and it is unlikely that any of his disciples wrote anything down. The Gospels are also pretty clear that the disciples misunderstood the mission of Jesus. They just did not get it. By and large, the early disciples expected Jesus to establish a political kingdom on earth. They expected that Jesus would overthrow Rome. They certainly did not expect that Jesus would be killed. After Jesus's death, the disciples were disheartened and disillusioned. They did not expect that Jesus would rise from the grave a few days after his death, though the Gospels record that Jesus had forewarned them. Even after Jesus ascended into heaven, the disciples probably did not write anything down right away since they expected that he would soon return. So how did the writing of the Gospels come about? Why would somebody write a book about Jesus?

Jesus did not come back as soon as early Christians expected. This delay caused people to begin to collect stories about Jesus and his sayings. The stories and sayings would have served a variety of purposes. They would have been used for missionary preaching, teaching new converts, or possibly even to entertain. The stories and sayings would have been passed down without regard to their context in the same way that similar stories, sayings, and even jokes are passed around today. The Gospel of John also makes reference to a "signs source," referring to how the miracles of Jesus served as "gospel signs"; see John 2:11, which says that Jesus's first miracle was "the first of his signs." Eventually these stories were gathered together into larger collections or books.

These stories would be collected and shaped into a continuous narrative by one of the Gospel writers. While it is not universally accepted, a large number of biblical scholars think Mark was the first Gospel to be written, around the year 70. It is commonly believed that the authors of Matthew and Luke used Mark as one of their sources since much of the material in Matthew, Mark, and Luke is similar. The Gospel of John was probably written independently of Matthew, Mark, and Luke. Each of these Gospels, like the letters of Paul, was originally written to a particular community with a particular purpose.

The names for each of the Gospels represent names attributed to them by church tradition. None of the Gospels include the names of the authors. Evidence within the Gospels gives us clues to who the authors may have been, but no tangible evidence is given. Thus our references to the Gospel authors are a matter of convention rather than biblical data.

The four Gospels were not the only Gospels written. Other Gospels were written for various purposes—many apparently wanting to "fill in the gaps" about the life of Jesus. There were competing tendencies to expand the number of Gospels and to reduce these traditions to a single Gospel. Tatian, following the latter tendency, wrote his *Diatessaron* (ca. 170). The *Diatessaron* was an attempt to take Matthew, Mark, Luke, and John and weave them all into a single narrative. It is similar to what we see today with nativity scenes with shepherds (Luke) and magi (Matthew) all worshiping the baby Jesus in a manger. Irenaeus argued forcefully for four Gospels, incorporating such reasoning as the need for "four winds," thus the need for four authoritative accounts of the life and ministry of Jesus. By the middle of the third century, the four Gospels were largely accepted by most of the early Christian communities.

The book of Acts is related to the Gospel of Luke. Though there is some dispute, most scholars believe that Luke/Acts were two volumes written by the same author. There may have been a period of time between the production of these two volumes, though that is not perfectly clear. While Acts is often called the Acts of the Apostles, the work highlights the expansion of the gospel from Jerusalem to Rome, fleshing out the saying of Jesus in 1:8, "But you will receive power when the Holy Spirit has come upon you; and you will be my witnesses in Jerusalem, in all Judea and Samaria, and to the ends of the earth."

The author of Acts, traditionally thought of as Luke (though this is disputed), may have had access to certain sources for the composition of his work. Several "we passages" may be from Luke's diary (16:10–17; 20:5–21:18; 27:1–28:16). Some scholars argue, however, that the "we" reflects Luke's source. Still others have suggested that this is a literary convention. Luke may have had a copy of the decree from the apostolic council (Acts 15:19–21). The Jerusalem church may also have had archives. Much of Luke's material was no doubt from the oral tradition. Regardless of Luke's sources, he weaves his material together into a well-crafted theological narrative.

The General Letters and Revelation

The General Letters (or General Epistles) became a collection by the fourth century. The letters recorded in 1 Peter and 1 John were widely used in the second and third centuries. The other letters of James, 2 Peter, 2 and 3 John, and Jude were more local in their use. Eusebius of Caesarea was the first to use the term "Catholic Epistles" as a collection of the general letters, since the word "catholic" refers to their "universal" or broad Christian reception within the Roman Empire.

The book of Hebrews has an interesting history. As noted earlier, it was attached to Paul by the second century by the Egyptian church. By the fourth century it was included in the letters of Paul in the Latin Vulgate. Modern scholars are virtually unanimous that Hebrews was not written by Paul; though numerous authors have been suggested, none has won universal support.

The book of Revelation is also a letter, though it is composed largely of apocalyptic material. It had an interesting time making it into the canon. Eusebius wrote that some recognized it as genuine but others did not.[1] Some segments of the church did not accept Revelation until the ninth century. Its acceptance into the canon was among the more disputed books included in the Bible.

1. See Eusebius Pamphillus, *The Ecclesiastical History*, trans. Christian F. Cruse (Grand Rapids: Guardian Press, 1976), 110.

■ Christianity, Constantine, and the Bible

For centuries, Christians and churches increased in numbers. They developed ecclesiastical rites, rituals, and governance as well as spiritual disciplines, theological understanding, and writings. The writings were of several natures: devotional, liturgical, ecclesiastical, apologetic, and so on. Apologetic literature was intended to defend Christians from those who marginalized and, at times, persecuted them. Scriptural writings were also on hand, but they varied in number and availability depending on the particular locations and circumstances. In some churches, it was possible to gather large numbers of scriptural writings. However, in most places, their availability was hit-and-miss at best. Sometimes scriptural writings were circulated among churches, which helped to spread both what they said and their reputation among Christians. Since most people were still illiterate, knowledge of the Scriptures was dependent largely on the summaries written by Christian leaders, such as catechisms, "rules of faith" (for example, second-century doctrinal summaries as found in Tertullian and Irenaeus), and occasionally informal creeds. The Old Roman Symbol (or Creed), for example, represented a short summary of basic Christian beliefs. It is believed that the creed served as a prototype for what became known as the Creed of the Apostles in the fourth century and Apostles' Creed in the eighth century.

Marcion of Sinope was the first Christian to create a formal canon of Scripture. His second-century canon mostly included the writings of Paul, along with other writings deemed heretical such as a variation of the Gospel of Luke, later known as the Gospel of Marcion. Perhaps somewhat in response to Marcion, Christians and churches increasingly recognized the need for a widely agreed-upon canon, which would prevent heretical beliefs, values, and practices from creeping into Christianity. Not all Christians agreed with regard to what a growing understanding of orthodoxy (or "right beliefs") might include. Indeed, there existed competing schools of thought with regard to what orthodoxy might include. But study of Christians in the ancient church reveals that the canonization process of Scripture probably took place over several centuries rather than during a relatively brief space in time. No doubt the fact that Christianity was still a relatively new religious sect in the Roman Empire, which restricted the amount of public church activities, discouraged efforts in forming a biblical canon.

When Constantine became emperor of the Roman Empire in the early fourth century, life changed drastically for Christians politically, socially, and culturally, as well as in the development of churches. When persecution of Christians was outlawed, Christianity was legalized and legitimized through

Constantine's patronage, and churches could openly assemble and develop. Of course, development can be a two-edged sword. On the one hand, Christians could freely gather, worship, and develop institutionally, as well as in other ways. On the other hand, institutionalization led to the possibility of cultural accommodation, ecclesiastical excesses, abuse of power, and other distortions of biblical, historic Christianity. In fact, one of the divides between Roman Catholic and Protestant interpretations of church history has to do with whether the Constantinian era in the long run helped or hurt Christianity. Catholics tend to see the era favorably, whereas Protestants tend to see it as problematic. Regardless of how one interprets the Constantinian era, the emperor made it possible for Christians and churches to focus on the development of a canon.

In 331, Constantine is thought to have commissioned the publication of fifty Christian Bibles. Eusebius was among those given the task of preparing the Bibles for the bishop of Constantinople, which Eusebius wrote about in his *Life of Constantine*. It is not clear, however, what the Bibles contained and whether copies of them still exist. The *Codex Vaticanus* and *Codex Sinaiticus* may be examples of Constantine's fifty Bibles, though neither of them contains the same books found in the eventual canon. Regardless, Constantine no doubt encouraged fourth-century Christians to devise their own canon lists that might eventually win widespread acceptance among churches. Athanasius, for example, was among those commissioned to publish a Bible, and he became a principal leader in the process of canonization.

Constantine called for the first ecumenical, or churchwide, council of Christians in the eastern city of Nicaea, mostly to counter the perceived heresy of Arianism. Church leaders from around the Roman Empire—the known Christian world—were brought together for the first time, and a rough draft of what came to be known as the Nicene Creed was developed in the establishment of orthodox Christianity. After the Council of Nicaea, the draft of the creed was sent to churches throughout the empire for feedback for a second council, eventually held in Constantinople in 381. The canon of Scripture was not discussed per se, though later observers noted discussions at the council about the validity and authority of particular New Testament books.

■ Canonization of the Bible

Christians and churches increasingly gathered together the various Scriptures they had and openly discussed their nature, usefulness, and authority. There was diversity among the textual manuscripts they had; there was not unanimity with regard to which Scriptures were valid and which were not. In the third century, Origen wrote a list of Christian Scriptures with twenty-one of the books eventually included in the New Testament; in the early fourth century, Eusebius wrote another list, also with twenty-one books, but the lists were not the same. Numerous lists or catalogs of canonical books were written, but none of them gained consensual acceptance. The books of the Old Testament were largely accepted based on those books established by Jews as the Hebrew Bible. The books of the New Testament, however, continued to be debated. Some lists included books from the eventual New Testament canon, but not all of them were mentioned. Likewise, other books not contained in the eventual canon were sometimes included—for example, the *Didache*, *Epistle of Barnabas*, *Shepherd of Hermas*, and so on.

Athanasius, bishop of Alexandria, is credited with being the first person to have listed all twenty-seven books eventually included in the New Testament canon. His list appeared in an Easter letter written in 367, which is also referred to as his 39th Festal Letter. With regard to the list, Athanasius refers to the books as "being canonized." His list actually included more than the twenty-seven books of the New Testament, and Athanasius rearranged some of the Old Testament books, along with the Deuterocanonical Writings. But his list was confirmed by Pope Damasus I, who in 382 issued his own canonical inventory, including the same books identified by Athanasius. When Damasus commissioned Jerome to undertake the Latin Vulgate translation of the Bible (ca. 383), the pope helped establish a final canonical list.

In northern Africa, synods (or councils) met in Hippo (393) and Carthage (397) in order to discuss, among other things, the Christian canon of the Bible. The former synod left out the letter to the Hebrews, but the latter synod articulated the complete list of New Testament books. Of course, the Synod of Carthage also included Deuterocanonical Writings, but the overall canon list finally included all of the books in the Old and New Testaments accepted by Christians thereafter as their Bible. Notably, Augustine gave leadership as bishop during the synods in Carthage in both 397 and 419, and he considered the canon closed. That is, Augustine believed that the process of canonization had concluded and that no additional books or writings should be included in the Bible. By the early fifth century, references to the Bible overwhelmingly sounded as if the canon was well established among the writings of Christians. The canon of the Bible was no longer debated but was promoted among the churches.

We can only imagine the interaction that took place between individuals and parties of individuals, advocating on behalf of the inclusion of certain books into the New Testament canon, and those rejecting other books. Lamentably, the issues and debates were not recorded, so no historical account is available to help us understand what the ancient Christians went through in determining sacred Scripture. Still, Christians since then have distilled the historical criteria most likely used for deciding which books should be included in the canon, and which books should not be included. James I. Packer, for example, lists the following three criteria for canonization:

1. apostolic authorship or authentication;
2. Christ-honoring doctrinal content, in line with known teaching of other apostles; and
3. continuous acknowledgment and spiritually fruitful use of the books within the church.[2]

Of course, these criteria represent a contemporary summarization of canonical criteria. The actual, historical process in all probability was not as nice and neat as the criteria suggest. But they give helpful insight into the kinds of considerations—rigorously or flexibly understood—in the process of canonization.

Assumed throughout the entire process of canonization is belief in the ongoing presence and work of the Holy Spirit in both the formation and canonization of the Bible. This assumption or theological presupposition is not always stated explicitly, but it is necessary for historic and contemporary beliefs about the Bible. Later Christians were more explicit in articulating this belief, but it was thought to undergird all individual and church efforts in determining an ecumenical, orthodox understanding of the inspired nature, authority, and consequent trustworthiness of the Bible. Of course, the role of the Holy Spirit—to greater and lesser degrees—is not important only for the canonization of the Bible. It is also relevant to the Bible's transmission through copying procedures and other means of reproduction throughout the centuries. After all, what good would a Bible be if, after its inspired origin, it became subject to human finitude and fallibility in its transcriptions, translations, and interpretations?

■ The Bible after Canonization

After consensus was reached about the biblical canon, remarkable consistency occurred among Christians and churches with regard to maintaining it. Only occasionally have people of note challenged the canon. Martin Luther, for example, considered certain books of the New Testament to be contrary to the teachings of the Protestant Reformation, such as *sola Scriptura* (Latin

2. James I. Packer, "Scripture," in *New Dictionary of Theology*, ed. Sinclair B. Ferguson and David F. Wright (Downers Grove, IL: InterVarsity, 1988), 627–31.

"Scripture alone") and *sola fide* (Latin "faith alone"). He wanted to eliminate the books of Hebrews, James, Jude, and Revelation from the New Testament, but did not. Instead, Luther chose merely to list them at the end of his German translation of the Bible.

In reaction to Luther and the other Protestant Reformers, the canon of the Bible became, perhaps, more debated and dogmatically avowed than ever before. For example, the Roman Catholic Council of Trent (1545–63) made its doctrinal beliefs about the Bible and Deuterocanonical Writings required affirmations for church membership. Protestants followed suit by articulating their own dogmas about the biblical canon, which included rejecting the canonicity of the Deuterocanonical Writings in subsequent statements of faith, such as the Thirty-nine Articles (1563) for the Church of England, the Westminster Confession (1647) for British Calvinists, and the Synod of Jerusalem (1672) for Orthodox Churches.

Other Christians in church history, of course, have been dissatisfied for one reason or another with particular books in the Bible. More often than not, people prefer to minimize or disregard portions of the Bible rather than reject their canonicity. Sometimes this preference for certain books of the Bible over other books (or portions of books) is called a "canon within the canon." However, before people become too upset or indignant over such disregard, they should keep in mind that most people function with a sort of select canon. For example, Christians may regard the New Testament more highly than the Old Testament, and Protestants may regard the writings of Paul more highly than other writings in the New Testament. If individuals harbor the belief that they have no such "canon within the canon," then they should take a look at their oldest, most used Bible. If one were to look at the oil stains on the sides of the pages in the Bible, caused by the touch of fingers, would there be portions of its sides more oil-stained due to frequent handling by the owner? If so, then one has discovered their "canon within the canon," regardless of whether one is consciously aware of it.

Overall no one, including Christians and non-Christians, has successfully argued on a wide-scale basis to either eliminate from or add to the canon. Some variations do exist among various Christian traditions with regard to how they view the Bible, Apocryphal/Deuterocanonical Books, and so on. Still others argue for an "open canon," believing that God is free to contribute additional revelation to people, should God choose to do so. After all, do Christians not believe that God continues to work in the world, communicating God's will to people and empowering them to act in accordance with that will? Yet given the undeniable diversity that occurs between the Christian traditions, the canon of Old and New Testaments has remained remarkably intact.

Perhaps more problematic have been the numerous manuscripts of the Bible that have been found from the eras of the ancient and medieval churches. After all, Bibles had to be transcribed by hand, and much of it was done by clergy, especially those sequestered in monasteries throughout the world. During church history, clergy and scholars have been limited by the number and quality of manuscripts they had available for copying. They also had the problem of discrepancies or errors made—consciously or unconsciously—in biblical manuscripts. Although precautions were instituted in the transcription of biblical texts and how copiers were motivated by their faith in God, numerous textual differences occurred in manuscripts. We know this because extant (or surviving) Hebrew and Greek manuscripts that were discovered from the ancient and medieval eras contain thousands of discrepancies or errors. On a textual level, such differences become a matter of investigation and fascination with the realities of biblical transcription, transmission, and so on. On another level, the preponderance of discrepancies or errors can become—for some—a potential crisis of faith, since their beliefs about the Bible preclude discrepancies or errors of any nature. The presence of these differences will be a matter of lengthy discussion in chapters 8 and 9.

■ English Translations

It lies outside the scope of this book to talk about all the translations of the Bible. Even narrowing a discussion to English translations of the Bible would be difficult to cover. Nowadays there seem to be so many new Bible translations being published that it is easy for a book about them to quickly become out of date. Still, let us talk a little about some of the more notable English translations in church history and criteria used for the translations.

Although earlier attempts at translation occurred in Great Britain, resulting in partial translations, John Wycliffe is credited for first translating the Bible into English, in the fourteenth century. His Bible became known eventually as the Wycliffe Bible. Wycliffe and his Lollard associates translated the Bible from the Latin Vulgate, so it was actually a translation of a translation. Wycliffe translated the Bible due in part to his attempts to reform the Roman Catholic Church, including resistance to papal authority and the magisterium (or teaching office). Wycliffe's body was exhumed by Pope Martin V in the fifteenth century and burned for heresy.

In the sixteenth century, the Protestant Reformation occurred in Continental Europe through the leadership of Luther, Ulrich Zwingli, and others. In England, William Tyndale was inspired by Luther's translation of the Bible into German. After making his intentions known to Roman Catholic leaders, Tyndale was declared a heretic. So he moved to Germany, where he may have met with Luther and began his translation of the Bible into English. His Bible eventually became known as the Tyndale Bible. He printed the New Testament in 1525 and the Pentateuch in 1529. Tyndale was unable to complete a translation of the entire Bible, but his scholarship was innovative for his use of Hebrew and Greek texts and for its publication by recently created printing presses. Tyndale's translation was influential in preparation for the British Reformation, and it provided the scholarly foundation for subsequent English translations.

After the British Reformation, several English translations of the Bible were published and widely used. The Geneva Bible (1559) was very popular because it divided books of the Bible into verses, which made it easier for people to read. It also included commentary that aided readers in study of the Bible. Queen Elizabeth I commissioned the Bishops Bible (1566) in order to create a national "authorized version." Eventually, King James I commissioned an Authorized Version of the Bible (AV; 1611), due in part to concerns by Puritans about previous translations and also to concerns he had about past translations and commentary considered subversive toward the monarchy and Church of England. The Authorized Version, also known as the King James Version (KJV), became the dominant English translation, eventually surpassing the influence of other Bibles and becoming the biblical source for the Anglican Book of Common Prayer (1662). By the eighteenth century, the King James Bible dominated biblical usage in the English-speaking world and continues to be a bestseller into the twenty-first century.

■ Translation Approaches

English translations (or retranslations) of the Bible occasionally occurred, such as the British update of the King James Version called the Revised Version (RV, NT 1881 and OT 1885) and its counterpart American Standard Version (ASV, 1901). But in the twentieth century, English translations proliferated, and new translations continue to be published in the twenty-first century. As more translations were created, increased consideration was given to the criteria used for translation. Several approaches, or philosophies, of translation exist, and they have all been used to greater and lesser degrees in church history. No Bible translation perfectly embodies any one of the philosophies of translation; instead, particular translations tend to reflect one philosophy more than others. Sometimes continua (or spectrums) have been diagrammed in order to compare and illustrate differences between English translations of the Bible. Such comparisons can be misleading, however, due to who creates the continua. Care should be used not only in studying such comparisons but also in knowing who created them and why.

Generally speaking, there are two main approaches to, or philosophies of, Bible translation. At one end of the spectrum is verbal-equivalence (or formal-equivalence) translation, which tries to write a literal, word-for-word translation from the original language to English. At the other end of the spectrum is dynamic equivalence, which tries to write a meaningful, thought-for-thought translation from an original language to English. As one might suspect, each approach would argue for its benefits over the other approach, pointing out the other's liabilities. For example, one might think that a word-for-word translation would come closest to the original meaning of a biblical text. However, anyone who has done translation from one language to another knows that word-for-word translations can also distort meanings, especially when idiomatic expressions are used that employ similes, metaphors, irony, or other linguistic and cultural expressions. Likewise, one might think that a thought-for-thought translation would come closest to the original meaning of a biblical text. However, straying too far from word-for-word translations runs the risk of projecting meanings on biblical texts more reflective of the translators than that of the original authors.

In practice, Bible translations rely on both approaches to translation, though to varying degrees. So it is not so much a matter of *if* an English Bible uses both approaches but *when* it uses them. Also, in practice, choices people make with regard to particular Bible translations may not have so much to do with their approach to translation as to their readability, use of common or contemporary language, religious background, or personal preference. It is nearly impossible to prevent the beliefs and values of the translators from affecting the final product of their translations, especially given the concerns of postmodernism with regard to the personal and cultural influences that affect Christianity. Still, most translators would argue that their particular approach least distorts the original meaning of the biblical texts.

Another approach to Bible translation is called paraphrastic (or idiomatic) translation. Basically, such an approach produces a paraphrase, rather than a translation, of the biblical texts. Paraphrases do not intend to provide exact equivalence of words or thoughts in the Bible but of the meaning behind the texts—for example, emphasizing their spiritual teachings. A popular paraphrase of the Bible titled *The Living Bible* (1971) was written by Kenneth Taylor. Eugene Peterson also wrote a paraphrase titled *The Message* (NT 1993; OT 2001). Of course, paraphrases may result in quite novel, perhaps poetic, renderings of biblical texts, taking great liberties in what is said—liberties especially susceptible to the beliefs and values of those paraphrasing them. If readers like the poetic license used in communicating the message of the Bible, then such liberties are considered worthwhile. Paraphrases are popular among people who find it difficult to read and understand long-established translations of the Bible.

Another factor that influences the translation of the Bible is the manuscripts used for translation. The King James Version of the Bible, for example, uses the textus receptus (Latin "received text"), which was the 1550 edition of the Greek New Testament. The textus receptus was thought to contain the most reliable biblical manuscripts when the King James Version was completed in 1611. Since then, however, thousands of manuscripts of the Bible have been discovered, many of them thought to be hundreds of years, if not a thousand years, older than the textus receptus. Since older manuscripts are thought by translators to be more reliable than more recent ones, translations after the late nineteenth century have used ancient manuscripts other than the textus receptus as their starting point for translation of the New Testament. Different manuscripts may not seem like a problem, except that there are differences between them, including the absence of numerous passages in the earlier manuscripts that are found in the textus receptus. The differences and omissions, especially to those who advocate against the King James Version, are crucial since they make the textus receptus seem less reliable, less truthful. In response, advocates of the King James Version argue that the textus receptus is more reliable and that other translations weaken the Bible as the Word of God due to their differences and omissions.

Today only the King James Version and New King James Version (NKJV, 1982), which updated the language into modern English, use the textus receptus. Other common translations do not, including the Revised Standard Version (RSV, 1952), New American Standard Bible (NASB, 1971; updated 1995), Good News Bible (1976), New International Version (NIV, 1978; updated 2011), New Jerusalem Bible (1985), New Century Version (NCV, 1991), and New Living Translation (NLT, 1996; updated 2007). As we will see in chapters 8 and 9, the presence of discrepancies and omissions in any of the biblical manuscripts challenges historic Christian beliefs about the authority and inspiration of the Bible as well as claims to its trustworthiness.

Another consideration in translation we will mention has to do with the use of inclusive language in referring to men and women in the Bible. Historically, the English language has considered male-oriented language to refer to males in some contexts but to males and females in other contexts. For example, references to "mankind" and "men" may refer to men and women as well as to men only. However, male-oriented language can become confusing with regard to when women are or are not included in the meaning. Even the context of some statements makes it difficult to decide. Correspondingly, speakers of the English language have increasingly preferred to use generic language when referring to both men and women so that less confusion occurs in communication. For example, inclusive uses for "mankind" are replaced by "humankind" or "humanity"; and inclusive uses for "men" are replaced by "people." Examples of inclusive Bible translations include the New Revised Standard Version (NRSV, 1990) and Today's New International Version (TNIV, 2005). Although the original manuscripts of the Bible may contain male-oriented language, it is thought that their meaning is best communicated through the dynamic equivalency of inclusive language in describing people.

■ The Importance of the Bible's History

If people want to become better students of the Bible, they need to learn more about its history. The Bible did not fall from heaven in its final form; it expanded and developed over hundreds of years. The final canon of Scripture did not occur all of a sudden, without issues raised and debates about the final list of books. The process of canonization took centuries before consensus arose among ancient Christians. Even after its canonization, the Bible continued to be a topic of contention among Christians in the East and West, and among Catholics and Protestants. There is also contention concerning which specific translation should be used. Knowing the history of the Bible helps us to better understand and appreciate its content. It also helps us to avoid far-fetched views of the Bible that may hurt, more than help, Christian beliefs, values, and practices.

Let us use an analogy to emphasize the importance of learning about the Bible's history: How do we get to know *you*? Is it possible to understand and appreciate the fullness of who you are without some understanding of your past? Certainly we can learn a great deal about you by observing who you are now—how you look, how you act, what you say, and so on. Indeed, lots can be learned from a present encounter with you. But to gain greater depth in knowing who you are, it is necessary to learn about your background, life-shaping experiences, key relationships, and other information about your past. Of course, people may not always like revealing their pasts, since there can be negative as well as positive things learned about them. The same is true, of course, for learning about the history of the Bible. Some people would prefer that we do not study too closely the history of the Bible, since it might reveal embarrassing facts about its chronological accuracy, scientific worldview, theological variations, and questionable morals. However, if in-depth understanding and appreciation of you is to occur, then a critical and historical approach needs to be taken in getting to know you. The same is true for the Bible.

Knowing the history of the Bible is also crucial for interpreting it. How can one rightly discern the Bible's teachings without information concerning its background, development, debates over its composition and ultimate canonization? Knowledge about subsequent issues of transcription, translation, and ecclesiastical authority—relative to the various Christian traditions—aid in the interpretive process.

In the next three chapters, our attention will turn to interpretation of the Bible. We will offer a commonsense approach to the topic. We will not provide step-by-step instruction with regard to how biblical interpretation occurs, but we will provide insight into key issues related to the history of the Bible. Such issues include the variety of genres found in the Bible, the importance of knowing the historical context of passages, and literary sources of the biblical texts. It is our hope that this brief history of the Bible, coupled with the principles of interpretation found in the following chapters, will reinforce the need for studying all its levels of meaning in order to understand rightly and apply effectively the teachings of sacred Scripture.

INTERPRETATION
OF THE **BIBLE**

3

Genre

A friend of mine (we'll call her Ann) used to work at a major university hospital and was routinely involved in open-heart surgery and heart and lung transplants. This stuff is way out of my league. I (Keith) grew up on a farm in South Dakota and have had some interesting experiences with animals. (Have you ever done a C-section on a cow? I helped the vet do that once out on our farm.) Ann is the only person I know who can literally rip a person's chest open and massage his or her heart. I did not know this happened until I met Ann. After surgery doctors will monitor a person, and if the person's heart stops beating and does not respond to the traditional shocks, then they will rip open the person's chest and literally reach in and massage the heart. And sometimes I think *my* job is stressful.

One day Ann came home from work and her six-year-old son (we'll call him Sammy) asked her about her day. I suppose the conversation started in a normal way, "Hey Mom, how was your day?" Ann probably responded, "Fine, Sammy, how was yours?" There was probably some exchange of chit chat—the usual banter that occurs between a mom and a six-year-old boy. Then the conversation became really interesting.

Sammy said, "Mommy, did you see Jesus today?" Now Ann is a very spiritual woman—a fine Christian woman. She prays a lot and is very much in tune with God. So this question, while a bit unusual, was not the sort of question that would catch her off guard.

Ann answered Sammy's question, "Honey, I feel Jesus is with me sometimes when I work."

Sammy, however, was six years old, and Ann did not answer the question that he had asked. So Sammy came back, "But mommy, did you *see* Jesus today?"

Ann, not understanding the question, again responded, "Honey, I feel Jesus's presence with me sometimes when I am working. Sometimes when things get really crazy I sort of feel that Jesus has his arms around me."

Sammy, however, had not asked *that* question and came back a third time, "But mommy, did you *see* Jesus?"

Ann, now somewhat bewildered, finally asked for clarification, "What do you mean, Sammy?"

Sammy asked, with all the sincerity and inquisitiveness of a six-year-old, "Mommy, when you are working, and you open up a person's heart, do you see Jesus?"

Sammy was raised in a Christian home and had attended Sunday school and church all of his life. No doubt he had heard many times people say that you must accept Jesus "into your heart." Sammy simply took what he had learned and wanted verification from his mother—a trained medical professional. Sammy imagined that if you looked inside a person's heart you would be able to see Jesus.

Before Ann could respond, Sammy continued with his theological inquiry, "Mommy, if a person accepts Jesus into his heart, and then he dies and gives his heart to somebody else, does that make the other person a Christian?" We face many tough ethical questions in the medical field today, but I doubt if this is a question medical ethicists have thought about much.

Does Jesus live in your heart? Does Jesus *really* live in your heart? What do we mean when we ask a question like this? How should we understand it? This question, like many other questions, is a matter of biblical interpretation.

■ Biblical Interpretation

Many books have been written on the interpretation of the Bible. Sometimes you will come across words like "hermeneutics" or "exegesis." Hermeneutics is simply the science of interpretation. Exegesis intends to "lead out" the correct meaning. They are fancy words, but the goal of good biblical interpretation is simply to discover the plain meaning of the text—nothing more, nothing less.

What is the "plain meaning" of the text? Is this the "obvious meaning"? What is the difference between the plain meaning and the obvious meaning? As I am using the term "plain meaning," it refers to the meaning that the original reader, or possibly the original hearer, would have ascertained. The "obvious meaning" might be what you—the contemporary reader—thinks. However, they are not necessarily the same. Your understanding of the obvious meaning might be miles apart from the plain meaning. Why is this?

The primary problem is that of distance. The biblical materials were written over a thousand-year period in at least three different languages in multiple cultural contexts. The biblical writers all intended to be understood, but they wrote to a different audience than a contemporary Western audience. If we want to understand, for example, what Isaiah said to his eighth-century contemporaries, we need to try to imagine as much as possible how to hear like eighth-century Hebrew people. The same is true if we want to understand the words of Jesus. We try to locate ourselves in the world of a first-century Jew living under Roman occupation. We may never have perfect interpretation, but good biblical interpretation makes its best effort. Even contemporary people sometimes have difficulty understanding one another. I have been married for over thirty-three years, and I still do not always completely understand the communication process. But we do our best.

This book does not attempt to give detailed instructions on the interpretive process. For that, one should consult one of the myriad books on the topic.[1] Rather, we will simply sketch in broad outline the types of questions people need to keep in mind if they want to discover the "plain meaning."

The great interpretive questions can usually be narrowed down to three:

1. What is the genre (literary type)?
2. What is the historical context?
3. What is the literary context?

Detailed analysis of the text will follow from those, but if these three "big" questions can be answered well, over 90 percent of the questions regarding biblical interpretation can be answered. The questions are interrelated, so our explanations will be as well.

■ What Is Genre?

The first question one needs to ask in interpreting any work of literature, the Bible included, is, what is the genre? The term "genre" is nothing more than a fancy French word that means "kind" or "type." Most American students are introduced to this term by the seventh grade, though many have forgotten

1. For example, see David R. Bauer and Robert A. Traina, *Inductive Bible Study: A Comprehensive Guide to the Practice of Hermeneutics* (Grand Rapids: Baker Academic, 2011); N. Clayton Croy, *Prima Scriptura: An Introduction to New Testament Interpretation* (Grand Rapids: Baker Academic, 2011); Gordon Fee and Douglas Stuart, *How to Read the Bible for All Its Worth*, 3rd ed. (Grand Rapids: Zondervan, 2003); see also the select bibliography at the end of this book.

the term by the time they arrive at college. As the students learned, the term is usually applied to literature or art. Thus a poem is not the same kind of literature as a telephone listing. Furthermore, there are dozens of types of poems, each having a different genre. A person trained in literature can easily tell a limerick from a sonnet, though to the untrained eye, the differences may not be apparent.

We make genre decisions every day, though most of the time this is done unconsciously. A native reader of a language usually has no difficulty recognizing genre. Thus typical Americans might buy a newspaper and immediately turn to the "sports" or "business" section. They would have certain expectations of the materials on those pages. People would turn to the business section to find economic news or market updates. If they wanted a box score of the baseball game, they would not expect to find it in the business section. In like manner, people wishing to bake a cake would look for a recipe in a cookbook.

We simply do not struggle with genre recognition on a daily basis. Nevertheless, we have all been caught by a joke when we have failed to see it coming. Certain types of jokes work because they are disguised as simple stories. When the punch line comes, we realize that it was not a story at all, but a joke. These types of jokes work because they intentionally mislead on the genre.

Genre recognition can be difficult when the literature we are looking at was written two or three thousand years ago in a different language by people with a completely different worldview than we possess today. Even when we are sensitive to the genre, our twenty-first-century Western assumptions often cloud our vision.

In the study of the Bible, genre recognition is probably the most important issue in matters of interpretation. It is probably not an overstatement to say that the biggest errors in interpretation result from failure to recognize genre.

For many Christians, the Bible is thought to contain only one genre: "Bible." The term "Bible," however, is simply another old French word that means "book." In English usage the term "holy" was appended to "Bible" signifying that this was no ordinary book, but a special book. In recent English usage, "Holy" is often dropped from the term "Holy Bible" for the more common expression "Bible." The Bible, or "the Book," is composed of sixty-six works that are commonly called "books." Only a few of the thirty-nine "books" of the Old Testament or the twenty-seven "books" of the New Testament could even remotely be considered books. The Gospels and Acts are the closest things we have to books in the New Testament. The letters of Paul are just that, letters. The same is true of the works that are traditionally called the General Letters (also called General Epistles). For the most part they are letters, though 1 Peter and Hebrews might constitute something slightly different. The last "book" of the New Testament, the Revelation of John, is the most misunderstood "book" of all. It too is a letter, though the bulk of it is written in the genre of apocalypse, a very popular style in the first-century Roman world. Each "book" of the New Testament is furthermore composed of many different genres.

It is probably helpful to give several examples of how genre recognition can aid interpretation. Let us approach this by giving several examples from different sections of the canon of the Bible. Understand that this is a very limited introduction. There are numerous books that can give more detailed information on genre.

■ The Old Testament

The Law

As noted earlier, the Hebrew Bible is composed of the *Torah* (Hebrew "Law"), the *Nevi'im* (Hebrew "Prophets"), and the *Ketubim* (Hebrew "Writings"). What about the Torah? Unfortunately, the Hebrew term *Torah* is often translated by the English word "law." The term really means "teaching" or "instruction" and is much broader than what we understand by "law" today. The Torah is a diverse collection that is composed mostly of legal material and narratives about the early fathers and mothers of Israel.

How should we interpret the legal material? Simply put, we must understand that these laws were not written for us. They were written for a particular people at a particular time and a particular place. It is obvious to most Christians that Deuteronomy 25:11–12 should not be part of our current legal system: "If men get into a fight with one another, and the wife of one intervenes to rescue her husband from the grip of his opponent by reaching out and seizing his genitals, you shall cut off her hand; show no pity." Yet many Christians would argue that the Ten Commandments should be followed, though in reality few actually observe the Sabbath (Exod. 20:1–17, esp. 20:8). Ceasing labor from Friday at sundown until Saturday at sundown is simply not a part of most Christians' regimen (though some Seventh-Day Adventists and others might observe the Sabbath in this way). How, then, should Christians deal with the legal material? As best as possible we should endeavor to understand the intent of the law and then determine if meaning or relevance can be extracted for today's time and place. The Sabbath law, for example, can instruct us on the value of work as well as on the value of rest from that work. Thus it can speak to the lazy and the workaholic in addition to those seeking gainful employment.

The Torah also includes narratives about the early fathers and mothers of the faith. Let us be clear here. Simply because somebody does something in the Bible does not mean that it should be an example for contemporary Christians. Children's Bibles have many stories about heroes of the faith, yet the editors of these Bibles wisely leave out many stories that are offensive to the contemporary reader (for example, the story of Lot and his family in Sodom; see Gen. 19:30–38). Typically we use value judgments, based on Christian principles, about the various characters in the story.

One cannot discuss the Torah and avoid the first chapters, the creation narratives. Here an understanding of genre is important, as we are dealing with language at a very basic level. In Genesis 1:6, we read that God places a "dome" (or "firmament" in other translations) in the middle of the sky to separate the waters above the dome from the waters below the dome. What exactly is this dome? How does it separate the waters above the heavens from the waters below the heavens? It is generally accepted among most people today that we live in a vast expanding universe with lots of galaxies and space. To our knowledge, there is no dome. What type of literature is this? One could argue, as some writers of the past have, that there used to be some sort of a dome, but the dome is now gone. Let us think about this, though. If you look up at the sky, it appears to be blue (except on a bad day in August in Los Angeles, near where I live, when the sky looks brown). Imagine a Hebrew father and his son out herding sheep three thousand years ago. The sheep are munching the grass, so the father and son lie down to rest for a bit and look up at the sky. The son asks the father, "Dad, why is the sky blue?" The father responds, "It looks like water to me. The sky must be blue because of the water God has in the heavens." "Ah," the boy replies, "but what keeps the water up there?" "God has put a dome up there to hold the waters in place," Dad says. "And he has put windows in the heavens to let the rains come down."

What you have in Genesis 1:6, then, is not a scientific treatise on the structure of the universe, but a description of how things *appear*. Did the writers of the Hebrew Bible actually believe this about the world, or did they simply describe it that way? We do not really know, and it does not really matter. They were not attempting to give a precise scientific definition of the origin of the universe. To ask that question of the text is looking for an answer to a question that was never asked.

Let us imagine, again, a contemporary young couple walking along the road in the early evening as the sun is about to set. The young woman makes an observation, "Look at the beautiful sunset." The young man responds, "Well, actually, the sun is not really setting; the earth is simply rotating on its axis and the sun is dropping below the horizon out of your range of view." While the young man may be more scientifically correct than the young woman, it is unlikely his comments will win any favor with the young woman. In fact, most of us would think the young man needs to be schooled on dating etiquette. This is obvious to a contemporary reader.

Unfortunately, some Christians approach the Bible in the same way as that young man. They may think they are holding up the veracity of the Bible by arguing for a literal dome in the sky, but in reality they simply come off looking rather naive. They are just like Sammy. Maybe Jesus *does* live in a person's heart, but not in the way Sammy imagined it.

The Prophets

Let us look at a couple examples from the second section of the Hebrew Bible where genre recognition will be useful as an aid to interpretation. The "Prophets" in the Hebrew Bible, as we have already seen, include what can be considered historical material as well as collections of writings such as the "book" of Jeremiah. What was said about the Torah is still true. Simply because a character did something does not mean that character should be emulated.

Let us look at the book of Jeremiah to learn something about how this book was formed. Jeremiah, like most of the prophetic books (what are sometimes called Major Prophets and Minor Prophets in the Christian canon), is composed primarily of two types of materials. It contains collections of speeches that Jeremiah delivered on various occasions. It also has some narrative sections that give a window into the historical context of the prophet. According to chapter 36, Jeremiah had his scribe, Baruch, write down words on a scroll that he had received from the Lord (Jer. 36:4). Because Jeremiah was restricted from entering the temple, Baruch entered the temple and read the scroll on a "fast day" (Jer. 36:6, 10). Micaiah, apparently a court official, heard this message and reported it to the palace (Jer. 36:11–13). Palace officials, in turn, instructed Baruch to come to the palace and deliver the message to them (Jer. 36:14–16). When the palace officials heard it, they were alarmed (Jer. 36:16) and determined to deliver the message to King Jehoiakim. When the king had the scroll read to him, however, he cut pieces off and threw them into the fire (Jer. 36:23). Later Jeremiah had Baruch write a similar scroll that had "all the words of the scroll" that King Jehoiakim had burned as well as "many similar words" (Jer. 36:32).

Jeremiah illustrates to a certain degree how this "book" came together. Jeremiah, like most of the prophetic books, is a collection of speeches given at various times and in various situations. The more we know of these situations, the better we can understand the speeches. Again, the speeches are not aimed directly toward the contemporary reader. When people or nations misbehave in the way that Israel, Judah, or other nations of the world misbehave, then the words of the prophets can clearly be relevant. Likewise, when the prophets give a message of hope to people who are in dire straits, it may be appropriate to apply those materials to our contemporary context.

The Writings

The final section of the Hebrew Bible is the "writings." This includes literature such as Psalms, Proverbs, and Job, but also books such as Song of Solomon (or Song of Songs), Ruth, and Daniel. Again, it will be impossible to look at all the genres in this collection, but a few examples will suffice to demonstrate the importance of genre recognition.

Every year I begin my Bible classes by showing a picture from the magazine titled the *Wittenburg Door* depicting the woman described poetically in Song of Solomon 7:1–9. However, the picture shows a "literal" rendition of the author's female love interest described in the biblical text. The visual of the woman includes thighs that look like jewels, a navel drawn the size of a bowl, a belly that looks like a "heap of wheat," two breasts that look like "two fawns, twins of gazelles," a neck drawn like a soaring tower, eyes that look like pools, a pronounced nose that extends like a "tower of Lebanon," and purple-colored hair. I show the picture, read the text, and ask, "What's wrong with this picture?" Aside from the fact that this is one ugly woman, it clearly illustrates the problem with reading a text literally that was not intended that way. This illustration demonstrates how romantic poetry is completely destroyed when it is understood literally. Indeed, sometimes a "literal" approach to interpreting the Bible is the worst way to understand it. Furthermore, the language used clearly demonstrates the distance between the poet and the contemporary reader. Telling a young woman that her "belly is a heap of wheat" (Song 7:2) might invoke a slap across the face. Furthermore, noting that a young woman's breasts are like "gazelles" (Song 7:3) might be grounds for a reprimand from the dean of students if not outright dismissal. As I instruct my male students, "Don't try this at home."

The writings also include the "book" of Proverbs. Interpretation of the various proverbs has its own issues. When I was in seminary, I had a fellow classmate who believed that a Christian could never starve to death. We had a fairly long conversation in the hallway on this issue. His appeal was Proverbs 10:3, "The LORD does not let the righteous go hungry, but he thwarts the craving of the wicked." Thus my friend concluded that the righteous could not starve to death based on this text. I argued that he was clearly wrong, and that Christians die everyday in some rather horrible circumstances. So what about Proverbs?

The book of Proverbs contains conventional wisdom. It was the sort of teaching that was passed from parent to child or that originated in the court. Literature such as this is generally true, but it does not present absolute truths that are always true at all times. Thus in the same book we can find sayings that appear to be contradictory: "Do not answer fools according to their folly, or you will be a fool yourself" (Prov. 26:4). This is paired with, "Answer fools according to their folly, or they will be wise in their own eyes" (Prov. 26:5). Which is it? How shall one answer a fool? It should be fairly obvious that both of these sayings cannot be true at all times. Each gives wisdom that is appropriate for a particular occasion. The truly wise know when to answer fools according to their folly and when not to do so.

Apocalyptic Literature

When we say "apocalyptic literature," we primarily mean the book of Daniel, which is part of the *Ketubim*. The word "apocalypse" (Greek *apokalypsis*) means "revelation"—indicating a disclosure. Apocalyptic is a much-abused genre, however, and deserves its own special treatment. Part of the problem with the term "apocalyptic" is that it is used in multiple ways. Sometimes apocalyptic refers to a social-political movement; sometimes it refers to a particular way of thinking about the future; and sometimes it refers to a particular type of literature. Rather than give a precise definition of apocalyptic—which is probably impossible—we will talk about apocalyptic literature in general and discuss other elements as they are relevant.

The monarchy of David was considered the "golden age" of Israel. Every king after that was measured against David and came up short. Thus the hope of Israel was that a new king would arise who would be like David and who would restore the kingdom to its Davidic glory. This king never showed up, however. Consequently, people began to be more pessimistic about the future. The belief that a Davidic king would arise within history was eventually replaced with the belief that God would need to intervene in a direct and decisive way.

Apocalyptic thought developed during the period of the Babylonian exile and flowered during the Persian period after the exile (sixth to fifth centuries BCE). It reached its full bloom during the Hellenistic (or Greek) period, after the time of Alexander the Great (fourth century BCE). In addition to the book of Daniel, we see apocalyptic expressions in Ezekiel 38–39, Isaiah 24–27, and Zechariah 9–14. Other apocalyptic material not included in the canon includes 1 *and 2 Enoch*, *Sibylline Oracles*, *Ascension of Moses* (mentioned in Jude 9), 2 *Esdras*, 2 *and 3 Baruch*, *Testaments of the Twelve Patriarchs*, and *War Scroll* from the caves of Qumran. The book of Revelation is the primary New Testament apocalypse.

Apocalyptic literature was, in large part, an answer to the problem of evil. Wisdom literature taught that God rewards the righteous but punishes the wicked. After the exile, this simply did not square with reality. Even when Israel kept the law, it was not prosperous and passed from subjection under one nation to subjection under another. The present experience of domination, sorrow, and disturbance caused the pious to look to the future for the fulfillment of God's promises. The fact of foreign domination produced an emphasis on the cosmic aspect of God's universal sovereignty. God was no longer simply the God of Israel but the God of the entire world and of all history.

Apocalyptic literature tends to be dualistic. It involves the cosmic struggle of good versus evil. The present evil age will ultimately give way to a future age of bliss. Apocalyptic literature was written to encourage the righteous to be faithful during interim times of persecution. The ultimate message of apocalyptic is quite simple—God wins.

A large portion of apocalyptic material, but not all of it, is visionary. In these visions, the writer is given inside information on the future state of the world. While some apocalyptic visions are no doubt authentic, the use of visionary features soon became a literary device used to gain authority for the work.

Apocalyptic material uses symbolism. These symbols are drawn from biblical traditions, but also from the cultural context surrounding Israel. Thus, in apocalyptic material, we see hints of Canaanite mythology, Zoroastrianism, neo-Babylonian astronomy, and Greek myth. For example, composite beasts, including dragons, are a staple of apocalyptic writing.

How should one interpret apocalyptic literature? One can say many things, but three items are worth highlighting here. First, the original readers of apocalyptic literature knew what they were reading. It made sense to them. Any interpretation of apocalyptic literature that involves helicopters or computer chips is reading things into the text that simply are not there. Second, this genre follows a set of conventions. The best way to understand these conventions is to read broadly in the literature. Many popular treatises on Daniel and Revelation, and so-called prophecy conferences, are often unaware of, or choose to ignore, the noncanonical literature. Knowledge of this literature gives insight into these conventions. Third, while many of the images in apocalyptic literature are stock images and have direct meaning that the ancient reader understood, other elements simply give color to the images. In other words, not every detail needs to be interpreted.

■ The New Testament

The Gospels and Acts

Much of what we said about the Hebrew Bible is intuitively understood by most Christians. Thus rarely does one find Christians building a parapet around their house, in spite of the injunction in Deuteronomy 22:8. Nor do Christian parents routinely kill their children for disrespect, though they may have felt that way at times, in keeping with the passage in Deuteronomy 21:18–21.

In the New Testament, the issue is not as clear. One needs only to think back on the popularity of WWJD (What would Jesus do?) paraphernalia that was very popular in the late 1990s. The implication of these various and sundry bracelets, bookmarks, Bible covers, and miscellaneous materials was that one simply had to ask, "What would Jesus do?" in order to solve all questions of behavior. While this is certainly commendable in some situations, it probably is not a good idea to make a lifestyle of it. It would simply cause a great deal of confusion, and you might be put in jail if you routinely walked around spitting on the ground and making mud globs to put in the eyes of the blind as Jesus did (John 9:6).

The stories about Jesus in the Gospels are just that—stories about Jesus. Why were they told? To look at each story and ask this question is beyond the scope of this book. One school of biblical interpretation, form criticism, does just that. Form critics look at the individual stories in the Gospels and determine if a story was used for evangelism, missionary teaching, discipline, instruction, encouragement, or various other activities.

The evangelists themselves, particularly Luke and John, give some indication of why they tell particular stories. In Luke's introduction (Luke 1:1–4), the author tells Theophilus, his benefactor, that he is writing "an orderly account . . . so that you may know the truth concerning the things about which you have been instructed." The writer of John tells his readers that he writes "so that you may come to believe that Jesus is the Messiah, the Son of God, and that through believing you may have life in his name" (John 20:31). Thus we see that Luke writes his Gospel for further instruction in the truth, while John writes to bring "belief."

The stories in the Gospels were originally passed on orally. At a later period of time, the stories were collected and put into an arrangement in order to convey the author's intent. Again, just because Jesus did something does not necessarily mean that the contemporary Christian should do what Jesus did.

The other primary type of material in the Gospels is the "sayings" of Jesus. Multiple volumes have been written categorizing these various sayings. Jesus primarily spoke in parables. A parable is simply a story with a point, often a single point. Examples of parables are the lost sheep (Luke 15:3–7), the lost son (Luke 15:11–32), the workers in the vineyard (Luke 20:9–19), and the rich man and Lazarus (Luke 16:19–31). Jesus also spoke using other literary forms such as metaphor, simile, similitudes (extended similes), proverbs, and allegories. A common problem of interpretation arises when a person reads a parable as an allegory. The classic example of this is Augustine's interpretation of the "good Samaritan." Augustine interprets the Samaritan as Adam. Jerusalem represents the heavenly city. Jericho represents the moon, which is to be understood as immortality. The thieves are the devil and his angels. The thieves strip the man of potential immortality by encouraging him to sin—and so it goes. Augustine's interpretation, however, tells us far more about Augustine's imagination and his own moral struggles than about the meaning of the original text.

The book of Acts is similar in many ways to the Gospels. What is interesting about the narrative of Acts is that roughly half of the material is in the form of speeches. Biblical scholars analyze other types of history writing of the period and are influenced by the work of the historian Thucydides (ca. 460–400 BCE). Thucydides makes a statement about methodology in his work *History of the Peloponnesian War*. He states:

> I have found it difficult to remember the precise words used in the speeches which I listened to myself and my various informants have experienced the same difficulty; so my method has been, while keeping as closely as possible to the general sense of the words that were actually used, to make the speakers say what, in my opinion, was called for by each situation.[2]

Bruce Metzger summarizes interpretation of Acts from a similar standpoint:

> In short, the speeches in Acts are literary masterpieces and deserve the most careful attention from the historian and the literary analyst. Those that occur in the "we" sections may embody notes made by Luke at the time; others are no doubt based on information derived from eyewitnesses whom Luke sought out as informants; still other speeches may well be Luke's own free composition, drawn up in accord with what he judged to be appropriate for the occasion.[3]

Acts, then, is history-writing with a purpose. The arrangement of the material is not necessarily chronological, but theological. It is best understood when one attempts to understand Luke's purpose in arranging the material as he has.

2. Thucydides, *History of the Peloponnesian War* 1.22, trans. Rex Warner (Baltimore: Viking Penguin, 1980), 47.
3. Bruce M. Metzger, *The New Testament: Its Background, Growth, and Content*, 2nd ed. (Nashville: Abingdon, 1990), 177.

The Letters of Paul and the General Letters

The letters of Paul are in some ways the easiest works to understand, but in other ways they are some of the hardest. They are letters, but they are not written to us. Contemporary Christians often use Paul's letters for explicit moral instruction. Again, sometimes this works fine, while at other times following an instruction in one of Paul's letters would simply be silly. So what can we say about Paul's letters? To begin with, we can say that Paul's letters are just that—letters. Paul wrote many letters to individuals and to churches. Some of these letters were collected and later included in what we call the New Testament, but others were not. We know, for example, that Paul probably wrote at least four letters to the church in Corinth since he makes reference in what we call 1 Corinthians to a previous letter (1 Cor. 5:9). Paul also makes reference to a previous letter in what we call 2 Corinthians (2 Cor. 7:8), though he clearly does not have what we call 1 Corinthians in mind.

How should we understand these letters? What surprises many students of the Bible is that Paul never set out to write Scripture—that is, sacred writings. He did not decide one day to write the Bible. He wrote his letters to address current issues in the churches of his day.

Let us briefly consider the situation in Galatia. Paul had visited a group of churches in the locality of "Galatia." The exact location is a matter of debate, but these churches were likely in the south central part of what is known today as Turkey. Paul had preached the gospel saying that those who trust in what God had done in Jesus would be put into a covenantal relationship with him—they would be "justified" (Gal. 2:16). He was clear that these people did not need to get circumcised, one of the requirements of the Jewish law. Later missionaries came in and preached that faith was great, but that the Galatians needed to complete themselves and get circumcised. Paul heard about this and wrote to the Galatians, telling them: "Just say no!"

What is the point? Paul's letter to the Galatians was not written to *us*. He was writing to the Galatians. The advice and instruction that he gives to the Galatian Christians is advice to them and may or may not be relevant to us. As such, Paul's letters are not eternally valid theological propositions or chapters in a theological argument. This statement alone often causes grief among shocked pious college students who have been raised to believe that Paul's letters are "the Word of God." But do not head for the exits yet! Paul's letters may contain eternally valid theological propositions, though that is a matter of interpretation. The reader must recognize, however, that calling something an eternally valid theological truth is making a faith statement. It is not something that a student of the Bible can either prove or disprove. Thus one might affirm that Paul's statement in Romans 5:6, that Christ "died for the ungodly," is true. At the same time, few Christians have felt obliged to search for Paul's cloak at Troas (2 Tim. 4:13), recognizing that this exhortation is addressed only to the original reader and has no bearing on any of us today.

It is important to know a little about first-century writing practices in the ancient Roman Empire. Letter writers in the first century, just like letter writers of today, followed certain conventions. Sensitivity to those conventions aids in the interpretation of the letter. It was common practice in a first-century letter, for example, to include a thanksgiving after the opening salutation. Paul himself routinely followed this practice. Thus we see in Romans, Paul writes, "First, I thank my God through Jesus Christ for all of you" (Rom. 1:8). While writing to the Galatians, however, he eliminates the customary thanksgiving. He clearly is not very thankful when he is writing.

Within the letter we can make other observations about genre. Some years ago, I heard a children's sermon where the pastor asked: "Boys and girls, what is the fruit of the spirit?" Enthusiastic responses followed with the usual answers: love, joy, and peace. One little boy said, "Honesty." This caught the pastor off guard, and she responded, "Well, honesty is a good thing, but it's not a fruit of the spirit." I was sitting in the pew listening to this, and my immediate internal reaction was, "Yes it is!" How so? Honesty does not occur on the list. Again, this involves understanding the genre.

Paul's letters typically included five parts:

1. salutation,
2. thanksgiving,
3. body,
4. paraenetical (or advisory) section, and
5. conclusion.

In the paraenetical section of Paul's letters, he includes three types of materials:

1. advice specific to the community,
2. maxims, and
3. vice and virtue lists.

Let us explore these in some detail. Advice specific to the community is just that. These are instructions to a particular group of people at a particular time in history, and they may have no necessary relevance to us. For example, Paul urges Euodia and Syntyche to be of the same mind in the Lord (Phil. 4:2). We would probably have a hard time even finding ladies named Euodia or Syntyche, though we could probably agree that "being of the same mind" is a good thing. However, I doubt if too many people have lost sleep over Paul's injunction to bring a cloak to Troas.

The second type of material is maxims. Maxims are short sayings that tend not to be bound by time or culture. "Let love be genuine," for example, does not require interpretation (Rom. 12:9). This is not a hard saying to understand, though it certainly may be difficult to do at times. Mark Twain, for example, is widely attributed to have said, "It ain't those parts of the Bible that I can't understand that bother me, it is the parts that I do understand."

The third type of material Paul includes is vice and virtue lists. They served to instill in the readers' minds what proper behavior looks like. Vice and virtue lists were a popular teaching tool among the philosophers of Paul's day. I grew up with a vice list: "You don't smoke, drink, dance, or chew." My children also picked up a vice list from their friends, "No fighting, no biting, no hitting, no spitting, and no bad words." These lists serve to ingrain into our minds the sorts of behavior that are not acceptable to our parents and our faith community.

Paul used these lists in the same way. The last element of the "works of the flesh" (Gal. 5:19–21) is "things like these." In like manner, the last element of the fruit of the Spirit (Gal. 5:22–23) is "such things." Paul's point about "fruit" is not that "love, joy, peace, patience, kindness, generosity, faithfulness, gentleness, and self-control" are all there is. Rather, the person who walks by the Spirit will bear fruit that looks like this. Thus if you asked Paul, "Paul, is honesty a fruit of the spirit?" he would probably respond in the affirmative.

Pretty much all of what has been said about the letters of Paul is true of the General Letters also. Each of them has a particular audience. The instruction given in them, as a result, may or may not be relevant for contemporary Christians.

The Revelation of John

In the earlier section on apocalyptic literature, we gave some broad outlines about the nature of apocalyptic and some clues to its interpretation. Those also apply to the book of Revelation. John was writing a letter to Christians in Asia Minor who were facing persecution. The overarching theme is clear: God wins! The images would have been clear to the original recipients. The beast (the Roman Empire) is under the control of the dragon (Satan), but to those who endure salvation will come (Rev. 13).

It would take far too long to go into particular details about interpreting the book of Revelation. However, we should keep in mind that, no matter how literally, allegorically, or anagogically (in an eternal, metaphysical, or eschatological way) one approaches the interpretation of it, the book remains highly symbolic. We must avoid the false dichotomy that says Revelation must be interpreted either literally or symbolically. Everyone interprets it, at least in some measure, symbolically. For example, even those who claim most to interpret Revelation literally and as predictive of future historical events may relish in speculating about the symbolic identity of the "beast," which is not thought to be the Roman Empire (Rev. 13:1); the symbolic meaning of the beast's number—666 (Rev. 13:18); and the beast's relationship to or identity as the "antichrist" (1 John 2:18–22; 2 John 7). Christians throughout church history have speculated about these topics, accusing countless popes, kings, politicians (usually from a rival political party), and other religious figures of being the antichrist. Such speculation may sound harmless, but it has led to gross caricatures of individuals and groups of individuals, resulting in bigotry and persecution that has no resemblance to biblical Christianity. Thus extreme care must be taken in interpreting apocalyptic literature, and people must refrain from wanting to know more about the future than what God has revealed.

■ Check Your Assumptions

So, if genre recognition is so important for meaning, then how do we learn to do it? The topic cannot be exhausted in one chapter. Part of the skill in genre recognition comes from simple common sense and from reading broadly. We noted earlier that apocalyptic literature is widely misunderstood because interpreters are simply unaware of the breath of apocalyptic literature. Entire books have been written on genre recognition, so some time spent with those books might be useful.

If there is one point to emphasize in genre recognition, then it would be to check your assumptions. What do you assume to be true? All of us have assumptions or presuppositions. They are a necessary part of life. Everyday decisions are so much easier because we have hundreds of assumptions that we make based on our previous experience. "Heuristics" is the fancy name for this sort of behavior—namely, the commonsense steps people take in their learning, decision making, and problem solving. When we see a traffic light go from green to yellow, we assume that shortly thereafter it will go to red. All of our lives we experienced this and rightfully conclude that it will happen again. Thus, in most parts of the country, when people see a yellow light, they slow down and prepare to stop in anticipation of the red light. (However, I have lived in Southern California for almost twenty years and notice that some folks routinely accelerate when they see a yellow light!)

Assumptions are absolutely necessary, yet sometimes they need to be questioned. When I was a child, growing up in church, I assumed that everything I read in the Bible was "literally" true. Thus, if I was reading the book of Amos and came to the phrase, "Thus says the Lord," I would assume that God had audibly spoken to Amos, and he was simply repeating to the people what God had told him (for example, Amos 1:3, 6, 9). Today, if one of my students walks up to me and says, "I feel like God is telling me to . . . [fill in the blank]," then I do not assume any audible voice. Rather, I assume that the student feels some sort of inner desire for action. If the actions seem reasonable, then I might assume that the desire comes from God. I am pietistic enough to believe that God does sometimes work inwardly in people to direct them on some course of action. At the same time, I have been around long enough to know that often God gets blamed for lots of selfish or simply stupid courses of action.

Ken Fisher has written a book on behavioral finance titled *The Only Three Questions That Count*, which asks three questions relevant to this topic. The questions are:

- What do you believe that is actually false?
- What can you fathom that others find unfathomable?
- What the heck is my brain doing to blindside me now?

Fisher's goal is to help investors purchase stocks that others miss. Yet his discussion is a fascinating review of how we make incorrect decisions every day based on incomplete or inaccurate knowledge, and how stepping back to ask these questions will help us make better decisions.

I regularly tell a story of a 1953 study done at Yale University. In this study, students were asked how many of them had long-term goals. The response was 3 percent. Twenty years later, the same students were surveyed, and it was discovered that the 3 percent who had goals were happier and more productive than the 97 percent who had not set long-term goals. In fact, as the story goes, the net worth of the 3 percent who had long-term goals exceeded the net worth of the other 97 percent combined.

It is a great story, is it not? Well, it did not happen. I was sitting in church a few years ago when my pastor debunked this story. He said it was made up. Since I am an academic by nature, I went home and did what my students do—I did a Google search. To my great disappointment, I found out that the story was urban legend. Lawrence Tabak traced the history of the story, and he argues that the story was told by many motivational speakers, many attributing the story to other motivational speakers in a circular fashion. Thus

Tony Robbins attributed the story to Brian Tracy, who attributed it to Zig Ziglar, who in turn attributed it back to Tony Robbins.

I had told this story in class many times and had believed it was true. I had acted as if it were true. I think my life was actually improved because I believed it to be true, yet all those years I had believed something to be true that was actually false. Information such as this is painful to process, as our brains are resistant to change, and we do not want to believe things that cause a paradigm shift. Nevertheless, sometimes a paradigm shift is the only way we can accommodate new information that comes to us. Fisher's book is worth the read, but simply reflecting on his questions will greatly aid you as you check your assumptions.

What is the point? Check your assumptions. Do you have an accurate sense of the biblical genre that you want to interpret? Do not be misled by false assumptions about the kind (or type) of literature you are trying to understand. Does Jesus *really* live in your heart? Well, spiritually yes, but not literally.

4

Historical Context

If understanding the genre is the most important element of biblical interpretation, understanding the historical context is a close second. The two cannot really be separated, as certain genres were only used at particular times in history. Thus one can understand the Revelation of John only if one recognizes that the genre of the revelation is a combination of letter, apocalypse, and prophetic literature. But one must also understand the historical context.

What do we mean by historical context? Anybody who has ever gone to a children's Christmas play knows that King Herod was not the person you would want to be married to or have as your father, since most of his wives and children ended up dead. Most Christians also have a reasonable idea of what type of attire a Roman soldier wore. Hollywood has done more than its share of first-century movies, and while they do not always get the facts straight, they usually look pretty good. And every fifth-grade church kid knows that if you want to be a shepherd in the Christmas play you need to have a bathrobe. Politics in the first century and the clothing styles of shepherds are elements of what we mean by historical context.

On occasion, I will get a student paper that contains the expression "Bible times." I always circle this expression and note that it is vague and unhelpful. There is no such time as "Bible times," since the Bible was composed over millennia. It is important to pay attention to the exact time of events, if they can be discerned. Contemporary readers will often compress the time horizon of ancient texts, due to the distance we have from the events. However, Jerusalem in the year 30 (during time of relative peace) was significantly different than it was in 66 (during Roman oppression), just as the United States is different today than it was in 1970 (or any other country in a thirty- to fifty-year period). Things change.

■ Historical Overviews

Every introduction to the Bible begins with a general historical overview. Understanding political history, for example, helps us to understand the broader political context and people's attitudes. Why is political history important? Significant people and events shape the culture. For example, Americans' views toward government were profoundly changed in the early 1970s after the Vietnam War and the events of Watergate. Trust in the government was profoundly shaken. Consequently, Christians today have differing views toward political authority than did their parents or grandparents. While some still have a great deal of trust in the government, many others are quite skeptical.

Diverse attitudes among Christians toward the government existed in the first century also. The apostle Paul, on the one hand, could write of the emperor Nero in the mid-50s CE that "those authorities that exist have been instituted by God" (Rom. 13:1). Paul's positive attitude toward the state reflects both his general Jewish understanding that the state as a whole is beneficent and the fact that Nero's leadership in his early days was quite promising. Paul lived during the *Pax Romana* (Latin "Peace of Rome") and was free to travel as a citizen of the Roman Empire and could even appeal to the emperor to save his own life (Acts 25:11).

John, on the other hand, writing toward the end of the first century during the reign of the Roman Emperor Domitian, sees the government as a beast under the control of Satan (Rev. 12:18–13:18). Christians were being hauled before the courts and put to death for their faith. A very important letter from the early second century illustrates this point. Pliny, the governor of Bithynia, writes to the emperor Trajan around 112. In this letter, Pliny asks the emperor for his advice on how to deal with Christians. Pliny tells Trajan his current practice:

> In the meantime, this is the procedure I have followed, in the cases of those brought before me as Christians. I asked them whether they were Christians. If they admitted it, I asked them a second and a third time, threatening them with execution. Those who remained obdurate I ordered to be executed, for I was in no doubt, whatever it was which they were confessing, that their obstinacy and their inflexible stubbornness should at any rate be punished. Others similarly lunatic were Roman citizens, so I registered them as due to be sent back to Rome. Later in the course of the hearings, as usually happens, the charge rippled outwards, and more examples appeared. An anonymous document was published containing the names of many. Those who denied that they were or had been Christians and called upon the gods after me, and with incense and wine made obeisance to your statue, which I had ordered to be brought in together with images of the gods for this very purpose, and who moreover cursed Christ (those who are truly Christian cannot, it is said, be forced to do any of these things), I ordered to be acquitted. Others who were named by an informer

stated that they were Christians and then denied it. They said that in fact they had been, but had abandoned their allegiance, some three years previously, some more years earlier, and one or two as many as twenty years before. All these as well worshipped your statue and images of the gods, and blasphemed Christ.[1]

This letter gives tremendous insight into the situation facing John's readers. Some Christians had denied the faith, according to Pliny, as much as "twenty years" earlier than the time of Pliny's writing. Thus the apostasy that Pliny mentions occurred during the reign of Domitian, who ruled from 81–96.

Clearly the view of the government that both Paul and John exhibit is influenced by their historical context, and interpreters take those contexts into account when they interpret the text for the modern reader. On the one hand, when the government is fulfilling its proper function, it is the "servant of God" and will "execute wrath on the wrongdoer" (Rom. 13:4). On the other hand, when the government exalts itself, grasps too much power, and has its citizens bowing down to serve it, then the government truly can be seen as a beast (Rev. 13). Huge interpretive errors, and major tragedies, have resulted when Christians have used these texts in inappropriate ways. Some German Christians under Hitler, for example, felt it was their obligation to serve the government, not realizing that the government in control was much closer to the government in Revelation 13 than that in Romans 13. Christians will disagree on their individual responses to government authority and to how expansive the role of government should be in everyday life, but there can be broad agreement that there is a legitimate role for government. Likewise, it can be clearly recognized that sometimes governments go beyond their legitimate function. Then, like Peter and John, Christians must declare: "We must obey God rather than any human authority" (Acts 5:29).

We have seen how the writers' context can influence their attitude, but it is also true that the recipients' context can influence the writers as well; the writers change language to suit the audience. Paul's letter to the church in Philippi, for example, illustrates this well.

The church at Philippi was the first church that Paul had founded in Europe. During his time there, he had faced some difficulties. We do not know all the problems that took place after that, but Paul was now in prison and the Christians at Philippi had sent Paul a gift through Epaphroditus (Phil. 4:18), who had been ill while staying with Paul. He wrote to the Christians at Philippi to thank them and to encourage them. What is interesting is that Philippi was a Roman colony, so Paul's language contains numerous terms that would

---

1. Pliny the Younger, "Gaius Pliny to the Emperor Trajan" X.96, in *Complete Letters*, trans. P. G. Walsh, Oxford World's Classics (Oxford: Oxford University Press, 2006), 278.

be immediately recognizable to that context. Thus Paul tells the Christians at Philippi to "conduct themselves as good citizens" (Greek *politeuesthe*; Phil. 1:27 author's translation) because ultimately their "citizenship" (*politeuma*; Phil. 3:20) is in heaven.

It is important, then, for the interpreter to have a broad understanding of the political history as well as an adequate grasp of the immediate historical context for proper interpretation. It is also important to know how events of the past influence the events of the present.

The casual reader of the New Testament might wonder why issues of the Jewish law were so controversial in the first century. Jesus, for example, routinely raised the ire of the Pharisees over such simple actions as allowing his disciples to pick and eat a few heads of grain on the Sabbath (Mark 2:23). Paul's letter to the Galatian Christians instructs them to refuse the Jewish rite of circumcision, and the narrative of Acts also wrestles with the question of what gentiles must do to become people of faith. What is behind the intense controversy we see in these texts?

We can only sketch this in broad outlines. A casual read of the Hebrew Bible will let the reader see that, throughout the period of the monarchy (after King David), the average person who lived in Israel did not take the law too seriously. The prophetic literature is full of failed attempts by the prophets to convince the people to follow the law. Samaria (capital of the northern kingdom of Israel) fell to the Assyrians in 722 BCE, and Jerusalem (capital of the southern kingdom of Judah) fell to the Babylonians in 587, after which the elite of Jerusalem were carried away to Babylon in what is known as the exile. The exile was formative, since the people had lost the primary institutions that were dear to them. God had promised Abraham the land (Gen. 12), but they no longer possessed the land. God had promised that a son of David would rule on the throne forever (2 Sam. 7), but Jerusalem had been destroyed. The temple, which represented the very presence of God, had been destroyed as well (1 Kings 8:12–21).

The three institutions that gave the people their identity—land, king, and temple—were all gone. This crisis caused the people to refocus on the law, which now became central to their faith. This focus on the law became even more intense during the Hellenistic period, with its intense persecution. Antiochus IV (ruled 175–164 BCE), in an effort to promote loyalty, banned circumcision and forced the Jewish people to eat pork that had been offered to idols. When the people resisted, Antiochus responded with intense persecution. As is often the case, the intense persecution by Antiochus resulted in the Jewish people intensifying their focus on the law, and particularly on those items that Antiochus had made illegal: circumcision and food laws.

In many ways, the persecution under Antiochus could be compared to the American Revolution. Just as Americans value freedom as one of their highest virtues, so also the Jewish people in the first century valued observance of the law. It is difficult for the casual reader of the New Testament to appreciate this passion. Time spent on some of the literature of the period, such as 1 and 2 Maccabees, will greatly aid the modern reader of the Bible in gaining a sense of the importance of this issue.

In addition, a good student of the Bible should use maps of different time periods in biblical history. Tracing the journeys of characters in the Bible is a great aid to interpretation. While I am writing this chapter in Azusa, California, I know from experience that Los Angeles is much closer than New York, and that a trip to Accra, Ghana, requires a plane flight, though there would be no language barrier. As you read about wars and movements of peoples in the Bible, you should trace these on an atlas to give you an idea of the time and distances involved.

■ Understanding Historic Worldviews

Knowledge of the historical context clearly requires knowledge of political history, but it goes far beyond that. One needs to know who ruled whom, when, and under what conditions. The modern twenty-first-century reader needs to attempt to get into the thinking patterns of the biblical writers. We need to understand the worldviews of the authors.

What are a few important things to know? Obviously, the more one learns about the first century, the more one is able to understand the writings of the New Testament. Likewise, the more one knows about ancient Israel, the more one is able to understand the Old Testament. It is clearly easier to understand the New Testament than the Old Testament, since the sources are far more extant and the time frame is closer to our own.

Students of the Bible have a wealth of material available, so we will give only a few examples of things that might not appear obvious to the general reader. Historical context also includes understanding how people perceived their world. This is known as cosmology—the study of the "cosmos" or "world." Understanding how the world came into existence is known as cosmogony. It is important to realize that the cosmology of the ancient world was understood largely from a phenomenological perspective, or how it appears. Earlier in the chapter on genre, we began to describe the shape of the world in the Old Testament. Remember, this is how they described the world, or pictured the world. The writers were giving a picture of what the world looks like, just as a sunset describes what the sun appears to do every evening. The earth possessed a "dome" (or "firmament," Gen. 1:6), which would hold out the water. This dome was blue due to the water that was above it. The Hebrew term *shamaim* is typically translated "sky" or "heavens." It could refer to the immediate area just above where the birds fly (Gen. 1:20). It could also refer to the dome itself, which separated waters above from waters below (Gen. 1:8). As such, the sky had windows through which the rain could fall (Gen. 7:11). The stars were affixed to this dome (Gen. 1:15), and the heavens were also where God dwelled in the highest heaven (1 Kings 8:30). Thus "the heavens" were thought to be in layers. The earth was flat and supported by pillars. Under the earth was a pit known as Sheol. Sheol was not at all like some modern conceptions of hell. Rather, Sheol was where all the dead went when they died. Popular conceptions of the world had changed by the first century, during the time the New Testament was written. Greek influence can clearly be seen. It was commonly believed that the earth was round and surrounded by seven planets. The planets revolved around the earth in ever-increasing concentric circles. The lowest planet, the moon, had the greatest influence on human life, often exerting an evil influence.

These ideas are still with us today. Thus the English language has words such as "lunacy" and "lunatic," terms that denote a type of temporary insanity, originally thought to be brought on by phases of the moon. One can be "moon-struck," a term that may also convey romantic connotations but that originally referred to temporary insanity or epilepsy. And what about those persistent werewolf traditions? Modern folklore is still fascinated with the full moon.

It should be obvious to modern readers that we do not conceive of the shape of the world in this way. Yet knowledge of it can inform our understanding of a biblical text. For example, in 2 Corinthians 12:2, Paul states that he was caught up into the "third heaven." What does he mean by this? Paul states that he does not know if this was a visionary experience or if he was actually transported there. In any case, it should be clear that Paul was not thinking that he was floating somewhere between Venus and Mars, using our contemporary worldviews. Nor was he using one of the popular Greek worldviews of his day. Paul was a Jew, and he brought his Jewish worldview to bear. He was no doubt conceiving of the world in the fashion we often see in the Hebrew Bible, where the third heaven would have been that highest heaven—the place where God dwells. Paul clearly understands it this way. He was in God's presence.

■ Contrasting Worldviews

One must be aware of elements of the historical context that are popularly believed to be true but that clearly are not true. As we asked in the chapter on genre, what do you believe that is actually false? Jesus tells his disciples, "Indeed, it is easier for a camel to go through the eye of a needle than for someone who is rich to enter the kingdom of God" (Luke 18:25). Clearly, it is not simply difficult; it is impossible for a camel to go through the eye of a needle. This explains the disciples' bewildered response, "Then who can be saved?" (Luke 18:26). In the disciples' understanding of the world, riches were a blessing from God. This saying of Jesus presented difficulty for early interpreters, so eventually a tradition arose that there was a gate in Jerusalem called the "needle's eye." This gate supposedly was shorter than a normal gate, and a camel had to get down on its knees to go through. It is an interesting story, but it has no basis in fact. The story first appears in the late Middle Ages as an attempt to lessen the difficulty of the saying of Jesus. The point Jesus made was that it is impossible for a camel to go through an eye of a needle—but with God all things are possible.

The previous story raises another interesting question. Why does the New Testament apparently have such a negative view of wealth? How is it possible that we have sayings in Deuteronomy that talk about the lavish material blessings God will shower on his people (28:1–14), and a saying in James that states, "Is it not the rich who oppress you? Is it not they who drag you into court?" (James 2:6). These sayings appear to be almost diametrically opposed to each other. Again, knowledge of the historical context will shed light on the issue here.

In the ancient world, land was a means of wealth production. Those who controlled land controlled wealth. Thus God's promise to Abraham that he would give him land is an implicit promise to give him wealth (Gen. 12:1). Ancient societies were also dependent on the weather and were subject to devastating forces such as drought and locust plagues, but the land was foundational. Possession of the land was central to Israel's identity and understanding of its relationship to God. Possession of the land is a major theme in the book of Deuteronomy, and the books of Joshua and Judges deal extensively with this theme.

At the end of the Jewish monarchy, the book of Ezekiel wrestles with the question of the land. Ezekiel writes to a people who have been conquered and exiled from the land—a land they believed had been promised to them in perpetuity by God. One question that some were asking was, "Since we are no longer in the land that God has promised us, has God failed?" No, was Ezekiel's response. You are here because of your wickedness. Ezekiel describes God leaving the temple in a glorious chariot (Ezek. 1:4–28). Later readers were often lost in Ezekiel's imagery, since they did not understand the historical context. But Ezekiel's original readers understood his message. According to

Ezekiel, the actions in the temple were simply disgusting to God. So God took a chariot, carried by cherubs, left the temple, and went to be with his people in Babylon. The irony is clear. Cherubs, a customary part of Babylonian mythology, were believed to guard the temple of Marduk, the leader of the Babylonian pantheon. Ezekiel turns the image on its head, however, and tells his readers that these cherubs, rather than protecting Marduk, are servants of the God of Israel.

So aside from its centrality to ancient Israel's identity, what else do we need to know about land? There is a saying among folks in real estate: "God isn't making any more land." The idea here is that the supply of land is limited. There is a finite supply, and more cannot be created. Ancient economies understood this concept and lived accordingly. Since land was limited, and the land was a means of production, it was understood that goods were limited as well. This idea of limited goods lies behind the New Testament and many of the prophetic texts of the Old Testament. There was only so much to go around. So if you have the goods and I do not, the only place I can get those goods is from you. You either have to share them with me, or I may be required to take them by force.

While some people may still believe such ideas today, modern economies do not function on those principles. A fundamental principle of modern economic thought is the idea that wealth can be created by the work of the entrepreneur. One does not need land; one simply needs a good idea. The entrepreneur is the individual who takes an idea and creates wealth from it. The laptop computers we type this book on are nothing more than sand, oil, and ideas. The cases are made primarily of plastic, a petroleum product, and most of the inner workings are made of silicon—nothing more than sand. One person had an idea and was able to create plastic. Another person had an idea and was able to create glass. Still other people had ideas, and they were able to create the microchip. We still believe that certain goods are limited. Not everybody who wants a new BMW can have one. Yet we no longer conceive of land as the primary means of wealth creation. Today we understand that an entrepreneur can create wealth, out of virtually nothing. People do not need land; they need an idea.

When one reads the Bible, the idea that land was how one created wealth and how one possessed wealth needs to be kept in mind. Deuteronomy was written with the idea that the people would possess the land that God had given to them. In turn, they would leave a portion of the produce for the landless (Deut. 24:19). In this way abject poverty would be averted. When the book of James was written, however, there was a different situation. We do not know the exact historical situation behind James, but it is clear that the recipients are not part of the wealthy class. The writer tells them to make do in the situation in which they find themselves. Thus it would not be fair to take James 2:6 and make universal application that all who are rich are oppressors. The historical context does make a difference.

Understanding ancient business practices can aid in understanding the text as well. Scholars have long been perplexed by Jesus's parable of the unrighteous manager (Luke 16:1–13). There are several difficulties in understanding this passage, not least of which is Jesus's commendation of the man's actions. Recent scholarship has shed some light on this passage, though. Apparently it was a common practice for a manager to run a little business on the side. It might be similar to an auto mechanic for a major dealership offering to fix a customer's car on the weekend for less than the customer would pay at the dealership. In this case, the "rich man" would be like a bank and would provide most of the money and goods that would be lent (Luke 16:1). The manager may possibly loan some of his own goods also, at a better rate of interest than that provided by the "rich man." So, if a creditor owed "a hundred jugs of olive oil," it may be that fifty of those jugs were owed to the owner and fifty were owed to the manager (Luke 16:6). When the manager tells the creditor to "take your bill, sit down quickly, and make it fifty," he is in essence eliminating his profit but getting back what is owed to the master (Luke 16:6). The manager is now penniless, but he has settled the master's debts and made some good friends in the process.

■ Religious Environments

So politics, cosmology, and economics are important elements of understanding the ancient world. What else does one need to know? The more one knows about the religious environment, the better one is able to understand the Bible. The writers of both testaments were immersed in rich religious environments. Often deities are named, and a student can do research in a good Bible dictionary. In Leviticus 20:2, for example, the people of Israel will be punished for giving their offspring to Molech. A quick trip to the library (or a Google search) will reveal useful information about Molech and the sacrificial rituals associated with that deity. It can be a greater challenge, though, when the deity or deities are not named.

Paul has a practice of not naming the deities he confronts on a regular basis. We know that much of his critique is against the goddess religions. The goddess religions were extremely popular and widespread. Worship of a goddess probably lies behind Paul's critique in Galatians 4:25, when he talks about Hagar being a mountain in Arabia. It is an allusion to the goddess worship that occurred on the mountain. Ancient temples were typically located on the highest point in the area. Paul's comment in Galatians 5:12, "I wish those who unsettle you would castrate themselves," is not simply a sarcastic comment on his part. Rather, the priests of the goddess religion practiced ritual castration in public festivals. Paul is simply warning the Galatians that, if they accept circumcision, then it is a rejection of faith in Jesus Christ. It is no different from going back to the religions out of which they came. Goddess worship probably also lies behind Philippians 3:2, where Paul warns of the mutilators of the flesh. It is also behind Paul's scathing critique of idolatry in Romans 1. These goddess festivals were public events, and the ancient writer Lucian notes that these festivals involved hundreds of worshipers at a time.

In Acts 14:8–18, we read a fascinating story where Paul and Barnabas are on a journey through Asia Minor. Paul heals a man in Lystra (Acts 14:8–10). Immediately the people begin to worship Paul and Barnabas as the Greek gods Zeus and Hermes. Why is this? The Latin poet Ovid tells a story about the gods Zeus and Hermes that lends insight into the narrative in Acts.

Ovid's story is worth telling. One day Zeus and Hermes were wandering through the land dressed as ordinary travelers. They wandered from house to house looking for hospitality. They found none. As the gods grew increasingly angry at the selfishness of the people, they came across a small cottage on the outskirts of the village. They knocked on the door and were greeted by an old man in tattered rags. When the gods explained their desire for food and lodging, the old man, Philemon by name, quickly invited them in. Philemon introduced the gods to his wife, Baucis. Philemon and Baucis busied themselves feeding the gods from their meager stores. As they sat down to eat, it soon became apparent to the elderly couple that no matter how much they ate, or how much they drank, the pitcher never emptied and the plate was always full. Upon the realization, Philemon and Baucis murmured a prayer to the gods for forgiveness for the meager meal and for their unpreparedness. Baucis told her husband, Philemon, to fetch the goose to kill, but when Philemon tried to catch it, the goose ran to Zeus for safety. At this the gods declared, "We are gods, and this neighborhood will receive punishment for its impiety, but you will be spared if you follow us up the hill." When they had all walked up the hill, they looked back and saw that the whole area was flooded. The humble cottage had been turned into a beautiful temple. The gods also granted to Baucis and Philemon their request that they would grow old and die together. When the couple reached their time to die, one of them was turned into an oak tree, and the other was turned into a linden tree near the temple.

The story is entertaining, but this was reality to the people that Paul and Barnabas met in Lystra. In their understanding, disaster had happened when the gods were not received properly. They wanted to make sure it did not happen again. Barnabas was treated as Zeus, the chief god of the pantheon, while Paul was treated as Hermes, the messenger god. It is also important to know that the word commonly translated "angel" in English translations (Greek *angellos*) is also often translated as "messenger." This lies behind Galatians 1:8 and 4:14 as well, which talk about Paul and others (including angels) as those who proclaim the gospel. Of course, those who proclaim the gospel may pervert it, and such false prophets are accursed.

Historical Context of Sickness and Evil

An area of historical context worth noting relates to the problem of sickness and evil. We are wading into some controversial areas here, but a brief overview can be a helpful window into the types of issues facing Christians as they read the Bible. Demonic activity in the New Testament is largely connected with sickness. Thus demons cause people to be mute (Matt. 9:32–34; 12:22). They cause blindness (Matt. 12:22–24). They cripple people (Luke 13:10–17). Even asceticism is blamed on demons (Matt. 11:18).

One of the more interesting stories is about an epileptic boy whom Jesus healed (Matt. 17:14–21). The term translated "epilepsy" is literally "to be moonstruck," since it was believed in the ancient world that epilepsy was associated with the powers of the moon. The story is interesting because what today we might think of as a disease due to a brain injury is connected with a demon that is also connected with an astrological phenomenon.

How do Christians deal with this? Well, it depends a great deal on your assumptions. Some look at the demonic activity as simply part of the ancient worldview that existed in the first century and attribute stories that deal with demonic activity to sickness, including mental illness. Others look at the demonic activity as being responsible for every event out there. So, in addition to the proverbial "demon rum," there is a demon for just about any activity that is considered illicit. Still others would attempt to separate what they considered a "regular" illness from one caused by demonic activity. As we said, this is a controversial area. From a purely pragmatic standpoint, though, most Christians, given a perceived physical illness, make their first call to the doctor rather than to a pastor, priest, or exorcist.

Where does evil come from? Again, views in the Bible changed over time. In some of the older texts of the Hebrew Bible, we see that both good and evil come from Yahweh. Thus we read that God sends an evil spirit to torment Saul (1 Sam. 16:14). The solution to this is not exorcism but acquiring the services of David to play music so that the evil spirit will depart from

Saul (1 Sam. 16:14–24). Likewise, God is angry with Israel. Consequently, he incites David to do evil by imposing a census on the people (2 Sam. 24:1). God is also the father of falsehood, as he puts lying spirits into the mouth of the prophets (1 Kings 22:23).

Historical Context of Satan

In later texts, we see that God acquires a helper, so to speak, to do his dirty work. This is where the "accuser" enters the picture; this "opposer" or "adversary" is called a "satan." Understand, though, that "satan" is not yet a proper name. "Satan" is simply a Hebrew word, which is not translated but transliterated. A "satan" is simply an "adversary." This adversary may be a human adversary or, as we shall see, a member of the divine court. We see, for example, that David is a potential "adversary" against the Philistines (1 Sam. 29:4). Some of David's political opponents are "adversaries" against him (2 Sam. 19:22). Other humans are referred to as "adversaries" as well (1 Kings 5:4; 11:14). These are all cases in which the "satan" or "adversary" is simply an opponent.

At other times, "satan" is used of a divine being. This divine being is a helper to God as he functions as a prosecuting attorney or sergeant at arms. In Job 1–2, we see that "satan" is a member of the divine court (Job 1:6), who is responsible to make certain that God's people are not getting off too easy (see also Zech. 3:1–7). At times, we see that the "satan" has the exact same duties as God himself. The classic example of this is in 1 Chronicles 21:1, where "satan" incites David to perform a census on Israel. The careful reader will have noted that this is a parallel passage to 2 Samuel 24:1, mentioned earlier. In the Samuel passage, Yahweh is the source of evil. In the Chronicles passage, "satan" is the source of evil. They have exactly the same job! In fact, they are the same. Is it God, or is it satan? Remember, "satan" is here portrayed as working for God. The "satan" has not yet gone freelance.

Another fascinating passage is found in Numbers 22. Here we read that Balak, a Moabite king, seeks to acquire the services of Balaam, a noted Babylonian sorcerer, to come and curse the Israelites. Balaam sets out on his way but is hindered by a divine messenger: "God's anger was kindled because he was going, and the angel of the Lord took his stand in the road as his adversary" (22:22). The English reader may not see that the divine messenger here is identified as an "angel" of the Lord as well as a "satan" (translated as "adversary").

By the time of the New Testament, the adjective "satan" had become a proper name for a personal being: Satan. Evil and sickness are still sometimes attributed to God, as the disciples' question in John 9:2 reveals, "Rabbi, who sinned, this man or his parents, that he was born blind?" By and large, however, Satan is now seen as God's ultimate adversary.

The point of this brief sketch about "satan" is simply to show that theological ideas change over time, so it is important to learn about their historical context. This is true about the problem of evil, the afterlife, and other ideas too numerous to mention. The Bible is not a static map of theological ideas. Views changed over time and were influenced by the surrounding cultures. How do Christians deal with this? Some scholars will talk about the development or evolution of religious ideas. Others will use the term "progressive revelation"; the idea is that God revealed himself gradually over time to his people. Hebrews 1:1–2 would be used to support this idea: "Long ago God spoke to our ancestors in many and various ways by the prophets, but in these last days he has spoken to us by a Son." The point is that the revelation in Jesus is more complete than that which had come before. So be aware of the differences in historical context, however you account for them.

■ Problem of Mistranslations

These are only a few examples in which knowledge of the historical context can aid understanding of the Bible. With some biblical texts, the historical context is difficult to pin down. At other times, the historical context can be known with relative certainty. The more one can learn about the historical context in all its facets, the better one will understand the text.

When we discuss historical context, we are usually looking at the historical context of the original authors and how that influenced them. Sometimes a lack of knowledge of historical context influences a translation as well. The term "Jehovah," for example, has an interesting history and came about due to misunderstandings of translation processes. Those of you who grew up on the King James Version of the Bible learned "Jehovah" as God's name. But let us be clear, "Jehovah" is just one big translation mistake (please wait for the context of this accusation before you condemn us as heretics). The name of God in the Old Testament is YHWH, which represents four Hebrew letters transcribed into Roman letters, also known as the *Tetragrammaton* (Greek "a word having four letters"). This word is typically translated in English Bibles as "LORD" and should probably be spelled in English as "Yahweh." So how did we get from Yahweh to Jehovah? There are several things to know. Hebrew, the language of the Old Testament, was originally written with only consonants, no vowels. Pious Jews did not say God's name, since one of the easiest ways to not take God's name in vain was simply to not say it at all. Rather than saying God's name, they would simply say "the name," "the blessed," or even "heaven." In Matthew's Gospel, for example, the term "kingdom of heaven" is a pious way of saying "kingdom of God" (for example, see "kingdom of heaven" in Matt. 5:3, 10, 19, 20; 7:21 and "kingdom of God" in Matt. 6:33; 12:28). A pious Jew would also often say the word "Adonai," which was the generic term for "lord" or "master," whenever they came across YHWH in the biblical text. As time went on, this practice became fixed. When reading the Bible, Jews would see the word YHWH, God's name, but they would instead say "Adonai."

In the eighth or ninth century BCE, the biblical texts were being copied by Jewish scribes called Masoretes, who were scribes and scholars located in Israel. Hebrew was no longer the native tongue, and Jewish students needed help to learn how to pronounce Hebrew. The Masoretes developed a system of vowel points that were written under the consonants. As part of this practice, when they came across the word YHWH, they would put the vowels for the word "Adonai," since the practice had become customary. They would see "YHWH" but say "Adonai."

When the Bible was translated into English, the translators did not understand this convention. The translators saw the consonants of God's name "YHWH," and they combined them with the vowels from Adonai and created the term "Jehovah." So that is how we can say Jehovah was simply one big translation mistake. Because the King James Version was such a popular and enduring translation, the term "Jehovah" is still widely used today.

■ Archaeology and the Bible

A tremendous aid to learning about the historical context of the Bible is the modern development of archaeology. Modern archaeology came of age during the nineteenth century, largely motivated by those who wanted to find archaeological evidence that confirmed information in the Bible. William Albright was a leader of the twentieth-century biblical archaeological movement. He became known to the public largely through authenticating the Dead Sea Scrolls in 1948. Archaeology employs many methods of investigation, including surveyance of ancient biblical sites, excavation of artifacts, and analysis of the data collected. In addition, archaeology makes use of anthropology, art history, ethnology, geography, geology, linguistics, and other scientific disciplines.

Archaeological discoveries have been a great boon for biblical studies, as they have at times been used to corroborate texts in the Bible. For example, discovery of the Dead Sea Scrolls showed that the biblical texts that had been copied over the years were strikingly true to the older texts. The Dead Sea Scrolls represent Hebrew texts more than one thousand years older than other texts available, with remarkable consistency between them. Archaeologists also found a stone fragment (called a "stele") in northern Israel with an inscription that mentions King David's dynasty—"the house of David." It provides the oldest confirmation of people and events in the Bible from a nonbiblical source (ca. ninth century BCE). To these examples, others could be added: Caiaphas's ossuary, or stone bone box (ca. first century), a Pontius Pilate inscription (ca. first century), a Galilean boat (ca. second century), and so on. Perhaps some of the most helpful insights from archaeology have been information about the day-to-day lives of people who lived during the various times and places mentioned in the Bible. This includes information about people and cultures in lands surrounding Israel, such as the Chaldeans, Canaanites, Egyptians, Hittites, Assyrians, Babylonians, Greeks, Romans, and so on.

However, archaeological studies can be a two-edged sword. While they may serve to corroborate the trustworthiness of biblical texts in certain cases, archaeological studies may challenge them in others. For example, excavation and historical data has challenged the numbers of Israelites (and others) who participated in the exodus from Egypt, as well as when or whether the event occurred at all. Details of the Israelite conquest of such cities as Ai and Hebron have been challenged based on disconfirming archaeological evidence. Here biblical scholars who use archaeology are often selective in their use of the data. Archaeology (and other scientific disciplines), for example, suggests that people—Homo sapiens—have been around for up to two hundred thousand years, while other scientific disciplines suggest that the universe is approximately fourteen billion years old. Some Christian interpreters of the Bible would argue that God's creation is only six thousand to ten thousand years of age, though others accept the idea of an old earth, created by God. So, as we see, archaeology can be a two-edged sword. Finally, the term "biblical archaeology" is rejected by some contemporary archaeologists who study the Bible. They argue that archaeology is a discipline in its own right and that it is a mistake to combine these two disciplines.

During the past two centuries, many Christians enthusiastically welcomed archaeology as proof positive of the historical information contained in the Bible. While notable corroborating evidence has been found, Christians should be wary about placing too much faith in archaeology. Archaeological evidence, after all, must be analyzed and—indeed—interpreted. Such interpretations may read into the evidence more than the evidence can prove, historically speaking, and can be pro-Bible or anti-Bible. After all, archaeological artifacts can communicate only so much with regard to authenticating or contradicting biblical data. So critical thinking must always be used in analyzing, evaluating, and interpreting data, and people ought not to be Pollyannaish, or unrealistically optimistic, in their expectations of archaeology. Despite these cautions, archaeology remains an invaluable resource for investigating aspects of the historical context of the Bible and the ancient Near East, which in turn helps us become better interpreters of them.

■ Importance of Historical Context

Like the archaeologists who have examined only small portions of the ancient sites, we have only scratched the surface of historical context. Students of the Bible can go as deep, historically speaking, as they have time to investigate it. Every civilization mentioned in this brief chapter has hundreds of volumes written about it, and study of them can be a bit overwhelming. It can take people more than ten years of formal academic study simply to get started in the field of biblical studies.

Fortunately students do not need to learn everything at once—even the experts do not. If you have not studied the Bible before, then it would be good to read a good Old Testament or New Testament introduction. Students are sometimes overwhelmed, however, when they see a five-hundred- to six-hundred-page "introduction." "Introduction" is a technical term for biblical scholars, and such an introduction usually includes a detailed historical overview of the whole era, as well as technical questions about biblical authorship, chronological dating, and so on. In this volume, we have not attempted that degree of detail but simply have given the types of questions people should ask as they read the Bible. Of course, Bible commentaries, dictionaries, and atlases can be used when people want to read a section more critically.

While the studying of historical context can be never ending, and one must stop at some point, the more the better, we say. To be sure, consideration of the Bible's historical context must take place if people want to mature in their interpretation, understanding, and application of the Bible.

5

Literary Context

Some years ago I (Keith) received a call from a *Los Angeles Times* reporter. He wanted my opinion on a book that had been recently published. I told the reporter that I had not read the book. He then proceeded to give me a quick summary of the author's positions, and then he asked me what I thought about them. As the editor described them, all of the author's positions seemed valid and were within the mainstream of biblical scholarship, and I said as much. The editor thanked me, and I went on about my work, oblivious to what might have just happened.

The next Sunday's paper included the reporter's book review on the author's work. As he laid out the author's positions, they looked different than he had described them to me on the phone. In fact, the author's book looked a little bit wacky.

The reporter then proceeded to list all of the reputable biblical scholars who had challenged or dismissed the author in question. Many of these authors were authors I had read and respected. Then came a line that hit me like a truck: "[author] is not without his supporters, however. Keith H. Reeves of Azusa Pacific University states. . . ." The reporter then proceeded to summarize a couple of my points on the telephone. Interestingly, what he quoted me as saying in the paper was essentially true. I had not written in support of the controversial author, however, and as the quotes stood, it appeared that I had. I had been misquoted.

What a person says may be true in its original context, but it might be clearly wrong when it is applied to a different context. That incident with the *Los Angeles Times* reporter was not the first time that I have been misquoted, and it was not the last time either. People who have an agenda will often mis-quote someone in order to move their agenda forward. One simply needs to look at our current political system. Unfortunately, it often happens in our churches as well. Many pastors and religious leaders have been damaged by manipulative or mean-spirited people who take their comments out of context and misuse them.

Well and good, but what does this have to do with interpreting the Bible? The story is told of a man who wanted to hear a word from the Lord, so he decided to look in the Bible to see if he could find some direction. The man really did not know how to read the Bible, so he decided he would simply open it up and read the first text he saw. He proceeded with his plan. He opened his Bible, put his finger on a text, and then read the text. In this case the text was Matthew 27:5, "Throwing down the pieces of silver in the temple, he de-parted; and he went and hanged himself." Not feeling particularly enlightened or encouraged, the man thought he would try this again. Now he opened his Bible and pointed at the first text he saw, which was the last part of Luke 10:37, "Go and do likewise." The man, clearly frustrated, flipped a few pages and put his finger in again. This time his finger rested on John 13:27, "Do quickly what you are going to do."

■ Introduction to Literary Context

It is easy to see the "proof texting" that has taken place in this story—that is, the use of biblical texts to "prove" something they do not say. The story is old and probably fanciful, but it serves to illustrate the point. Biblical texts can be understood only in their larger literary contexts. One of my seminary professors was known constantly to say, "CIE," which was short for "context is everything." I often tell my own Greek students, "A word means what it means when it means it." Words only have meaning in sentences. Sentences only have meaning in paragraphs, and paragraphs only have meaning in the literary context of complete works.

Most people will understand this in theory, and many will attempt to avoid this sort of proof texting. But it is still very prevalent today when it comes to the Bible. Many do not realize how important the literary context is beyond the simple avoidance of proof texting.

Example: Agape

Let us illustrate this by looking at the Greek word *agapē*. Unless you have never been in a church, you have probably heard sometime in your life that *agapē* means God's special love, God's unconditional love, or something similar. Is this really true? Does *agapē* really mean some sort of special "God love"? How would we know? You might be tempted to turn to an English dictionary to try to find *agapē*. In fact, if you look up *agape* on Dictionary.com, you find the following definitions:

1. the love of God or Christ for humankind
2. the love of Christians for other persons, corresponding to the love of God for humankind
3. unselfish love of one person for another without sexual implications; brotherly love[1]

For many people this would be the answer. Case closed. They would simply pick the word that best fit their own ideas and run with it. But is this the best way to find the meaning of a word? In short, no! A dictionary simply summarizes and reports how most people use the word. What if most of these people are wrong? Again, how would we know?

Our first problem is that people are using an English dictionary to give the meaning of a Greek word. While it may be true that the majority of English speakers use *agape* to refer to God's love, it does not follow that the Greek term means that—at least, all the time.

The word itself only has meaning in a particular context. The Greek word *agapē* always means God's love when God is the subject. So *agapē* does refer to God's love in John 3:16, "For God so loved the world. . . ." *Agapē* is a very versatile word, however. It was used more broadly than to simply refer to God's love. Furthermore, it is not a distinctively "biblical" word, as it was used by writers other than writers of the Bible, including non-Christian writers who wrote long before the time of Jesus.

One of the more interesting uses of *agapē* is found in the Septuagint account of 2 Samuel 13:15. The Septuagint is the first and oldest translation of the Bible. Here is the quote from the New Revised Standard Version (NRSV): "Then Amnon was seized with a very great loathing for her; indeed, his loathing was even greater than the lust he had felt for her. Amnon said to her, 'Get out!' "

This verse is part of a larger tragic story of how Amnon, the son of David, devises a ruse to entrap his half-sister Tamar (2 Sam. 13:1–22). Tamar is a very beautiful woman, and Amnon is completely infatuated by her. Amnon is unable to "do anything to her" (2 Sam. 13:2). Amnon is so obsessed by

1. Dictionary.com, "agape," http://dictionary.reference.com/browse/agape, accessed July 27, 2011.

Tamar that his friend, Jonadab, asks him why he is so "haggard morning after morning" (2 Sam. 13:4). Amnon confesses his desire for his half-sister, and Jonadab helps Amnon devise a ruse. Amnon pretends to be ill. When his father comes to check on him, Amnon directs his father, "Let my sister Tamar come and give me something to eat" (2 Sam. 13:5). So Tamar, dutiful sister that she is, makes some food for Amnon and brings it to him. Amnon sends out all the help and then grabs Tamar, making his appeal: "Come, lie with me, my sister" (2 Sam. 13:11). Tamar refuses, "for such a thing is not done in Israel" (2 Sam. 13:12). Tamar pleads with Amnon to seek permission from the king, "for he will not withhold me from you" (2 Sam. 13:13). Amnon is undeterred by Tamar's plea, and he rapes her. This story may not have been familiar to you; it did not make the cut in the children's Bibles.

Astute readers will immediately point out that the English word "love" does not occur in this passage in the NRSV, and they are correct. The NRSV translates *agapē* with the English word "lust." Feel free to compare several versions on this. The New International Version (NIV) renders the verse this way: "Then Amnon hated her with intense hatred. In fact, he hated her more than he had loved her. Amnon said to her, 'Get up and get out!' " We see that the NIV does use "love" for *agapē* in keeping with popular English convention, but no thoughtful person would argue that Amnon's feelings toward Tamar can in anyway be construed as what we commonly think of as love—certainly not something such as God's love. It should be obvious that the third definition from Dictionary.com, "unselfish love of one person for another without sexual implications" does not apply here. The NRSV is clearly correct in rendering *agapē* as "lust" in this context.

So what can we learn from this? We can come away with two points:

1. Do not use only an English dictionary to define a Greek word, and

2. *agapē* can mean "lust."

Hebrew, Greek, and English Languages

Some might object that we are dealing here with the Septuagint, which is a Greek translation of the Hebrew text. Maybe the translators used *agapē* incorrectly here. (The writer does not know of anyone who actually objects for this reason, but it did come up in a class session once, and you have to cover your bases.) This objection fails for two reasons. First, the translators of the Septuagint spoke Greek as their native tongue. It is much more probable that their understanding of Greek is better than the pastor who had one year of

Greek in seminary and who uses it in a sermon on occasion. As a professor of Greek for over twenty-five years, I can tell you I have heard many sermons that have badly misused the Greek language. I often tell my students that a little bit of Greek is a dangerous thing. The second reason I do not think the translators got *agapē* wrong is that the Septuagint became the Bible of the early church, including most of the writers of the New Testament. Thus the Septuagint was for them authoritative Scripture.

Since Paul used the Septuagint as his Bible, he was fully aware that *agapē* did not always mean "God's love." In fact, in one of his letters to the Corinthians (our 1 Corinthians), Paul has to define what he means by *agapē*. Paul tells the Corinthians that he is using *agapē* as something that is patient and kind among other things (1 Cor. 13:4). If *agapē* so obviously means God's love, then why does Paul have to tell the folks in Corinth what he means by it? (Though many biblical scholars think 1 Corinthians 13 may not have originally been written by Paul but may have been a poem he adopted for his purposes, for our argument here it does not really matter.) Paul has to tell the Corinthians what he means by *agapē* because the most popular goddess in the city, Aphrodite, the goddess of love, has her temple on a very high hill overlooking the city. Many of the men in Corinth are quite happy to claim to be followers of Jesus Christ while they continue to visit the temple of Aphrodite to spend time with the temple prostitutes. The Corinthians think that they know what "love" is. Paul tells them, "It's not that!"

We see, then, that Greek words, like English words, can have diverse meanings based on the context. The English word "love" is similar to the Greek term *agapē*, in that meaning is derived from context. When I was in college, I remember one of my friends saying that he loved pizza. He was quickly corrected by a fellow student who said, "You don't love pizza." She wanted to restrict the term "love" to a particular meaning and use "like" instead. Yet we see that the English term "love" has a broad range of meanings from the sublime to the crude. So we can say "God loves the world." At the same time, the English language can accommodate a young man driving down the street yelling out at a young woman, "Hey baby, let's make love." The English term "love" is broad and diverse in its meaning. Greek terms are the same.

Words typically have a range of meanings. Sometimes the meaning of one word will overlap with the meaning of another word. In our illustration (concentric circles of "love" and "like"), we see that the English words "love" and "like" can on occasion be used interchangeably. At other times, however, they are very distinct in their meaning. When I talk about pizza, for example, I can say, "I love pizza." I can also say, "I like pizza." Essentially, I am simply noting that I have a preference for pizza over certain other types of food. Unless my tone of voice indicates otherwise, I am essentially saying the same thing. Thus, in this context, "like" and "love" mean essentially the same thing. They are synonyms.

Now imagine a romantic Italian café. John and Martha are seated, having finished a wonderful meal. They are eating their dessert and drinking their coffee. The light is subdued, coming from the candles on the table. Martha looks into John's eyes and says, "John, I love you." John, emboldened by Martha's comment, looks deeply into her eyes and says, "Martha, I like you." It does not work, does it? Neither will John and Martha's relationship, but that is another story. Here we see that the English terms "love" and "like" have completely different meanings. The terms have a range of meanings that sometimes overlap but that are sometimes distinct.

■ The Meaning of Words

An individual Greek word often can have a range of meanings. A common error among neophyte interpreters is "semantic loading." This simply means to force a range of meanings into a single use. Recently I was at a dinner, and a woman was talking about a particular Bible verse to a friend. I heard her say, "The original Greek word means" and then proceed to give about five or six meanings and attempt to force all those meanings into the particular verse she was discussing. This does not work either.

Let us illustrate this point, first with an English term, and then a Greek one. A young woman is getting ready to play basketball, so she takes a backpack and fills it with the equipment that she needs to play: shoes, clothes, ball, water bottle, and so on. She then throws her *gear* into her truck, starts the truck, puts it into *gear*, and drives away. We have used the English word "gear" here in two distinct ways. A native English speaker knows the difference and would not confuse the meanings of the terms. A nonnative, however, could potentially confuse these meanings.

Let us now consider a second illustration—the Greek word *sarx*. Its meaning is more complex linguistically and theologically.

Example: Sarx

Paul uses the Greek word *sarx* in broad and diverse ways. This term presents particular problems for the translator and the interpreter, since the term has diverse meanings and can be theologically loaded. *Sarx* is traditionally translated "flesh," but this is where problems start. Paul sometimes uses the term simply to refer to literal flesh or meat, as in "tastes like chicken." So he states, "Not all flesh is alike, but there is one flesh for human beings, another for animals, another for birds, and another for fish" (1 Cor. 15:39). Paul also uses the term *sarx* to refer to natural human descent; so Jesus is a descendent of David according to the flesh (Rom. 1:3). Paul also uses the term *sarx* to refer to humanity in a morally neutral way where "all flesh" simply refers to all people (Rom. 3:20 author's translation). Paul has a distinctive use of the term "flesh," however, that has decidedly negative connotations. Thus, in Galatians 5:16–17, Paul writes, "Live by the Spirit, I say, and do not gratify the desires of the flesh. For what the flesh desires is opposed to the Spirit, and what the Spirit desires is opposed to the flesh; for these are opposed to each other, to prevent you from doing what you want." Here flesh is humanity that is opposed to God. It is living life without the Spirit of God. One lives life according to the flesh, or one lives life according to the Spirit. Flesh and Spirit are seen as two opposing forces.

It is a huge mistake, however, to see flesh here as referring to the physical body. This can lead to all sorts of ascetic practices that are not warranted— at least, not based on this passage. Paul proceeds to give a list of what is traditionally called "works of the flesh" (Gal. 5:19–21). While some of these "works" clearly refer to the physical body, the majority of terms have nothing to do with what is often thought of by "flesh." Thus "enmities, strife, jealousy, anger, quarrels, dissensions, factions, envy" are terms that in popular conversation are often thought of as sins of the Spirit (Gal. 5:20–21). We thus seriously misinterpret the text when we think of "flesh" in Paul in strictly bodily terms.

A Little Bit of Greek Is a Dangerous Thing

Some years ago we were discussing the "works of the flesh" in a Romans– Galatians class that I teach. One of the items listed is "sorcery" (Gal. 5:20). A student in class informed me that he had been told, either by his pastor or his youth pastor, that "sorcery" here meant "drug use." The Greek word, which is translated "sorcery," is *pharmakeia*, from which we obviously get the English word "pharmacy." A pharmacy is a place where one may purchase drugs. Thus my student had been told that "using drugs" was what was behind this word here.

As I noted earlier, a little bit of Greek is a dangerous thing. It is true that our modern English word "pharmacy" does derive from the Greek word *pharmakeia*, but it is completely wrong to say that the word *pharmakeia* in Galatians 5:20 is a condemnation of "using drugs" (as my student stated it). (Legal disclaimer: I do not endorse the use of illicit drugs, or legal drugs for that matter, for recreational purposes. I would hate to be quoted out of context.)

Sorcery in the ancient world often did use rather strange concoctions that we might identify as "drugs" today. Sorcery and magic in the ancient world is a fascinating topic, but it is beyond the scope of this book to give an adequate introduction here. Suffice it to say, "sorcery" in the ancient world has very little to do with recreational drug use in a twenty-first-century American context.

While we are on the topic of "works of the flesh," here is one more example. In Galatians 5:21, Paul lists the word "carousing." What image comes to your mind when you think of carousing? Well, when I was in high school, my mom thought "carousing" was young men driving around late at night looking for things to do. Or as some of the older folks would say, they were "looking to get into trouble."

Let me first say that, when I was driving around late at night in high school, I was not necessarily looking to get into trouble. Usually we were just looking for things to do. But as a parent of three daughters, I have to say that I have become more like my mom and have a little more suspicion of young men driving around at night.

What does "carousing" mean? The Greek term here is *kōmoi*. It is related to the word "village" and literally means "village festivals." But what is a village festival? Well, it did not look much like the current farmer's markets. Village festivals were celebrations to the various deities of the time, including some famous ones such as Dionysus. They were essentially worship celebrations, which involved a whole lot of activities that cannot be described in a G-rated introduction. Yes, it did involve lots of alcohol, lots of sex, and lots of other things your parents would not approve of.

Beware also the etymological fallacy. People routinely mention that the Greek word *hamartia* (translated as "sin" in most versions) means, etymologically, to "miss the mark." They will tell you that the term was used in archery or spear throwing, and that when the archer missed the target, it would be called *hamartia*. Thus they explain that sin is "missing the mark." If only life were that simple. While it is true that the etymology of the word was connected with spear throwing and meant "missing the mark," it is completely irrelevant for biblical interpretation. The important question is not the original meaning of the word but the meaning intended by the author. Paul, for example, typically uses the term *hamartia* in the singular to refer to a force or realm of existence one is found in. Thus a person is in "sin" and only through an act of Jesus Christ can one be moved from the realm of sin into the realm of eternal life. Thus the dominant metaphor of Christian existence in the writings of Paul is that one is "in Christ." Other writers use the term *hamartia* in other ways, though a full study is beyond the scope of this introduction.

Generally speaking, when biblical authors use a particular word, they have a precise meaning in mind. It is not different from today; when we write or speak, we intend to be understood. The more significant our message, the more carefully we choose our words.

■ Multiple Meanings

There are occasional exceptions to this rule, for example when the author of John uses terms with multiple meanings. The story of Jesus and Nicodemus is a classic example of double meaning. You may remember the story from John 3. We read of a certain ruler named Nicodemus who approaches Jesus at night. John 3:2–8 describes some of their conversation:

> He came to Jesus by night and said to him, "Rabbi, we know that you are a teacher who has come from God; for no one can do these signs that you do apart from the presence of God." Jesus answered him, "Very truly, I tell you, no one can see the kingdom of God without being born from above." Nicodemus said to him, "How can anyone be born after having grown old? Can one enter a second time into the mother's womb and be born?" Jesus answered, "Very truly, I tell you, no one can enter the kingdom of God without being born of water and Spirit. What is born of the flesh is flesh, and what is born of the Spirit is spirit. Do not be astonished that I said to you, 'You must be born from above.' The wind blows where it chooses, and you hear the sound of it, but you do not know where it comes from or where it goes. So it is with everyone who is born of the Spirit."

What is the problem? The New Revised Standard Version translates the Greek term *anōthen* as "from above" (John 3:3). The translators have a bit of a challenge here, as there is wordplay in the Greek text. The term *anōthen* can mean "from above." That is how it is used here. Jesus tells Nicodemus that he needs a heavenly birth. He needs to be born "from above." The term *anōthen* can also mean "again." That is how Nicodemus understands it. Jesus tells Nicodemus that he must be born from above. Nicodemus, however, is completely in the dark. He understands Jesus to be saying that he must be "born again." Thus Nicodemus asks a rather silly question, "Can one enter a second time into his mother's womb and be born?" (John 3:4). Nicodemus fails to understand Jesus's comment and continues to be confused. The reader of the Greek text would see the wordplay and chuckle. The English reader, however, is left confused, just like Nicodemus.

We see similar confusion in John 4. Jesus has a conversation with a woman from Samaria while he is sitting by a well. It is a familiar story. Jesus is tired, and he sends his disciples into town to grab some food. Meanwhile, Jesus is sitting by the well in the middle of the day. It is hot, and as the woman approaches, Jesus asks her for a drink of water. During this conversation, Jesus makes mention of "living water" (John 4:10). Jesus is speaking metaphorically, but the woman does not grasp the metaphor and thinks that Jesus is referring to "running water." It is a legitimate way to understand the expression, but not the way that Jesus uses it here. Jesus speaks metaphorically; the Samaritan woman hears literally.

People still fail to see metaphors today. Some time ago Don was traveling on a plane. On this particular day, he was reading a book by C. S. Lewis, a noted Christian author. The person sitting next to him on the plane noticed what Don was reading and almost immediately asked him if he was "born again." If you have ever flown much, you know that sometimes you would like to strike up a conversation. At other times, you just like to keep to yourself and read a book. For whatever reason, Don did not give a yes or no answer. He responded by saying, "I have drunk the living water." The person sitting next to Don either did not like his answer, did not understand it, or required further clarification. He came back and asked him again, "But have you been 'born again'?" This started a theological dialogue. I am not sure how long the conversation lasted, but the interrogator continued to press Don. He wanted to hear Don say the words, "Yes, I have been born again." Don, however, tried to explain to him that he was only choosing a different metaphor to express his relationship with Jesus. Don said, "I am simply using the metaphor from John chapter 4, while you are using the metaphor from John chapter 3." This fellow passenger was so locked in to that one metaphor that he could not understand or recognize that Don had genuine Christian faith. When Don and he parted ways at the end of the plane trip, the man said to Don, "I'll pray for you." He simply could not understand (or accept) that the metaphor of "drinking living water" was a valid way to speak of one's redeemed relationship with God. It was as valid as the metaphor of being "born again." In fact, it is more so, since—as we have seen—Jesus never asked anyone if they had been "born again."

The Gospel of John is one case where the author routinely uses terms that have double meaning, and he does so intentionally. Generally speaking, however, an author will use a term with a precise meaning in mind. A good interpreter will endeavor to identify that particular meaning and not load multiple meanings into a particular context.

What have we learned thus far? Proof texting is not a viable approach to biblical interpretation; the meaning of a word is determined by context; and words can have diverse meanings.

■ Arrangement of Literature

The literary context goes beyond simple words and paragraphs. Paying attention to the literary context reveals that entire narratives are constructed in ways that show meaning is derived from the whole, not simply from the individual parts.

The Gospel of Luke serves as a good example of how an author arranges the material to convey meaning that might not otherwise be obvious. Multivolume works have been written on Luke's literary artistry. We will give a few examples that show how attention to literary context informs the reader.

Luke states his purpose in the prologue (Luke 1:1–4). In one of the most elegant Greek sentences in the New Testament, Luke writes to his benefactor, Theophilus, that he is writing an "orderly account" (Luke 1:3) so that "you may know the truth concerning the things about which you have been instructed" (Luke 1:4). What does Luke mean by an "orderly account"? The modern Western reader might assume that "orderly" means chronological. A careful reading of Luke, however, indicates that something other than chronology drives Luke's narrative. For example, in Luke 4:23, the crowd at the synagogue in Nazareth asks Jesus: "Do here also in your hometown the things that we have heard you did at Capernaum." However, Luke has made no mention of Jesus doing anything in Capernaum—yet. In fact, immediately after this story, Jesus goes to Capernaum and casts out a demon (Luke 4:31–37). This is the sort of thing that might cause the people of Nazareth to say, "Do here also in your hometown the things that we have heard you did in Capernaum" (Luke 4:23). So has Luke gotten his stories out of sequence? Interestingly, a careful reading of the Gospel of Mark shows that these stories are indeed reversed in Mark. In Mark's Gospel, Jesus goes to Capernaum first and casts out a demon (Mark 1:21–28). Later he goes to Nazareth. The welcome he receives in Nazareth in Mark's Gospel (Mark 6:1–6) is less friendly than the reception he receives in Luke.

Why the different sequence of stories in Mark and Luke? Most biblical scholars think that Mark was written first and that Luke used Mark as one of his sources. In fact, Luke acknowledges that others had written "orderly accounts" before him (Luke 1:1). It is likely that one of these "orderly accounts" was Mark's Gospel. Why would Luke reverse the sequence of Mark's stories? If we look at Luke's version of the events in Nazareth, we see several things that would indicate Luke's purpose. The event in Nazareth is the first public act of Jesus in Luke's Gospel. In this way its significance is highlighted. Nazareth is also where Jesus reads from the scroll of Isaiah and announces his mission: "The Spirit of the Lord is upon me, because he has anointed me to bring good news to the poor. He has sent me to proclaim release to the captives and recovery of sight to the blind, to let the oppressed go free, to proclaim the year of the Lord's favor" (Luke 4:18–19). On completion of the reading, Jesus announces, "Today this scripture has been fulfilled in your hearing" (Luke 4:21).

The events in Nazareth, then, function as a programmatic statement for Luke. This is the story Luke wants to tell first. This is the story that better than any other story encapsulates for Luke what Jesus is about. Joseph Fitzmyer, in his commentary on Luke, demonstrates how Luke rearranges the chronology of Mark on seven separate occasions. In each case, Luke is making a theological case. That is what Luke means by an "orderly account."[2]

Luke also has a large section of material in what is commonly called his "travel narrative" (Luke 9:51–19:44). At the beginning of this section, Luke makes an interesting announcement about Jesus, "When the days drew near for him to be taken up, he set his face to go to Jerusalem" (Luke 9:51). This marks an obvious transition in the narrative, but interestingly, Jesus takes almost forever to get there! Jesus had been in Galilee, and then he immediately entered a Samaritan village. This would be the most direct route to Jerusalem. Samaria is south of Galilee, and Jerusalem is south of Samaria. This would not be the normal path a Jew would take, however, since most Jews would skirt around to the east to avoid Samaria. But before you know it, Jesus is back in Galilee again. What is fascinating about Luke's narrative is that the reader is constantly being reminded about Jesus's journey to Jerusalem (Luke 9:51; 13:32–33; 17:11; 18:31; 19:28). So what does one make of these repeated references? Whole books have been written about Luke's travel narrative. Biblical scholars agree that Luke's placement of these references is significant. Various theories have been proposed as to why Luke does this, but a growing consensus is that Luke wants the reader to see Jesus as a prophetic figure—a new Moses. The repeated journey references would evoke the image of a new exodus.

2. Joseph A. Fitzmyer, *The Gospel according to Luke I–IX: Introduction, Translation, and Notes*, The Anchor Bible 28 (New York: Doubleday, 1982), 15, 287–98.

What have we learned? The literary context is very important; words only have meaning in context; and stories or sections of narrative must be read in their context to appreciate fully the point the author is making.

■ Excursus on Methods of Biblical Criticism

On page 57, we laid out three important questions for anyone who wants to read the Bible. We have called this a commonsense approach to biblical interpretation. It has focused on helping the reader gain understanding of what the authors were writing to their original audience. Consequently, it focused on understanding the authors' intentions. Many others have approached the Bible in other ways. Some have attempted to focus on what happened before the text came into its final form. Others have focused on the text as an independent entity removed from the authors' purview. Still others have focused on the readers and how they derive meaning from the text. In this excursus (that is, a digression or detour from the subject), we will highlight a few methods of biblical studies that have been used by scholars. As we have said repeatedly, this book is not an attempt to be exhaustive but simply to provide an overview of methods that have been used on the biblical texts.

We will use the term "historical-critical" at times in this work. Sometimes historical-critical is used broadly to cover a multitude of approaches. At other times, it is used more specifically to refer to those early works that attempted to get behind the text, so to speak, in order to see what actually happened in the original writings. Those works represented an attempt to get to pure history removed from any interpretive comment.

Source criticism, for example, determines to find original written sources that lie behind the documents we now possess. Early source-critical scholars note that at times in the Hebrew Bible, a writer would use God's personal name, "Yahweh." At other times a writer would use the term "Elohim" for God. At still other times, the writer would use a combination of divine names. The Hebrew Bible was further edited by one or more editors who brought the teaching in line with Deuteronomy (and its theological worldview) and another editor (or editors) who reflected the influence of the priests (and their theological worldview). Consequently, source critics suggested the theory of multiple sources: J source (Yahweh), E source (Elohim), D source (Deuteronomist), and P source (Priestly). Variations of source criticism are still used today, while other biblical scholars reject source criticism outright.

Form criticism attempts to reach beyond written documents to the oral tradition. Thus form critics isolate various types of stories and suggest that each of these types of stories had a particular life setting. Some stories were used for evangelism, while other stories might be used for teaching, discipline, apologetics, and so on.

Redaction critics look at the work of the editor, or redactor. Early source critics suggested that Mark was probably the first Gospel written and that Matthew and Luke had used Mark as well as another source, which they named Q (for *Quelle*, the German word for source). Whereas historical critics attempt to read the Gospels to find the historical kernel and form critics attempt to isolate the original stories, redaction critics are interested in determining how the individual evangelists shaped their material into a narrative and how the evangelist contributed to the message.

Literary critics are only mildly interested in the preliminary history of the text, if at all. They focus on the text as it stands independent of its history of origin. Literary critics look at such things as narrative settings, characterization, and plot development to see the meaning of the text.

Other approaches focus on the readers and how the readers create meaning from the text. *Reader-response* and the plethora of various ideological (or theological) methods would be included in this category—for example, deconstruction, liberation criticism, postcolonialism, feminist criticism, cultural criticism, and so on.

Ultimately, we see that some approaches focus on the intent of the authors, other approaches focus on the text itself, and still other approaches focus on the reader. What we have called a commonsense approach is eclectic to some degree but focuses primarily on the intent of the author. While we recognize that we all read the texts from our own social locations, a focus on authorial intent, no matter how difficult that task may be to execute, is a worthy endeavor.

■ The Importance of Literary Context

If authorial intent is important, then it is critical to pay attention to the literary context. When we speak or write, we expect our message to be received with integrity. Should we not give the same attention, if not more, to biblical writers? We must be extremely cautious when removing isolated verses from their contexts.

Those who have grown up in the church are familiar with many examples of verses that have been used outside of their original contexts. Sometimes this can be destructive, though, at times, clever or exhortative meaning can be derived by intentionally using a verse out of context. No harm can come of that as long as one is aware of it. One favorite example is the application of 1 Corinthians 15:51 on a church nursery door: "We will not all sleep, but we will all be changed" (NIV).

Problems arise, however, when students (and teachers and preachers) of the Bible naively understand and implement this technique in ways that misconstrue or blatantly distort the biblical content. Although the Bible talks about the virtue of simple, childlike faith (Mark 10:15; Luke 18:17), it does not intend that we should have simplistic, uninformed faith. The more mature we become in interpreting the Bible, the more mature we become in our understanding, words, and actions.

THEOLOGY
OF THE BIBLE

6

Religious Authority

In talking about the Bible, some consider it unnecessary—and possibly dangerous—to talk also about theology. But theology intends to contemplate complex Christian beliefs and values and present them in ways that are understandable and applicable. The same is true about wanting to talk theologically about the Bible.

What is theology? Simply stated, theology represents the study of God and all things related to God. The word comes from the Greek words *theos* ("god") + *logos* ("word," "discourse," "study"); theology has to do with the discourse, study, or logic of what Christians have to say about God and the works of God in the world. Throughout church history, Christians have done their best to describe their basic beliefs, values, and practices. They did this in order to teach converts and children about Jesus Christ, to defend themselves from critics, and to develop a more comprehensive understanding of God and Christianity.

Early examples of theology include the catechisms developed for teaching converts and children. Apologetics were written to defend Christians from those who condemned and persecuted them. Eventually, creeds were written in the attempt to describe the consensus of Christian beliefs and values. The Nicene Creed represents the first ecumenical—or churchwide—summary of Christianity. When the council of church leaders was convened in 325, a first draft was written. Afterward the church leaders returned to churches throughout the Christian world to discuss and debate the content of the creed. In 381, church leaders reconvened at the council in Constantinople and approved the Nicene Creed, also called the Nicene-Constantinopolitan Creed.

The Nicene Creed, however, says almost nothing about the Bible. The main reason for this is that the canon of the Bible, including the Old and New Testaments, had not yet been formally approved. The first councils—or synods—that approved a canon of Scripture were the Synods of Hippo (393) and Carthage (397). So the Nicene Creed could not say anything about that which had not yet been agreed upon by Christian leaders.

Interestingly, the Christians who were involved with the canonization of the Bible were also among the Christians who approved the Nicene Creed. When some Christians argue that the religious authority of the Bible should supersede that of church tradition, they forget (or perhaps ignore) that some of the same people responsible for the canonization of the Bible (393, 397) were responsible for the Nicene Creed (325, 381).

As churches developed after the formation of both the Nicene Creed and the canon, Christian leaders discussed the appropriate relationship between them and the longstanding religious authority of church leaders. Over time, different views arose with regard to the right relationship between the Bible and other authorities. Issues arose including the nature of religious authority, the inspiration of the Bible, and the Bible's trustworthiness. Not all these issues arose at once, but they continued to be discussed and debated. They are crucial for both Christian and church understanding today.

One of the goals of theology is to develop a more consistent and informed view of the Bible, including questions and concerns about it. Practically speaking, everyone has a "theology of the Bible," though they may not be consciously aware of it. People's understanding of the nature and applicability of the Bible varies widely, but most of them have an opinion, even if it is one of benign neglect.

Sometimes people have a theology of the Bible that is inconsistent. They view the Bible in contradictory ways. For example, they may acclaim the Bible to be their highest religious authority yet they seldom read it; they may say it does not err, yet they regularly disregard it.[1] So one of the goals of theology in general, and of this chapter in particular, is to present theologically identifiable views about the Bible. In order to accomplish this task, the discussion of the Bible will include some of the aforementioned issues: religious authority, the inspiration of the Bible, and the Bible's trustworthiness. These issues are not exhaustive; others could easily be added. But these issues represent some of the more basic and commonly asked questions about the Bible.

---

1. One may say that such inconsistencies are due to sin rather than to a lack of intellectual consistency or other behavioral scientific explanations. Speaking as Christians, we certainly must consider the pervasiveness of sin when discussing any topic theologically. But our present focus is on the intellectual, rather than spiritual and moral, challenges to how the Bible is understood. We want to talk about how people think differently about the Bible, not speculate about why they differ.

A variety of historical Christian views about the Bible will be discussed in subsequent chapters. We present these views with the intent of bringing greater clarity to their variety. Sometimes people do not want to do the hard, critical work of looking at options and then deciding for themselves. They would prefer to be told what to believe rather than deal with difficult and sometimes uncomfortable questions. Yet we consider it intellectually imperative and a sign of maturity for people to decide for themselves, after they have looked at the options Christians have held about the Bible.

Skeptics may wonder: If Christians have had multiple views, what is to prevent readers from believing anything they want? Does looking at diverse Christian views result in relativism, or a "lukewarm" view of the Bible, which displeases God (Rev. 3:16)? Of course such outcomes are possible. But we value making informed, rather than uninformed, decisions. Just as Christians are to love God with their minds as well as their hearts, souls, and strength, they should love and study the Bible with good intellectual judgment. So we want to provide historic views of the Bible that represent sincere beliefs and values that Christians have had, even those views that differed from one other. By looking at the variety of views, readers will, we hope, be able to understand what issues have caused differences of opinion and then make more informed decisions about what they believe. We think that people who make informed decisions about their theology of the Bible will be more confident about the Bible and more effective in applying it in their lives.

The following chapters in this section deal with crucial issues about a Christian understanding of the Bible. We begin with a chapter on religious authority (chap. 6) and how Christians' understanding of it developed historically. Views of religious authority did not just appear; they developed over time. The oldest views are not necessarily the best; likewise, the newest views are not necessarily the best. So, as always, critical thinking is crucial in reading and deciding one's own beliefs and values.

Chapter 7 deals with the inspiration of the Bible, which is probably the most important biblical term used to describe the divine origin of sacred writings. Understanding the biblical and historic Christian beliefs about inspiration is crucial for a contemporary theology of the Bible. Chapters 8 and 9 deal with the results of inspiration, specifically with regard to the trustworthiness of the Bible. To what degree is it reliable? To what degree is the Bible error free? To what degree are human questions about the trustworthiness of the Bible relevant to how God wants to work in and through the lives of people? Such questions have been among the most debated and divisive among Christians. It is our hope that the following chapters will help readers experience greater clarity and conviction about the Bible.

■ Preliminary Considerations

Before talking about the Bible from a theological perspective, it is important to mention several caveats, or cautions. Christian theologians have long been aware that they bring to their studies certain assumptions or presuppositions about theology. The same is true for any person and for churches, even if they are not consciously aware of them.

The purpose of this book is not to present an extensive investigation of people's theological assumptions and presuppositions. Nor do we as authors intend to present and evaluate all of our assumptions and presuppositions. Instead we want to present what we consider to be representative Christian views, based on our lifetime of biblical and theological studies. As such, our approach is both commonsense oriented when it comes to biblical interpretation and fair-minded in presenting various theological interpretations of the Bible. We do not intend to present some views positively and others negatively. We want to present each view as fairly as possible so that readers may feel more confident in deciding for themselves with regard to issues under investigation. We hope to help facilitate readers' confidence in learning about and assessing the different Christian beliefs about the Bible.

When people talk about the Bible, they may make it seem as if there is only one interpretation of it, when in reality there may exist one or more alternatives. This variety of interpretations has become more noticeable as Christians use different critical approaches (biblical methodology or criticism) to biblical texts. In so doing, the Bible's trustworthiness and morality and also its divine inspiration have, at times, been challenged. Of course, such challenges are not new, as some people think. The Bible's authority, inspiration, and trustworthiness were questioned almost from the beginning by those who opposed Jesus and his followers. Throughout church history, these same issues have arisen in various ways. Our contemporary ignorance of them, regrettably, may contribute to assumptions and presuppositions that hurt our theological understanding of the Bible.

When we make comments about the Bible and its interpretations, they are made with the understanding that complex questions persist about their theological legitimacy. Not everyone may agree with our presentations of the following viewpoints, since people sometimes have different slants on how they interpret the historical and theological data. So readers must always be on guard, critically speaking, in order to decide for themselves about the subject matter of this book. For example, when we will make biblical references, we cite the Bible not as proof texts (or "eisegesis") for the particular theological viewpoints but as typical verses in support of them. Thus they serve more as representative

Christian understandings rather than as definitive interpretations of the Bible. Likewise, when we make historical and theological presentations, we try to be fair in describing them rather than evaluating the different viewpoints presented. Again, it is our goal to aid readers to decide for themselves with regard to what they believe about the Bible's authority, inspiration, and trustworthiness.

■ By What Authority?

"By what authority?" was a question often asked of Jesus according to the writers of the Gospels. People were amazed that he spoke with authority (Mark 1:27; Luke 4:22, 32). Other Jewish leaders appealed to Abraham, David, prophets, or the Scriptures. However, Jesus uniquely claimed authority, which was confirmed by the performance of miracles, healings, exorcisms, and other signs and wonders (Matt. 8:23–27; 9:6–8; 15:29–31; Mark 2:12; Luke 4:36; 8:25). Detractors claimed that it was by the power of Beelzebul—Satan— that Jesus performed powerful deeds, such as the casting out of demons (for example, Matt. 12:24). Jesus countered by saying that it was illogical to say that "Satan cast out Satan" (Matt. 12:26). Besides, exorcism was a recognized spiritual practice among the Jews. So, Jesus's deeds as well as his words confirmed an authority unlike that to which the people of Israel were accustomed.

According to the Gospel writers, Jesus claimed that his authority was given by God the Father. "All things have been handed over to me by my Father," said Jesus, "and no one knows who the Son is except the Father, or who the Father is except the Son and anyone to whom the Son chooses to reveal him" (Luke 10:22). He also said, "All authority in heaven and on earth has been given to me" (Matt. 28:18). So Jesus seemed aware that he spoke and acted with divine authority—God-given authority—which was confirmed in both words and deeds (John 12:47–50; 14:10, 23–24).

God's authority would continue after the life, death, and resurrection of Jesus. The Holy Spirit would come in fulfillment of prophecy (Acts 2:16–21), indwelling Christian believers and empowering them to fulfill God's will in the world. According to the New Testament, the Holy Spirit of God continues to work in and through believers until the end times.

The question of authority is contested now perhaps more than ever. When I (Don) was a teenager in the 1960s, a famous bumper sticker read "Question Authority." In the midst of the Vietnam War, the threat of "mutually assured nuclear annihilation," the civil rights movement, and other cultural upheavals in the United States, people questioned every authority. They questioned the authority of the government, its leaders, longstanding cultural conventions, and—of course—religion. Christianity and its time-honored traditions were not accepted unquestioningly. On the contrary, people questioned many beliefs, values, and practices to the point of some famously declaring that "God is dead."

Decades later, the United States is still involved in military conflict, though now in other countries. The rise of postmodernism and its concern with the cultural relativism of people's beliefs, values, and practices has further caused people to question, question, question. No one thinks that the questioning will soon diminish. On the contrary, most think questioning will increase. Thus it is all the more important to talk about the nature of authority in general, and about religious authority in particular. In the context of this book's discussion of the Bible, it seems reasonable to think that its authority is challenged more than ever. Indeed, that might be the case. However, it is simplistic to think that the issue of authority involves only that of the Bible. Historically, the topic of religious authority has been complex. In order to discuss the authority of the Bible, it will first be necessary to investigate the historical development of Christian understandings of religious authority.

Early Christian Authority

Jesus gave authority to the disciples to continue in ministry (Matt. 10:1; John 20:21–22). According to Matthew, Jesus's final words bequeathed authority to the disciples to go, make disciples, baptize, and teach people to obey everything that Jesus commanded them (Matt. 28:18–20). Like Jesus, they exhibited authority to perform signs and wonders as well as preach and teach. In fact, a part of what it meant to be an apostle was to be someone sent out with authority.

In time, Christianity spread, and questions arose with regard to the growing number of gentile converts. When decision making became more complex, the apostolic council was held in Jerusalem (ca. 50). Were gentile converts expected to obey the Mosaic laws? The council concluded that they were not. Gentiles were exempt from most Jewish laws, except for a few pertaining to blood, eating meat containing blood, fornication, and idolatry (Acts 15). The apostolic council became a model for later conciliar decisions by churches.

Overall authority rested with the apostles and those they appointed to lead churches. Although Jesus was considered the head of churches (Eph. 5:23; Col. 1:18), elders and other overseers in churches were increasingly honored, giving leadership and being obeyed (1 Thess. 5:12–13; 1 Tim. 5:17; Heb. 13:17). Their authority extended to preaching the gospel, forgiving sins, overseeing the churches, and even excommunicating those who intentionally and habitually rejected Jesus and his teachings.

The Scriptures—the Hebrew Bible of Judaism—were considered authoritative. Jesus frequently appealed to them with the phrase, "It is written" (for example,

Matt. 4:4; Luke 4:4; 19:46). When Jesus was led into the wilderness by the Holy Spirit, and he was tempted by Satan, it is significant that Jesus responded with Scripture (Matt. 4:1–11; Mark 1:12–13; Luke 4:1–13). Even on the cross, at the time of Jesus's greatest testing, he responded by quoting Scripture, "My God, my God, why have you forsaken me?" (Ps. 22:1; see also Matt. 27:46; Mark 15:34). Like the psalmist, who began the lament in Psalm 22 with these words, Jesus went on to affirm God's will and ultimate good for his life as well as others.

Jesus often appealed to the Scriptures in his preaching and teaching. He chided listeners for knowing "neither the scriptures nor the power of God" (Matt. 22:29). Jesus revered the Scriptures and considered himself the fulfillment of them (Luke 4:16–21). Following Jesus, the disciples and other followers appealed to the Scriptures (Acts 1:15–17; 17:10–11). To them, the Scriptures were inspired by God (2 Tim. 3:16–17); no valid prophecy was given that did not come from God (2 Pet. 1:20–21). In time, this reverence spread not only to the Hebrew Bible but also to the writings of other apostles. Second Peter 3:15–16 refers to the writings of Paul. Verse 16 says, "There are some things in them hard to understand," yet Paul's writings are compared with "the other scriptures." This identification of early Christian writing with Scripture points to developing ideas about the extent of their authoritative nature.

Although growing reverence for the Scriptures developed within the New Testament, authority resided more in the disciples and their conciliar leadership. They represented the primary place the Holy Spirit dwelled and through whom the Holy Spirit worked. The Hebrew Bible also had authority, which aided the disciples in following Jesus. But God's chosen leaders, indwelled and empowered by the Holy Spirit, primarily exerted authority in the developing churches and their mission in the world.

The Bible does not provide a clear-cut and comprehensive theology of religious authority. Certainly God is the ultimate authority in all matters of Christian belief, values, and practices. However, the means by which people discern that authority developed progressively, reflective of particular times, places, and circumstances. Today we can discern trajectories within the writings of the Old and New Testaments, which aid us in understanding the nature and extent of the Bible's religious authority. Still, it is necessary to investigate the religious authority of the Bible in terms of how it functioned in the first and subsequent centuries.

Ancient and Medieval Churches

Similar to the first-century church described in the Bible, primary religious authority in ancient and medieval churches resided in the Christian leadership. When Constantine legalized Christianity in the Roman Empire (Edict of

Milan, 313), he led the burgeoning church and the clergy. Constantine called the first ecumenical council in Nicaea, and subsequent councils were called by the emperors in consultation with the clergy. Over time, the authority to lead the churches, including the right to call councils, resided in the clergy rather than in political leaders, though belief in the "divine right" of lead-ers—kings, caesars, emperors—pervaded the ancient and medieval churches.

As churches developed, religious authority was thought of in complex, dynamic terms that could not be reduced to a single entity. Church tradition represented the repository of decisions made by church leaders who guided Christians. It included the ecumenical creeds: Nicaea (325), Constantinople (381), Ephesus (431), Chalcedon (451), Constantinople II (553), Constanti-nople III (680–681), Nicaea II (787), Constantinople IV (869), and others.

The Bible was thought to be authoritative. It contained the "material" suf-ficient for knowledge of God, salvation, the Christian life, and other matters of theological and ethical importance. However, the Bible does not talk about every theological and ethical question people have. Likewise, there are portions of the Bible that require sophisticated interpretation because the meaning is not eminently clear. In such instances, it is necessary for Christians to appeal to church tradition and to contemporary church leadership—the magiste-rium (or teaching office)—to discern the meaning of the Bible, believing in the ongoing work of the Holy Spirit in them. Altogether these represent the "formal" sufficiency of God's revelatory work. The distinction between the material and formal sufficiency of the Bible means that the Bible contains all the material necessary for Christianity and that the past and present leader-ship of God's church are formally necessary for God's active presence and work in the world.

The Bible was considered inspired and authoritative for matters of Christian belief and practice. But the interpretation of it was not considered a private matter. It required input from those more mature—spiritually and theologi-cally—in understanding divine revelation. Thus churches and their leaders had authority along with the Bible when it came to "rightly explaining the word of truth" (2 Tim. 2:15).

Division arose gradually between the leadership of churches in the West and those in the East. When schism finally occurred in 1053, both Western and Eastern churches blamed the other for the severance between what be-came known as the Roman Catholic Church and the Orthodox Churches. The Western churches had gradually come under the leadership of a single cleric—the pope; Eastern churches were organized more regionally under the leadership of patriarchs. Due to various disagreements, both Western and East-ern churches ended up excommunicating one another. The disagreements are more complex than what will be discussed in this book, but one of the main disagreements had to do with who had final religious authority over matters of belief and practice. The Western church thought primacy belonged to the pope and magisterium; Eastern churches obviously disagreed.

Protestant Reformation Churches

The Roman Catholic Church was the dominant Christian presence in the West. However, there was not always agreement among the leadership about developments within the church. Attempts to "reform" the church occurred, but it was not until Martin Luther in the sixteenth century that theological and ecclesiastical issues came to a head. With regard to religious authority, Luther argued that the Roman Catholic Church, the pope, and the church's magisterium misrepresented and, at times, transgressed the teachings of the Bible. Among other changes, the notion of religious authority needed to be reconceived and reimplemented.

Luther advocated *sola Scriptura* (Latin "Scripture alone"). From his perspective, the Bible alone represents God's final authority in the world. If church leadership conflicted with clear teaching in the Bible, then the religious authority of the Bible superseded it. Of course, questions will arise about how to interpret the Bible, but the matter of final authority was certain. When challenged by leadership in the Roman Catholic Church, Luther famously said:

> Unless I am convicted by Scripture and plain reason—I do not accept the author-ity of popes and councils, for they have contradicted each other—my conscience is captive to the Word of God. I cannot and I will not recant anything, for to go against conscience is neither right nor safe. God help me. Amen.[2]

John Calvin and other Reformers agreed with Luther's affirmation of *sola Scriptura*.

They recognized that Scripture represented the only religious authority that arguably predated and theologically superseded ecclesiastical authority as it developed in Roman Catholicism. In his *Institutes of the Christian Religion*, Calvin formidably presented his theology of the Bible and how Christians need to focus primarily on reading, interpreting, and proclaiming the Bible rather than relying on the church and its traditions.

Both Luther and Calvin believed in the "sufficiency" of the Bible. That is, it is sufficiently understandable so that individuals may properly interpret

---

2. Martin Luther, quoted by Roland Herbert Bainton, *Here I Stand: A Life of Martin Luther*, A Hendrickson Classic Biography (1950; repr., Peabody, MA: Hendrickson, 2009), 180.

the Bible. People do not need the church and its traditions in order to com-
prehend the Bible's central teachings. In this regard, the Bible manifested not
only "material" sufficiency but also "formal" sufficiency. Individuals, aided
by the Holy Spirit, possessed all that is necessary for knowledge of God and
salvation and for attaining salvation. Another way of talking about the Bible's
sufficiency is its "perspicuity"—its clarity of thought with regard to matters
of Christian faith and practice.

Luther and Calvin did not naively read the Bible without any understanding of its historical development and the need for critical interpretation. As
we will see in later chapters, they considered the Bible to be divinely inspired
and trustworthy. Luther and Calvin further knew that the Bible needed to be
understood in light of the teachings of respected Christians and historic church
teachings. They were familiar with the patristics and medieval scholarship.
Augustine's thought, for example, was crucial in many of their interpretations
of the Bible. However, when traditions seemed to contradict the plain and
obvious teachings of the Bible, the Bible's authority prevailed.

Later, Anabaptists took the principle of *sola Scriptura* to certain logical
conclusions, focusing solely on biblical studies and challenging historical
studies of the Bible and church teachings as unnecessary for understanding
biblical Christianity. People alone, aided by the Holy Spirit, were sufficient
in comprehending what God wants to communicate to people about salvation and the Christian life. For example, creeds such as the Nicene Creed
were considered dispensable, since they distracted people from the primacy
of Scripture. A kind of primitivism pervaded Anabaptists traditions, leading
to the desire to re-create first-century Christianity, having no creed but Jesus
Christ and no book but the Bible.

British Reformation

The British Reformation occurred under quite different circumstances from
the one Luther led in Continental Europe. To make a long story short, King
Henry VIII of England was denied a divorce by Pope Clement VII. So Henry
followed the lead of Continental European Reformers and instigated a British
Reformation. The break with Roman Catholicism was complex, evolving long
after he died. But Henry initiated an Anglo-Catholic form of Protestantism
that developed differently from that of the Continental Reformation both
theologically and ecclesiastically.

In many ways, the Church of England—also known as Anglicanism—tried
to develop as a moderate form of Protestantism that balanced the religious contributions of Continental Protestantism and Roman Catholicism. Adherents

considered themselves to be a kind of via media (or "middle way") between perceived excesses of previous ecclesiastical developments. They drew on what they considered the best of Protestantism and the best of Catholicism, creating a hybrid that balanced the religious contributions of both.

With regard to religious authority, Anglicans emphasized the primacy of scriptural authority. But its authority was primary, rather than exclusive. Substantively, Anglican views may not have been all that different from Luther and Calvin, since the latter Reformers had sophisticated understandings of the Bible and its interpretation. Luther and Calvin knew that biblical interpretation was a complex undertaking aided by the wisdom of past interpreters and critical thinking. Anglicans also knew that the principle of *sola Scriptura* could be implemented naively in ways that led people to think that anyone could interpret the Bible as authoritatively as anyone else. While the salvific purpose of the Bible may indeed be available to anyone through the aid of the Holy Spirit, a complete understanding of the Bible requires prolonged study. Such study was aided by the faithful efforts of Christian interpreters, past and present.

In the spirit of the via media, Anglicans talked about the primacy of scriptural authority coupled with the genuine—albeit secondary—religious authority of church tradition and reason. Some refer to this threefold understanding of interdependent religious authorities as a kind of "three-legged stool," understood hierarchically with the Bible as primary. Reason, or the critical thinking of logic, was considered a God-given part of the *imago Dei* (Latin "image of God") with which people were created. If people are to love God with their "whole heart, soul, mind, and strength," then reason helps Christians make wise decisions with regard to biblical interpretation. Reason helps to discern how to balance the religious authority of the Bible along with the respected contributions of the church and its traditions. Thus Anglicanism intended to balance reasonably the contributions of the Bible along with the contributions of historic Christianity.

Deism

The Anglican emphasis on reason and critical thinking was encouraged by the growth of Enlightenment beliefs and values. The Enlightenment is not traditionally thought to have arisen in Great Britain. Rather, it is thought to have started with the intellectual musings of René Descartes in seventeenth-century France. Descartes wanted to have certainty about his beliefs and values. Although Descartes believed in God, he did not want to rely on any authority—religious or nonreligious—for the certitude he sought. Reason alone seemed the most reliable authority for his quest. Descartes wanted to establish a firm foundation of knowledge beyond doubt (or indubitability) by methodically doubting all past claims to truth until a rationally undeniable truth could be legitimately established. He doubted everything until he reached a thought or conclusion he could not doubt—namely, that he doubted, or that he thought. Hence, Descartes stated the famous dictum: *Cogito ergo sum* (Latin "I think, therefore I am" or "I am thinking, therefore I exist"). With this certitude, he developed his philosophy, which included the logical inference of God's existence. From Descartes's perspective, reason provided the legitimation of one's existence and of the existence of God.

Although Descartes claimed to be a devout Roman Catholic, his philosophy was accused of being deistic. Deism is the belief that God created the world to function as it does but does not continue to interact directly with it. Since God is not thought to interact with people, God does not listen to or respond to prayers. Instead, people must use their reasoning skills to understand the order of the world that God created. Rationally, people can understand the divinely ordained nature of the world and learn to live in it reasonably and thus happily. Deism claimed that God created the world like a clock and that it now runs according to the laws of nature created by God. As people study God's creation, they can discern its innate reasonableness and learn to live happily in accordance with it.

With regard to religious authority, reason alone becomes the authority people ought to live by. Christians in Great Britain became well-known proponents of deism. Lord Herbert of Cherbury and Matthew Tindal, among others, were deists who believed that reason coupled with observation of the natural world provided truth enough for genuine religion. Deists lived lives based on reason more than on a God who miraculously intervened on a day-to-day basis. Deists were among the first modern critics of the trustworthiness of the Bible, since the biblical world seemed antiquated and contrary to growing empirical studies of the natural world. The influence of British deism spread throughout the world, including in the United States, where people like Thomas Jefferson and Benjamin Franklin promoted deism.[3]

3. The Declaration of Independence of the United States was written primarily by Thomas Jefferson and edited by Benjamin Franklin. It mentions a "Creator" and "Nature's God," but these probably refer more to a deistic conception of God than to a more biblical, historic Christian understanding. As such the Declaration of Independence relies more upon the Enlightenment authority of reason, for example, as found in its references to "self-evident" truths and "unalienable rights," than to a traditional Christian understanding of God and religious authority. See the Declaration of Independence (1776), The Library of Congress website, http://www.loc.gov/rr/program/bib/ourdocs/DeclarInd.html, accessed April 3, 2011.

Evangelical Revivals

In the seventeenth century, a revivalist movement known as Pietism began in the Germanic states. Philipp Jakob Spener preached the importance of Christian piety, and he organized small discipleship groups called "little churches within the church" (Latin *ecclesiolae in ecclesia*). He promoted a more vibrant experience of Christianity that included a heartfelt devotional life. Spener's Pietism was not well received by the orthodox Lutheran leadership, but the vibrancy of his religiosity spread throughout the Christian world. Pietists influenced Christians during the eighteenth century in Britain with the development of Methodism and in the American colonies with the First Great Awakening.

In England, John Wesley had been influenced by the Moravians, who were Pietists from Bohemia. Wesley ministered with George Whitefield, who emphasized outdoor preaching and evangelism. Wesley led a widespread revival throughout England, and Methodism emerged with pietistic emphases on devotional living and small-group ministries. In the American colonies, Whitefield ministered alongside people such as Jonathan Edwards, who gave leadership to a revival known as the Great Awakening. Like the Pietists, Edwards preached and wrote about revivalist conversion and its experiential evidence, especially in his book *Religious Affections*.

Wesley represents a good example of how a new trajectory in understanding religious authority developed. With a growing emphasis on the experience of heartfelt religion, Wesley appealed not only to the primacy of scriptural authority but also to experience as a genuine—albeit secondary—religious authority. Having been schooled in Anglicanism, Wesley was aware of the via media of the Bible, tradition, and reason. He did not consider appeals to experience, along with tradition and reason, to be anything different from what had been done throughout church history. But the inclusion of experience as a religious authority represents a distinctive development in Christian understanding of religious authority.

Later scholars refer to Wesley's appeal to the primacy of the Bible, along with the religious authority of tradition, reason, and experience, as the "Wesleyan quadrilateral." The image unfortunately suggests a geometric image with equilateral sides, but for Wesley Scripture categorically was the final religious authority. In this regard, his views are complementary to those of the Protestant Reformation. The imagery, in point of fact, alludes to the Anglican understanding of the Lambeth Quadrilateral, which conjures up the image of fortress walls that defend cities. The Wesleyan quadrilateral is not intended to convey equal religious authorities or a static conception of their relationship, which discourages faith integration and other integrative applications. Instead, the link between the Bible, tradition, reason, and experience is thought to be dynamic, interdependent, and more realistic in describing the way Christians actually make theological decisions. Throughout church history, Christians have continuously used more holistic and integrative approaches to authoritative decision making than use of the Bible only.

Liberal Protestantism

In the nineteenth century, growing criticism of Christianity occurred based on persistent Enlightenment skepticism about the trustworthiness of the Bible, the church, and the church's traditions, the last of which Protestants had long doubted. In addition, the trustworthiness of reason, logic, and the certitude of innate knowledge was increasingly challenged. Modern people found that experience—people's basic data—was the most reliable starting point of knowledge.

In this context, Friedrich Schleiermacher defended Christianity, appealing to an absolute "feeling" of dependence on God, or conscious awareness of being in relationship with God. This feeling or experience was considered the most authoritative data point or foundation of one's Christian spirituality and theological reflection. Other religious authorities could be challenged, but one's immediate encounter with God provided the most certain starting point for Christianity.

During the nineteenth century, historical criticism of the Bible flourished. Christian scholars increasingly interpreted the Bible using the same historical and critical assumptions applied to other ancient texts. If one approached the study of Scripture without the assumption or presupposition that it is divinely revealed and inspired, then what are consequences of the investigation? The most immediate consequences were that the Bible no longer seemed historically and logically reliable. Whereas past Christian interpreters were generous in disregarding apparent discrepancies, those discrepancies now became the focus of biblical interpretation. Moreover, hundreds of ancient manuscripts had been found that were older and presumably more reliable than previous manuscripts used for biblical translations. Rather than resolve apparent textual discrepancies, these manuscripts seemed to make them more numerous, pronounced, and irreconcilable. Interpreting the Bible as one would any other text exposed it to increased scrutiny and skepticism as a trustworthy religious authority, much less an authority for historical and scientific investigation. The Bible appeared to be as fallible as other claims to knowledge and truth.

For Schleiermacher and other contributors to the burgeoning movement known as liberal Protestantism, the immediate experience of God seemed more trustworthy than alternative religious authorities. To the extent that the Bible enlightened and enhanced people's relationship with God, it was welcomed, studied, and applied toward the Christian life. To the extent that the Bible seemed inaccurate, anachronistic, self-contradictory, morally suspect, or counterproductive to nurturing love for God and others, the authority of the Bible was restricted. In practice, Christians regularly disregarded parts of the Bible, though they may have done so naively, unconsciously, or perhaps sinfully. However, now the Bible was not thought to be entirely trustworthy; people needed to use both historical and critical thinking in order to discern rightly the value of what the Bible has to say.

Responses to Liberal Protestantism

Numerous Christians disagreed with liberal Protestantism, especially its skepticism about the Bible and its diminished religious authority. One response was the development of the doctrine of biblical inerrancy. Basically, inerrancy argues that the Bible does not err. Although there are variations of the doctrine, early advocates argued for a dictation theory of divine inspiration. God dictated words to biblical authors, and they obediently wrote them word for word. The words of Scripture could not err, for they were the words of God rather than of people. The doctrine of inerrancy became a foundational belief of fundamentalist Christianity. Over time, this understanding of the doctrine became more nuanced and explanatory of apparent discrepancies in the Bible. Discussion of inerrancy will continue in subsequent chapters on the topics of the inspiration and trustworthiness of the Bible. However, in many ways, inerrancy was thought to return to ancient church and Protestant beliefs, if not also Roman Catholic beliefs. While some may consider inerrancy a novel contribution to the Christian understanding of the Bible, due to rational and evidential defenses of its errorlessness, its advocates did not think so.

Karl Barth mounted another challenge to liberal Protestantism in the twentieth century, advocating views that became generally known as neoorthodox or dialectical theology (also known as "theology crisis"). Barth emphasized that Jesus Christ, who lives and continues to relate with people, is the true Word of God (John 1:1). The Bible contains the words of Jesus and points to him, who is the living Word. So the Bible can be thought of as the Word of God only in a secondary way. It is authoritative to the extent that the Bible serves as the occasion by which God encounters people through the words contained therein. Thus God's divine self-revelation has more to do with people's personal encounter with God than with people's intellectual encounter with the words of the Bible per se. It is not people's reliance on propositional statements in the Bible (or about the Bible) that is important; it is their reliance on the living Jesus, who is God. The Bible does not save people; Jesus saves people. They are to worship him and not human thinking about propositional statements of truth. Jesus is indeed the way, the truth, and the life. But people ought not to confuse the person of Jesus with the book written about him along with other matters related to God and the Christian life.

Barth thought that biblical studies should be done with the same historical and critical methods of interpretation that had developed in the nineteenth century. There was no reason to avoid truths about the Bible, even if they included inconvenient truths about the Bible's fallibility. But Christians' trust placed in the words, propositions, and supposed certitude of the Bible was misplaced. Rather than trusting in God, trust was placed in something other than God. To be sure, Barth still believed that the Bible contains the words of God and points to the things of God. But it is God who gives insight from the Bible—that is, the insight and truth of eternal significance. People need to turn to the true Word, who is Jesus, rather than something with conferred authority, even if it be the Bible.

The nature of religious authority can be described dialectically. Although "dialectic" is defined a number of ways, its usage here communicates the belief that both God and the Bible are authoritative, though paradoxically, only God—ultimately speaking—is authoritative. The Bible has authority because God ordained that Christians live in accordance with it. The reason Christians live in accordance with the Bible, however, is not because it is considered free of errors or because of some rational or empirical legitimation of its truth. The human role in the writing of the Bible precludes it from such notions, due to observable limitations of the role finite people played in its creation. People abide by the Bible because God wants and commands them to do so. Their trust is in God rather than the Bible, and people trust that God will graciously honor their obedience to it.

Postmodern Views of Religious Authority

"Postmodern" and "postmodernism" are terms that have been variously used to describe a growing dissatisfaction with the Enlightenment and its affirmations, also known as modernism. Generally speaking, modernism emphasizes the rational and empirical legitimation of knowledge. Modernism has great confidence in people's ability to discover truth here and now through the scientific method, without reliance on historic traditions of science, philosophy, or religion. Hence, modernism tends toward human self-sufficiency and individualism. From a religious perspective, modernism tends toward secularism and at times is antagonistic toward religion because of how religious adherents have thwarted the progress of science, technology, and other Enlightenment ideals.

There is no single manifestation of postmodernism. Some trace the roots of postmodernist thinking back to Friedrich Nietzsche, while others consider the Continental philosophers Jean-François Lyotard, Jacques Derrida, and Michel Foucault to be the foremost advocates of postmodernism. Generally speaking, postmodernism emphasizes the limitations or "situatedness" of human knowledge. Since knowledge is culturally related to a particular place, particular time, and particular people, they question the rational and empirical legitimation (or foundation) of knowledge claimed by modernists. This does not mean that there is no truth, but it points out the limits of people's claim to know it comprehensibly and with certainty. Although people may claim to have certain knowledge, they are unaware of or unwilling to acknowledge the obvious aspects of their finitude. Rather than speak in terms of certain, propositional truth, advocates of postmodernism prefer to use the term "narrative" (or story) for how they discuss their beliefs, values, and practices. The concept of narrative conveys how situated, contextual, or culturally relative people's statements are. When people make claims of truth that they consider rationally and empirically certain, postmodernists call such statements "metanarratives," since they claim to possess knowledge that is not situated—that is not limited by human finitude. So-called metanarratives represent claims to universal knowledge and universal truth that transcends everyone else's particular narrative, story, or view of the world. According to postmodernists, claims to possess metanarrative (or absolute) truth may do injustice to the truth that others have, since alternative truth claims must, by definition, be denounced. As such, claims to having absolute truth may lead to the marginalization, oppression, or even persecution of people who do not submit entirely to those who claim to be the exclusive guardians of truth.

If metanarrative claims are advocated zealously to the point of marginalizing or excluding the views of others, those claiming the metanarrative run the risk of doing violence toward others, persecuting them intellectually if not also in other ways. In contrast, postmodernism wants to learn more about other people's stories and more about other groups of people's stories. By taking into account more and more information about other people, societies, and entire civilizations, a higher probability of truth may be established.

Postmodernists argue that rationalism and empiricism do not exhaust the knowledge people have. Such knowledge can be discussed in terms of propositional statements, and the truthfulness of those propositions can be debated.

However, it is doubted whether propositions can encapsulate the whole of what is true. A person, for example, can be described by propositional statements. Will those propositional statements be able to describe the whole of who the person is? Can the totality of who you are be reduced to sets of propositions? Likewise, a particular text—such as the Bible—may have authority, but that authority is not necessarily tied to the text's rational and empirical flawlessness or indubitability. The Bible may have a different kind of authority that has more to do with authorship, apostolicity, or divine inspiration than with legitimation through rationalism and empiricism. So postmodernism does not deny the existence of authority. It is understood differently, however, than how authority is advocated by modernism's appeal to reason and experience. As such, postmodernism rejects the kind of foundationalism that arose with Descartes, but not authority per se, including religious authority. Instead, postmodernism argues for authoritative appeals of a different nature.

Again, there is no single strand of postmodernism that can be easily defined. But whereas modernism tends to be confident in the legitimacy of its rationally and empirically argued claims to knowledge and truth, postmodernism tends to be skeptical of them. Whereas modernism tends to make declarative statements of propositional truth, postmodernism tends to relate narratives that include truth from the situated context in which it is spoken. Whereas modernism claims to have firm rational and empirical grounds on which to make truth claims, postmodernism tends toward a more relativist view of knowledge, at least with regard to the degree that people claim truth from the perspective of rational and empirical legitimation. Postmodernists frankly acknowledge the contextual or cultural influence on knowledge. It is not that individuals alone are situated; their sociocultural context also influences people's narratives. This does not mean that substantial amounts of information cannot be compiled, trusted, and applied to life, but humility must characterize human claims to it since people are in an ongoing process of learning more and more.

Keeping in mind that a variety of Christians claim to be influenced by postmodernism, it is difficult to make generalizations about how it influences their Christian understanding. Some would say that postmodernism emphasizes how, since biblical times, Christians have lived "by faith, not by sight" (2 Cor. 5:7)—that is, by belief and practice rather than by rationality or empirical investigation. Their faith was in a person—God, Jesus Christ, the Holy Spirit—rather than in a set of propositional statements. For example, when Jesus said, "I am the way, and the truth, and the life" (John 14:6), was he calling people to commit to the rational and empirical indubitability of his statements, or was he calling people to commit themselves to him, a person?

From a postmodern Christian perspective, there seems to be no necessary problem in agreeing with the apostle Paul, who said, "For we know only in part. . . . For now we see in a mirror, dimly" (1 Cor. 13:9, 12a). What is now seen dimly will be seen clearly when we meet God—when we personally and immediately encounter God: "But then we will see face to face. Now I know only in part; then I will know fully, even as I have been fully known" (1 Cor. 13:12b).

Some postmodern Christians suggest that cultural relativism unavoidably influences Christian understanding, so that they question whether exclusivistic claims to religious truth and authority are warranted. Of course, this degree of skepticism is what frightens Christians who want to affirm that Christian beliefs, values, and practices should have dominion over all dimensions of life and not just the spiritual one.

Critics of postmodernism argue that its skepticism may result in a kind of tribalism (or neotribalism) that says no one tribe (like-minded group, or social network) of people can claim more knowledge or truth than any other. If no one can claim to have more truth than others, then affirmations by a person or "tribe" must be enforced by power or cultural coercion rather than by rational or empirical argumentation. Relations between people reduce to power struggles, since truth plays a diminished role.

Despite postmodernist Christians' caution about the degree to which their claims can be rationally and empirically legitimated, they do not wholly throw out the possibility of making religious claims—even universal religious claims. But the authority by which they make such claims appeals more to personal, historic, and cultural authorities (for example, church tradition) than to those of reason and experience, rationalism and empiricism.

Some references by Christians to postmodernism, confusingly, have more to do with its cultural aspects than with its intellectual claims. In fact, they may celebrate what they consider to be the merits of postmodern culture, without understanding the theological implications of what they promote. For example, culturally postmodern Christians may like the freedom they feel in experimenting with numerous ways to worship, sing, dress, and go about the various church ministries. They may also like the use of narrative and story as a way to communicate God; they may nostalgically like to recover premodern expressions of church rites, rituals, and liturgy; and they may like more community-oriented dynamics and expressions of Christianity. However, while they may like to call themselves "postmodernists" or a "postmodern church," they may neither understand nor care about the intellectual challenges of postmodernism to biblical, historic Christianity. They might actually be appalled at the theological implications of calling themselves postmodern.

So, before Christians go about describing themselves culturally by what seems "new" or "different," they also need to do the requisite work of evaluating the intellectual implications of their claims. Given the intellectual concerns of postmodernism, Christians need to be, at least, more humble with regard to the truth claims they make about God, creation, humanity, sin, salvation, and the Christian life. There is indeed a "situatedness" or contextuality characteristic of all human knowledge; after all, Christians think of themselves as part of creation, which is both relative to and dependent on God (though there is not agreement with regard to the extent of that situatedness). Christians also need to be open to the prospect of conceiving religious authority less in terms of rational and empirical legitimation and more in terms of personal and historic legitimation. Such an approach may seem less certain, questioning the degree to which Christianity is based on rationality and empirical facts, but it may also seem more biblical, apostolic, and canonical.

■ Ongoing Issues

The issue of religious authority has been a question of great import from the time of Jesus onward. Of course, most Christians would say that God is their ultimate religious authority, and rightly so. However, with regard to the authorities readily available to people today, which ones function most authoritatively on behalf of God? Jesus's authority was challenged by religious leaders, and he defended it. As the first-century church developed, questions of authority again arose. The church met the challenges through apostolic leadership, a council, and, of course, the Scriptures. The Scriptures were unformed, since neither an Old Testament nor a New Testament had been formally canonized by Christians. Despite this lack of canonization, the Scriptures remained authoritative for matters of religious beliefs, values, and practices.

Apostolic leadership served predominantly as the final religious authority during the patristic era. However, as Christianity became established in the Roman Empire, so did the canon of Scripture. Its authority was considered unique, since its origin took place among the apostles during the first century. Nevertheless, scriptural authority was not thought to usurp the ongoing apostolic leadership passed on through the succession of clergy. Apostolic authority was first greatly challenged with the schism between the Eastern and Western churches. But the primacy of apostolicity persisted, despite competing claims to apostolic authority.

The Protestant Reformation brought the question of religious authority to a dramatic pivot point in church history. From the Protestant perspective, biblical authority superseded that of other ecclesiastical and historic authorities.

However, once the Reformation occurred, a variety of understandings of authority arose. Questions of authority became especially important in contrast to growing Enlightenment claims to authority of a more rational, empirical, and secular nature. Challenges to authority continue in light of postmodern challenges both to Enlightenment-oriented modernism and Christianity.

When considering the issue of religious authority from a Christian perspective, one ought not to think that newer is better, or that so-called premodern views are passé. Such assumptions may diminish the authoritativeness of the Bible itself, which few Christians would want to do. Instead, Christians need to think about what they value most with regard to the various views presented. They are presented not to confuse people but to help them understand some of the key alternatives that arose in church history. Greater understanding of the distinctive viewpoints may be helpful in making theological decisions for oneself.

The questions of theory and practice may be of help in assessing Christian views of religious authority. If one is unclear about one's particular theory (or theology) of authority, then begin by clarifying how one makes theological decisions in practice. For example, to what degree do your religious and personal decisions reflect the Bible? Does it directly affect your theological decision making, or are your decisions thought, at least, to be implied in the Bible? To what degree are your life decisions influenced by a religious leader or leaders, the local church, or a denomination? How do such authorities compare with the Bible? How historically and critically do you interpret the Bible? To what degree do logic and critical-thinking skills affect your theological decision making? What of relevant experience, and to what degree may it include personal experience, collective experiences, scientific investigation, and culture? How contextual is your theology; that is, to what degree do you consider theological decision making to be a complex, dynamic process that is not easily defined? To what extent is the Bible thought to be a sure foundation of truth that does not err? To what extent is the Bible subject to historical criticism? To what extent is all human knowledge susceptible to historical criticism and other contextual challenges to modernistic confidence in sure intellectual foundations of truth? Is all knowledge culturally relative? May Christians legitimately say that Jesus is "the way, the truth, and the life"? If so, how?

The questions above are not intended to overwhelm readers to the point that they freeze up or become incapable of deciding since the issues seem too complex. Issues related to religious authority are indeed tough questions. But they are questions Christians deal with almost every day in their lives, unconsciously if not consciously. Moreover, we have presented a number of Christian views that readers may use as examples to help develop their own theological understanding of the Bible and other religious authorities. Rather than let people make crucial life decisions without self-awareness, it is our contention that they are better off if they become increasingly aware of not only what they believe, value, and practice but also why they do so. We invite readers to become more aware and intentional about their theological decision making, and all decisions are potentially theological, if they want God to be part of their lives. In becoming more aware, we think that people will also become more successful and confident in how they make decisions about the Bible and all important life decisions.

7

Inspiration of the Bible

The apostle Paul served as mentor to a young pastor named Timothy, whom Paul had known since his youth. Paul mentions Timothy multiple times in the epistles. It is debated whether the two letters expressly written to Timothy in the New Testament were written by Paul. Because some scholars question the Pauline authorship of 1 and 2 Timothy, one should be prudent in utilizing their content. Be that as it may, from a canonical perspective, which has always included both writings in the New Testament, 1 and 2 Timothy have prominently influenced Christians throughout church history. Perhaps no verses have been more influential than those pertaining to the divine inspiration of Scripture.

Second Timothy is addressed to Timothy, and Paul claims to write the letter from prison, presumably in Rome. Facing imminent death, Paul writes with passion, sharing final advice to his pastoral apprentice. Amid various bits of advice, Paul wants to encourage Timothy in the face of suffering and persecutions. In chapter 3, Paul warns him about the godlessness of the last days (2 Tim. 3:1–9). He encourages Timothy by talking about the many persecutions he personally experienced, and how God faithfully helped him to persevere (2 Tim. 3:10–11). Paul uplifts himself as a role model in the face of false teachers as well as persecutions (2 Tim. 3:12–13). He exhorts Timothy to remember all he learned and believed since childhood, and how Timothy had "known the sacred writings that are able to instruct you for salvation through faith in Christ Jesus" (2 Tim. 3:15). Paul then comments on the nature of those sacred writings, producing the most powerful reference used by Christians to describe the inspired nature of

God's revelation. He says: "All scripture is inspired by God and is useful for teaching, for reproof, for correction, and for training in righteousness, so that everyone who belongs to God may be proficient, equipped for every good work" (2 Tim. 3:16–17).

These verses will be discussed more thoroughly later in the chapter. But the key concept is the divine inspiration of Scripture. No clearer statement is found within the biblical writings with regard to divine inspiration. However, despite its apparent clarity, these verses have been understood variously throughout church history. To what Scripture (or Scriptures) do Paul's words pertain? What is the nature of inspiration? What is the etymology of the word? How was the word understood in its sociocultural context as well as its religious context? Can the statement apply to itself; that is, can the affirmation about inspiration be applied to 2 Timothy? How has the concept of inspiration developed in church history? What ways has it been understood? Has there been a consensus in the meaning of inspiration? If not, then how ought Christians decide about the nature and extent of its meaning? Is the concept of divine inspiration still meaningful today?

These questions along with others have been crucial to Christians' understanding of the Bible. Other biblical passages have been used, of course, to reinforce and expand on the meaning of divine inspiration. So we write this chapter to help readers understand the nature and extent of Christian beliefs about the Bible's divine inspiration. Our discussion will begin with the Bible's self-portrait, so to speak, referring to the biblical references used to describe sacred writings. We will next look at ways that divine inspiration was viewed in antiquity and how ideas about it developed later in church history. Finally, we will present a summary of the ways divine inspiration has been understood by Christians. Although differing views of it exist, most Christians refer to divine inspiration in terms of how they understand both the uniqueness and authority of the Bible.

■ What Scripture Says about Scripture

Scripture—the Bible—does not provide a clear statement or theology of itself. It makes significant comments about the nature of "Scripture" or "sacred writings," but the Bible is not systematic in talking about them. As discussed earlier, the Bible developed over numerous centuries and in compound ways. So caution should be used in attributing a biblical or theological statement uncritically to all verses.

Let us look at a number of things found in the Bible to describe the nature of sacred writings (Scripture, or Scriptures), especially with regard to divine inspiration. The only two explicit references to divine inspiration are found in Job 32:8 and 2 Timothy 3:16. Job 32 recounts the story of Job, his three friends, and a fourth friend, named Elihu. Elihu had remained silent while Job and his other friends spoke, out of respect because they were older (Job 32:6–7). However, Elihu thought that Job was too heavily invested in justifying himself rather than God, and his friends had no constructive answers in response to Job's questions, though they considered Job to be in the wrong (Job 32:2–5). So, in anger, Elihu said, "But truly it is the spirit in a mortal, the breath of the Almighty, that makes for understanding" (Job 32:8). The reference to "breath of the Almighty" is sometimes interpreted as inspiration. According to the book of Job, it is God who gives true understanding rather than people's age, their wisdom, or other human qualities. The reference to the breath of God is not related to Scripture, so it does not directly help us with regard to our study of its divine inspiration. But the concept of the breath of God relates to how similar terminology is used in 2 Timothy 3:16.

The Greek word for divine inspiration used in 2 Timothy 3:16 is *theopneustos*, which is variously translated as "God breathed," "God breathed out," "God spirated," or "inspired." In fact, in some translations of the Bible, the word "breath" was used, rather than inspiration, in order to be more literal in translation. Historically, translators of the Bible have favored "inspiration" as the preferred wording, emphasizing a well-known expression for divine origin.

The concept of divine inspiration already existed within the ancient Near East. People were thought to be overcome by the gods and goddesses, inspiring them to speak or act in ways that accorded with the gods' and goddesses' will. The Greek muses, for example, were considered a source of knowledge. They were thought to inspire literature, art, and music of Hellenistic culture. Some people were actually considered the "oracles" or "soothsayers" of God, speaking and acting on behalf of the gods and goddesses. Others, such as Hercules, were considered half divine and half human. So the notion of divine inspiration was already present and known by the ancients.

Paul's reference to the divine inspiration of Scripture, of course, pertains to the Hebrew Bible—the Old Testament. Paul seems to have no problem with referring to the Old Testament as the "oracles of God," which includes the law (Rom. 3:2). Others in the New Testament tell of their belief in Scripture. Jesus repeatedly referred to Scripture, using variations of the expression "it is written" more than seventy times. He also talked about the prophecies and how they must be fulfilled, especially through his life, death, and resurrection (for example, Mark 14:49; Luke 24:44). In talking to the Jews, Jesus appealed to Scripture—the Word of God—in order to talk about himself as "God's Son."

> Jesus answered, "Is it not written in your law, 'I said, you are gods'? If those to whom the word of God came were called 'gods'—and the scripture cannot be annulled—can you say that the one whom the Father has sanctified and sent into the world is blaspheming because I said, 'I am God's Son'?"
>
> John 10:34–36

Jesus and others referred to Scripture as the Word of God. For example, Jesus ascribed Moses's words to God (Matt. 19:4–5). Other examples can be added about how Jesus, the disciples, and other followers of Jesus considered Scripture's originator to be God, mediated through people, and eventually through written record.

Without doubt, Scripture was considered unique, divinely inspired, and authoritative by first-century Christians. Questions arise, however, when we try to understand the nature and extent of that authority and to extrapolate their beliefs with regard to issues and concerns raised at later times and places. Like those in the first century, Christians have always had extraordinarily high regard for Scripture. But it is not easy to determine how Scripture should be specifically understood from the general comments they made. Hence a variety of Christian beliefs developed about its inspiration.

■ Historical Developments

During the first three centuries after the time of Jesus, Christians did not have the luxury of developing a theology of divine inspiration, since they were marginalized within the Roman Empire, unable to develop a widespread consensus of beliefs. They had not even been able to canonize the Bible, much less formalize theological claims about it. Eventually, Christians under Constantine were able to meet publicly and ecumenically for the first time. After the Council of Nicaea, which brought together Christian leaders from around the empire, a first consensual statement was reached about the nature of prophecy, which relates to the nature of Scripture. The first creed—the Nicene Creed—talks about the nature of prophecy in relationship to the person and work of the Holy Spirit. It says:

> We believe in the Holy Spirit, the Lord, the giver of life,
> who proceeds from the Father and the Son.
> With the Father and the Son he is worshiped and glorified.

He has spoken through the Prophets.
We believe in one holy catholic and apostolic Church.
We acknowledge one baptism for the forgiveness of sins.
We look for the resurrection of the dead,
and the life of the world to come. Amen.[1]

The Nicene Creed attributes prophecy to the Holy Spirit, who spoke through the prophets. The creedal statement alludes to the words of 2 Peter 1:20–21: "First of all you must understand this, that no prophecy of scripture is a matter of one's own interpretation, because no prophecy ever came by human will, but men and women moved by the Holy Spirit spoke from God." Many prophets claimed to speak for God. There were, of course, false prophets. Claims to be a prophet did not guarantee the authenticity of a person's prophecies. However, the prophecies of Scripture were not thought to be false, originating or interpreted by people, and thus subject to the limitations of human judgment. Instead, true prophecies, including those of Scripture, were thought to be from God through the Holy Spirit. Early views of divine inspiration relate to the belief that the apostles, and later the church, spoke prophetically, which represented truth "from God."

As the Nicene Creed suggests, Christians prior to and subsequent to the fourth century affirmed the divine inspiration of the Bible. Likewise, they generally affirmed its truthfulness. However, while Christians accepted the Bible's divine inspiration in theory, in practice they recognized numerous interpretive quandaries. Rather than talk about the Bible as if it erred or contradicted itself, different methods of biblical interpretation arose in order to harmonize the discrepancies. Early schools of biblical interpretation arose, centered in Alexandria (Egypt) and Antioch (Syria). On the one hand, the Alexandrians appealed to allegorical (or symbolic) interpretation of Scripture in order to find deeper meaning, which also resolved some of the apparent discrepancies found in the text. Clement of Alexandria and Origen were famous representatives of the Alexandrian school. The Antiochians, on the other hand, such as John Chrysostom, placed more value on the literal, historical interpretation of the Bible. They did not deny the presence and value of allegory, but they focused more on the historical meaning of the Bible than on its mysterious, mystical, or spiritual meaning. In time, the Alexandrian school became more influential in biblical interpretation. In

---

1. "Nicene Creed," International Consultation on English Texts translation, http://www
.creeds.net/ancient/nicene.htm, accessed April 23, 2011. Note: The phrase "and the Son" (Latin *filioque*) did not appear in the original version of the Nicene Creed, but it was formally added in the eleventh century by Pope Nicholas I, which contributed to the eventual split between Eastern Orthodox Churches and the Western Roman Catholic Church.

fact, the allegorical and symbolic interpretations of Scripture developed into related hermeneutical methods, since Scripture was thought to contain various meanings or senses.

The Bible was thought to contain at least four senses. Thus a fourfold approach to biblical interpretation arose that included the following herme-neutical methods:

1. literal, or historical interpretation;
2. allegorical, or symbolic interpretation (including typology);
3. tropological, or moral interpretation; and
4. anagogical, or eternal, metaphysical, eschatological interpretation.

Interpreters looked first for the literal, historical meaning of texts. How-ever, if historical inaccuracies or biblical contradictions were present (that is, Scripture contradicting Scripture), then there may be other interpretations that explain apparent discrepancies or errors in the text. For example, inter-preters might ask, is there allegorical or symbolic meaning in the text? For some interpreters, the latter type of interpretation may reveal deeper, mysti-cal meaning in the text that is not obvious to those who read only biblical texts with literal, historical expectations in mind. Typologies, for example, are clearly used in the Bible, and less straightforward typologies may reveal hidden meaning in the biblical texts. Likewise, some texts—such as parables, which are problematic when read only as literal historical stories—may be best understood with moral interpretations. Instead they represent a different type of genre, requiring a different hermeneutical approach, which provides more profound ethical teaching. Finally, anagogically oriented texts and, in-deed, entire books of the Bible may be best understood with a metaphysical or eschatological interpretation that does not readily lend itself to a literal, historical approach, which may mislead interpreters with regard to what can be religiously known now or in predicting the future. In some instances, a literal, historical approach to interpretation may be the worst way that people understand the biblical text.

This fourfold approach to biblical interpretation goes back in history as far as Jerome (ca. 347–420) and John Cassian (ca. 360–435). Others, such as Origen (ca. 185–253), thought of interpretation more in terms of body, soul, and spirit—a threefold approach to biblical interpretation—but promi-nently appealed to allegory in resolving historical inaccuracies and biblical contradictions. Thomas Aquinas (ca. 1225–74) and Nicholas of Lyra (ca. 1270–1349) utilized the fourfold approach of literal, allegorical, tropological, and anagogical interpretation. But they recognized that the fourfold approach to biblical interpretation, in and of itself, was not sufficient to explain the development of all church doctrines since some of them arose as articles of belief rather than rationally and empirically established beliefs, values, and practices.

During the ancient and medieval eras, Christians were not speculative about the nature of divine inspiration. It was generally accepted that the Bible was inspired by the Holy Spirit, without critical questioning about theological particularities. After the Protestant Reformation, however, more questions arose among churches about religious authority, biblical inspiration, and proper interpretation. Because of the priority placed on biblical authority by the Reformers, it was important for them to promote the Bible as much as possible, despite a similarly high view of divine inspiration of the Bible held by the Roman Catholic Church.

Roman Catholics argued that, as an article of belief, the canonical books of the Bible are inspired. Thomas Aquinas had talked about divine inspiration of the Bible in terms of instrumental causation, reflective of ancient and medieval discussion of causality. Presumably God used people as instruments through whom God inspired the writings of the Bible. However, the Roman Catholic Church did not specify a particular understanding of the instrumentality or mechanism of divine inspiration. According to the Roman Catholic Church, the inspiration of the Bible is not something deduced from the Bible alone. Since the church and its leadership, as well as the Bible, have religious authority, the nature and extent of the Bible's inspiration is also confirmed by the church and its apostolic leadership. The Holy Spirit is thought to work in the lives of Christians, individually and collectively, and the Holy Spirit has inspired prophetic proclamations throughout the Christian era and not just in the creation of the Bible.

The Roman Catholic Church thought it had the authority to confirm the inspiration of the Bible. Of course, this confirmation acknowledged the Bible's teachings about sacred Scripture; it also acknowledged the truthfulness of the Bible's teachings. As we will see, the Roman Catholic Church affirms that the Bible does not err, which further legitimates its divine inspiration. Of course, the views held among Roman Catholics should not be thought of as monolithic; there exist conservatively oriented and progressively oriented branches of Catholicism. Lively debate occurs among Catholics with regard to many theological issues, including that of divine inspiration. Despite the church's official statement about inerrancy, the proper interpretation of the Bible still requires input from the church, since not everything in it is thought to be plainly clear to individuals unaided by the guidance of apostolic authority, in turn aided by the grace of God's Holy Spirit.

Martin Luther agreed with the high view of the Bible held by the Roman Catholic Church, though he disagreed with the logic that its divine inspiration was confirmed through the legitimation of the church. His concern had more to do with how God revealed the gospel through Jesus, the Bible, and preaching; all represented the inspiration of the Holy Spirit at work for people's salvation. Luther mentioned the verbal inspiration of the Bible—namely, that the words of it were inspired by the Holy Spirit. However, Luther did not speak of a verbal theory of inspiration per se, which was developed later by Christians in the nineteenth century. To this extent, many consider Luther to be premodern in the sense that he did not ask the same kinds of historical and critical questions raised after the emergence of Enlightenment concerns. Caution must be used in trying to distill contemporary theological viewpoints in earlier Christians for whom the issues were different. For example, words and phrases used in one era of church history may not have the exact same meaning in another era. One risks projecting Christians beliefs and values on the past that distort, rather than clarify, biblical and theological views.

Luther also affirmed the trustworthiness of scriptural teachings and considered its content confirmatory of divine inspiration. He did not explicitly affirm a teaching of inerrancy, for example, but he was confident of truth contained in the Bible. The Holy Spirit bore witness to the divine inspiration of it, and like other aspects of Luther's theology, the Spirit's witness was available to individuals, just as was salvation, without the mediation of the church. Luther was aware of the fourfold approach to biblical interpretation, which he sometimes referred to as the *quadriga* or *quadruplex*. At first Luther opposed it since he thought that it contradicted his emphasis on the authority of the Bible alone (*sola Scriptura*). However, he vacillated in his appreciation of the fourfold approach, noting that at times multiple approaches to the interpretation of the Bible were necessary and beneficial to understanding the gospel. Biblical texts may not have multiple meanings, but they did contain obviously diverse genres.

John Calvin similarly affirmed the divine inspiration of the Bible. He sometimes referred to how God dictated the words of the Bible through the Holy Spirit. For example, when Calvin comments on 2 Timothy 3:16, he says, "The law and the prophets are not a teaching delivered by the will of men, but dictated by the Holy Ghost."[2] However, there is not unanimity among Reformed scholars with regard to whether Calvin would have understood these words in terms of a mechanistically oriented theory of dictation that disregarded all

---

2. John Calvin, quoted by J. I. Packer, "Calvin the Theologian," in *John Calvin: A Collection of Essays* (Grand Rapids: Eerdmans, 1966), 162.

human admixtures to creation of the Bible. Although Calvin did not articulate a formal dictation theory of divine inspiration, he clearly held a high view of the Bible's inspiration, authority, and trustworthiness. If the words of the Bible seem wanting in any way, according to Calvin, they appear that way because God made it so in order to communicate with people whose understanding is limited or unrefined. The content of the Bible functions as if a parent has to simplify words to a young child in order for the child to understand. The particularities of God's revelation to people in the Bible have more to do with people's immature understanding rather than with any deficiency in the texts.

Later Reformed Christians became more explicit than Calvin in talking about the Bible as verbally dictated. The Second Helvetic Confession (1562), for example, reflects the leadership of Heinrich Bullinger and other Continental Reformers. The confession clearly talks about how the very words of the Bible are inspired by the Holy Spirit and that they are without errors. Consider the section "Scripture Teaches Fully All Godliness":

> We judge, therefore, that from these Scriptures are to be derived true wisdom and godliness, the reformation and government of churches; as also instruction in all duties of piety; and, to be short, the confirmation of doctrines, and the rejection of all errors, moreover, all exhortations according to that word of the apostle, "All scripture is inspired by God and profitable for teaching, for reproof," etc. (II Tim. 3:16–17). Again, "I am writing these instructions to you," says the apostle to Timothy, "So that you may know how one ought to behave in the household of God," etc. (I Tim. 3:14–15). SCRIPTURE IS THE WORD OF GOD. Again, the selfsame apostle to the Thessalonians: "When," says he, "You received the word of God which you heard from us, you accepted it, not as the word of men but as what it really is, the Word of God," etc. (I Thess. 2:13). For the Lord himself has said in the gospel, "It is not you who speak, but the Spirit of my Father speaking through you"; therefore "He who hears you hears me, and he who rejects me rejects him who sent me" (Matt. 10:20; Luke 10:16; John 13:20).[3]

As Protestant scholasticism developed, more emphasis was placed on following the theology of its founders than on the Reformation principle of "always reforming." The creativity and fidelity to the Bible in Luther and Calvin lapsed into more and more meticulous investigation and preservation of the founders' writings as understood—rightly or wrongly—by their followers. Their scholasticism may have prevented them from anticipating the questions and challenges of the burgeoning Enlightenment and its influence on Christians' understanding of the Bible.

3. The Second Helvetic Confession, Christian Classics Ethereal Library, http://www.ccel .org/creeds/helvetic.htm, accessed April 23, 2011.

■ Views of Divine Inspiration

The Enlightenment encouraged Christians to view the Bible as a human book, without the presupposition of its divine inspiration. What does the content of the Bible suggest about itself, without prejudicing interpretations of it? How does a more inductive approach to biblical studies affect one's beliefs—one's theology? In particular, how does it affect the longstanding affirmation of the Bible's divine inspiration?

Once divine inspiration was no longer assumed, even by Christian interpreters, a variety of theological viewpoints arose. Some were decidedly skeptical about the nature and extent of divine inspiration. Scripture looked more like human inspiration than anything divine. In response (or reaction) to these progressively skeptical views, more conservatively oriented Christians devised very specific doctrines designed to defend historic affirmations of divine inspiration. There certainly was precedent in what ancient, medieval, and Reformation Christians had written, but their comments had not been theologically articulated as specific doctrines. Thus a variety of viewpoints arose.

Rather than looking at these views historically, we instead want to look at them relative to the degree to which they view Scripture as divinely inspired. Do not think of the following views as either advocating divine inspiration or not. Such either/or categories are far too limiting. For example, grouping theories into the categories of conservative/liberal or evangelical/mainline is woefully inadequate; too many issues are involved, including issues that may or may not relate to their views of the Bible per se. Instead think of the various theories as being on a spectrum or continuum between those tending more toward divine inspiration and those tending away from it, usually toward views that emphasize the human dimension of inspiration. If we think of the relationship between viewpoints more in terms of a continuum rather than either/or categories, we can be more critical in how we understand and relate them to one another. Just because a view is at one end or the other does not necessarily mean that it is better or worse. In fact, few Christians agree with the most extreme views. As we will see, the majority of Christians identify with views in between the extremes. Although views at the extreme ends of the continuum may seem more consistent, logically speaking, they reveal that logic alone is inadequate in determining biblical and theological beliefs.

Of course, views in the middle are not necessarily more balanced, correct, or—especially—biblical than other theological views. Most views, at least those on the divinely inspired end of the continuum, claim to be biblically based or demonstrable. Obviously, those who hold different views would disagree, claiming, for example, that a far more contextual approach to the question of divine inspiration is required. Because there is no consensus in church history with regard to particular theologies of divine inspiration, there is no ecumenical standard by which to arbitrate between views. Thus we will speak of the following views as theories rather than as views, theologies, or doctrines; they are theories that should be analyzed and assessed for how well they answer questions about the Bible, textually and spiritually.

Arguments that claim to be based on the Bible alone may not be automatically convincing. As already mentioned, most of the theories below would claim to be biblical or biblically based, depending on the particular ways they understand Christian decision making. Proponents of some theories will likely need to argue more persuasively than others, utilizing evidence—from church tradition, critical thinking, and relevant experience—that will be more persuasive than others in arguing for their theological point of view.

It is a judgment call on our part with regard to where each theory falls on the continuum. Consensus categorizations of theories of divine inspiration do not exist. So, rather than create arbitrary categories, we group related theories of divine inspiration together. We will try to give reasons as to why certain theories of divine inspiration are placed where they are in the order of discussion. Be advised that the theories mentioned do not reflect exact locations on the so-called continuum; some would actually be better put on entirely different continua, since not all of them deal with precisely the same issues related to divine inspiration. The order of discussion simply provides a comparative way to evaluate the different theoretical viewpoints. It is hoped that this exercise will help bring clarity to readers rather than confusion.

We realize that there are probably more views of divine inspiration than some readers imagined, and perhaps more than they realistically want to know. Complicating the discussion is that theories mentioned in the chapter are sometimes defined differently. Thus terms like "verbal," "plenary," "dynamic," "partial," "limited," and so on are not always understood the same way. In fact, if you want to read further about these various theories, there are scholarly treatises that go into far more detail and word parsing than we do. So readers must be patient in order to understand the particular definition for terms used in this book, which may not necessarily be the same as definitions found in other sources.

Dictation (or Mechanical) Theory

The dictation theory argues that God dictated words to the biblical authors to write. The mechanism of dictation prevents any admixture of

the authors' personality, lives, historical context, and other factors subject
to their human finitude and sinfulness. The mechanical or instrumental
emphasis of the dictation theory is why it is sometimes described as the
mechanical theory. The dictation theory of divine inspiration claims that
it represents the most truthful understanding of the Bible and is the least
susceptible to errors.

Advocates of dictation theory point to the numerous biblical references
to how God spoke to and through people, and how those conversations were
recorded in the Bible. The prophets often prefaced their comments with
the declaration, "Thus says the Lord." Other appeals are made to biblical
passages that talk about how all prophecies and Scriptures are inspired by
God, how excellent and trustworthy the resulting passages are, and how a
sovereign God would not allow the Bible to be written that was not entirely
in accordance with God's sovereignty. Thus every word—indeed, every letter—of Scripture is thought to be dictated by God.

Philo of Alexandria advocated an "automatic writing" theory of the Bible
that resembles dictation theory, and the First Vatican Council of 1868–70
used phraseology substantively the same as that of dictation.[4] Advocates
of dictation theory point to similar references in ancient, medieval, and
Reformation Christians who readily talk about how the Bible represents the
express words of God. To be sure, such references were frequently made.
However, references to God's words expressed in the Bible do not necessarily equate with the theory of dictation advocated formally in the nineteenth
century. Nineteenth-century Christians rejected the growing questions and
concerns raised by Enlightenment-oriented interpreters of the Bible who
used historical and critical methods of biblical interpretation. Although
advocates of dictation theory may appeal to previous Christians, whom they
claim as confirmation of their theological views, they may not unambigu-
ously claim them as clear-cut advocates of the theory. Since earlier writers
did not deal with the theological implications of divine dictation theory
per se, it is anachronistic to claim them as advocates. Such caution is true of
any relatively modern formulation of theology that attempts to legitimate
its beliefs by claiming uncritically the support of ancient, medieval, and
Reformation Christians for their theories.

Today few Christians advocate actively on behalf of the dictation theory.
Too much emphasis in biblical interpretation is placed on the personalities
of biblical authors, the significance of their life circumstances, and other

4. Bruce M. Metzger and M. D. Coogan, *The Oxford Companion to the Bible* (New York:
Oxford University Press, 1993), 302–4.

dimensions of their historical context to view every word and letter of the Bible to be simply the dictation of God. For example, the different personalities, backgrounds, and worldviews of the Gospel writers are generally distinguished with regard to the particular presentations they make about the life and ministry of Jesus. Although God could have had their personalities, lives, and historical contexts in mind when God dictated the words of Scripture to them, few Christians consider this theory adequate. Of course, in practice, Christians sometimes think about the Bible as if every word and letter are God's words, as if God dictated them. Christian preaching, teaching, and devotional comments made by Christians may suggest that the words of the Bible carry the weight of God's word-for-word instructions to people today. But a mature approach to biblical interpretation should be cautious as well as prudent with regard to making absolute claims about knowing the mind and will of God.

The concept of dictation can be found in other religious traditions. The Qur'an (or Koran; Arabic "the recitation"), for example, was claimed by Muhammad to have been dictated to him by Allah, the Arabic name for God. The words of Allah were thought to be dictated verbally to Muhammad by the angel Jibril (or Gabriel). Similarly, in the Church of Jesus Christ of Latter-Day Saints, founder Joseph Smith claimed that the *Book of Mormon* was given to him by the angel Moroni on golden plates, written in an ancient Egyptian language. Through divine inspiration, Smith translated the golden plates and published them as *The Book of Mormon: An Account Written by the Hand of Mormon upon Plates Taken from the Plates of Nephi*. Because both the Qur'an and the *Book of Mormon* are thought to be dictated by God, their followers are heavily invested in arguing for their word-for-word perfection and inviolability.

When Christians argue for the dictation of the Bible, they too must be heavily invested in arguing for its word-for-word perfection and inviolability, or what we will later describe as the doctrine of inerrancy. Some argue that inerrancy requires the theory of dictation; however, other Christians argue that alternative theories of divine inspiration equally support it. Ironically, one of the arguments used to defend the doctrine of inerrancy is the so-called slippery-slope argument; that is, if even one error is found in the Bible, then the entirety of its truthfulness is destroyed. Yet most proponents of inerrancy do not rely on the dictation theory to substantiate their beliefs about the Bible. Apparently, the slope is not so slippery or steep that an appeal to the dictation theory is necessary. Thus slippery-slope argumentation does not necessarily support (or refute) any particular view of divine inspiration.

Verbal and Plenary Theories

The verbal theory of divine inspiration argues that the very words and phrases biblical authors chose to write were inspired by God, while at the same time reflecting their particular personalities, lives, and historical context. However, the reflection of their lives in no way diminished the precision of what God wanted to communicate through them. The human element, although present, did not prevent the authors from choosing words and phrases that communicated exactly what God wanted communicated. The biblical authors in no way limited the divine control over (or superintendence of) and truth of what was written.

Sometimes the verbal theory of divine inspiration is associated with what is known as the plenary theory. "Plenary" basically means all (or full, unlimited) the words of the Bible, and not only some of the words of the Bible. The combination of verbal and plenary (or plenary and verbal, or verbal-plenary) views is intended to counter those who advocate a partial or limited view of God's inspiration of the Bible by saying that some portions of it were more inspired or reliable than other portions. Although the verbal and plenary theory may recognize that some parts of the Bible are more crucial for communicating the gospel, all of it should be thought of as inspired and worthy of being called the Word of God.

The verbal theory of inspiration is sometimes identified with dictation theory rather than plenary theory. So categorizations of the various theories can be misleading, and a critical approach to understanding them should be used. Although both theories claim the highest understanding of divine inspiration of the Bible, the verbal and plenary theories want to avoid the mechanistic limitations of dictation theory, which seem to view biblical authors as automatons and disregard their rich historical and cultural backgrounds.

It is easy to find examples of Christians who advocate verbal and plenary theories of inspiration. Advocates include such notable scholars as the so-called Princeton school, which included Reformed scholars at Princeton Theological Seminary during the late nineteenth and early twentieth centuries, such as Archibald Alexander, Charles Hodge, Archibald A. Hodge, and Benjamin B. Warfield. Advocates of verbal and plenary inspiration have widely influenced conservatively oriented Christianity in the United States and around the world.

The Fundamentals, or *The Fundamentals: A Testimony to the Truth*, was an anthology of essays edited by A. C. Dixon and Reuben Archer Torrey during 1910–15.[5] The publication became a focal point for the so-called

---

5. For an updated edition, see Reuben Archer Torrey and Charles L. Feinberg, eds., *The Fundamentals: A Testimony to the Truth* (Grand Rapids: Kregel, 1990).

fundamentalist-modernist controversy. Although *The Fundamentals* discussed numerous topics, later Christians used its title as a way of distilling five fundamental beliefs, which should be required of truly biblical Christians. The five fundamental beliefs were considered crucial in countering the progressively liberal and secularizing views of the Enlightenment among a growing number of Christians, especially within mainline Protestant denominations. The five fundamental beliefs have been stated in different ways, but basically they include the following:

1. the verbal inspiration and inerrancy of the Bible;
2. the virgin birth of Jesus;
3. belief in Jesus's death as the substitutionary atonement for sin;
4. the bodily resurrection of Jesus (and correspondingly of everyone); and
5. the historical authenticity of miracles, especially those of Jesus.

For the sake of our present discussion of divine inspiration, only the first fundamental belief is of importance. Some references to the first fundamental include only verbal inspiration, while others include plenary inspiration and inerrancy. Although the doctrine of inerrancy will be a topic of discussion in the next two chapters, its affirmation is considered inextricably bound up with the theories of verbal and plenary inspiration of the Bible.

One consideration (or caveat) that needs to be mentioned is the fact that most advocates of verbal and plenary inspiration would say that, technically speaking, their beliefs pertain only to the original writings or autographs of biblical authors. This qualification is noteworthy because, if their theories are challenged for any reason, then technically the challenges do not apply since we no longer have the original autographs of the Bible. While this may seem like an artful dodge, apologetically speaking it also works against those who believe in the verbal and plenary theory of divine inspiration. What good are their beliefs if there is no existent or known text that may be read and evaluated? Although appeals to the original autographs seems like a red herring argument (or distraction), advocates still argue that existing biblical manuscripts and indeed present-day translations are sufficiently truthful in their communication of God's divinely inspired revelation that designations such as verbal, plenary, and inerrant still apply. They apply, but always with qualifications with regard to technical discussions of the issues, which may perplex as much as clarify one's theology of the Bible. (More will be said about debate regarding the original autographs of the Bible in the following chapter.)

Dynamic, Concursive, and Sacramental Theories

Dynamic theories of divine inspiration argue that some dynamic occurs between the work of the Holy Spirit and that of people in the writing of the Bible. The nature of the dynamic is not always clearly or consistently articulated by its advocates, but it is inadequate to talk about divine inspiration alone without the simultaneous involvement of the authors of the Bible. Augustus Strong, for example, argued "that the Scriptures contain a human as well as a divine element, so that while they present a body of divinely revealed truth, this truth is shaped into human molds and adapted to human intelligence. In short it is neither natural, partial, nor mechanical, but supernatural, plenary and dynamical."[6]

In stringing together so many adjectives, Strong may be claimed by those who advocate multiple views of divine inspiration. This is why, in part, it is so difficult to claim past Christian scholars as advocates of a particular theory, since they lived before the theories became formalized. Be that as it may, Strong represents someone who considered it inadequate to think of inspiration (or creative involvement) only in terms of God's role in the writing of the Bible. The human authors must also be considered in more dynamic, interrelated, and interdependent ways together with the work of the Holy Spirit. Thus the need for the Holy Spirit's involvement extends beyond the writing of the Bible; the Holy Spirit continues to work in the lives of readers, guiding them in rightly interpreting, understanding, and applying divine revelation.

The *concursive* theory of divine inspiration represents, perhaps, an updated version of the dynamic theory, since the concursive theory intends to present a middle way (via media) between the divine and human dimensions of writing the Bible. The word "concursive" derives from the word "concur," which suggests that the Holy Spirit inspired the authors of the Bible simultaneously as they wrote and the authors utilized their particular human gifts and talents. That is, there is a "concursus" or confluent authorship between the involvement of the Holy Spirit and the involvement of people. Of course, the concurrence represents a mystery or paradox, which does not suggest a 50/50 or even a 99/1 split of inspiration. Like the longstanding doctrine of the incarnation of Jesus Christ, the concursive theory argues that Scripture can be understood as 100 percent divinely inspired while simultaneously being 100 percent human. This is not a paradox to be logically explained, but a paradox to be affirmed by faith. The concursive theory wants to affirm fully both divine and human participation in the writing of Scripture. Although

6. Augustus H. Strong, *Systematic Theology*, 2nd ed. (New York: Armstrong, 1889), 102.

this argument may seem like a sly attempt to claim the best of both divine and human participation, the concursive theory presents an incarnational understanding of the Bible that resembles the creedal, orthodox paradox of the incarnation.

An implication of the concursive theory is that the Bible can be viewed entirely as a divinely inspired writing. As such it can claim all the authority and trustworthiness one might expect of revelation from God. Simultaneously the concursive theory claims that Scripture can be understood and studied as other books written by people. For those who value most the divine inspiration of the Bible, the latter affirmation is problematic. Although advocates of the concursive theory may claim divine inspiration for the Bible, their study of it may engage the texts as if it is a human creation. As such, the Bible is subject to the same kinds of historical and critical investigation that led Christians in the past to question not only the trustworthiness of the Bible but also its legitimacy as divine revelation. Is it sufficient to affirm the divine inspiration of the Bible while at the same time subject it to the most rigorous and skeptical investigation possible? Is this, not a paradox, but a contradiction that defies logic as well as historic affirmations of the authority and trustworthiness of the Bible?

I. Howard Marshall represents an advocate of the concursive theory of divine inspiration, as do Benjamin B. Warfield and others. However, caution must again be used in terms of identifying past Christian scholars with more contemporary manifestations of particular theories. By intending to serve as a middle way between the polarities of divine and human authorship, it is possible for two very different interpretations of the theory to occur. For example, from the perspective of those who argue that Warfield represents the concursive theory, rather than a verbal or plenary theory, inerrancy might be claimed as a necessary conclusion of it because—after all—the Bible can be understood as being 100 percent divine. However, from the perspective of those who argue that Marshall represents the concursive theory, views of the trustworthiness of the Bible other than inerrancy might be claimed, since the Bible can also be understood as being 100 percent human. Indeed, those who read Warfield and Marshall would probably consider Warfield to fall further on the divine end of a divine-human continuum, while Marshall would fall further on the human end. Thus the concursive theory is not easily classifiable; that is, it may be interpreted in more than one way, thwarting those who claim to know the only way the theory may be interpreted.

Overall, proponents of the concursive theory of divine inspiration want to incorporate more of the human dimension in writing the Bible without excluding the Holy Spirit's role. Appeals to mystery and paradox sound appealing until particular questions of biblical interpretation arise. To what degree may the Bible be understood as human, fallible, susceptible to the sinfulness of authors? To what degree may historical and critical interpretive methods have free reign over the Bible?

Some Christians think about the authorship of the Bible in terms of its being a means of grace, in an almost sacramental way of understanding the Bible. Although there exist various understandings of the means of grace and sacramentalism, a *sacramental* theory of biblical inspiration emphasizes how God uses physical, material elements as signs of spiritual, immaterial realities. Correspondingly, God may use people as physical, material agents as signs of spiritual, immaterial truths in the Bible, which function in ways that are graciously efficacious in the lives of people. A sacramental theory will also rely on mystery and paradox to talk about how God effects salvation in the lives of people, including means of humble bread and wine. Likewise, it is thought that God effects revelation in the lives of people by the means of humble human authors—how God graciously, sacramentally reveals things in and through finite, fallible people. To the degree that people rely on the sacraments as means of grace, they likewise may rely on the Bible as a means of grace and divine revelation. Sacramentally speaking, greater divine revelation occurs as people read Scripture with the gracious aid of the Holy Spirit, unavailable through the mere reading of the Bible alone. The dynamic interaction between the Holy Spirit and readers results in a greater revelatory whole than occurs through reading of the individual parts of the Bible.

Since there is not uniformity among Christians with regard to their understanding of the sacraments (if they acknowledge the sacraments at all), a sacramental theory of the inspiration of the Bible may not be all that appealing. It is difficult enough trying to find agreement among Christians regarding the sacraments, so adding a sacramental view of the Bible may confuse matters more. Perhaps so, but the prospect of a sacramental view of the nature and extent of divine inspiration is intriguing for those who find existing—less mysterious and paradoxical—theories less appealing.

Partial, Limited, or Degrees of Inspiration Theories

Partial or *limited* theories of divine inspiration argue that parts of the Bible are divinely inspired. Advocates believe that the Bible contains divine revelation; however, one must use prudence and careful biblical study in order to sift out the "chaff from the wheat," so to speak. Contained within the Bible are eternally significant teachings, but it contains the admixtures of human, cultural, and moral qualities incompatible with God's self-revelation. The admixtures, of course, may have occurred at multiple points in the writing and transmission of the Bible. It may have occurred during the time of oral tradition, before writing occurred; it may have occurred during the writing, rewriting, editing, or redacting of the Bible; it may have occurred during the copying and transmission process of ancient texts. Who knows? But biblical texts contain obvious discrepancies and inconsistencies that are incommensurate with a pristine understanding of divinely inspired revelation. Such content must be weeded out in order that the excellences of the gospel may be revealed.

Advocates of partial or limited theories of divine inspiration arose primarily during the nineteenth century, as Christians began to use historical and critical methods of biblical interpretation. Not all approached biblical texts with the presupposition that all of it was a human creation, but neither did they approach texts with the presupposition that they were a divinely inspired creation. Otherwise, how does one account for the apparent discrepancies that biblical scholars had long given the Bible a pass on? That is, they no longer believed that they could in good conscience ignore obvious discrepancies and inconsistencies in the biblical text. Longstanding attempts at harmonizing them seemed like a devotional approach that lacked the kind of historical and critical rigor characteristic of other human endeavors. If God is truly the sovereign being described in the Bible, surely God's revelation ought to be able to endure such questions.

An example of those who advocate partial theories of divine inspiration is Adolf von Harnack who wanted to distill the "timeless kernel" of divine revelation from the "historical husk" in which the former was encased in the Bible. During the nineteenth century, Harnack was impressed by the scholarly results of historical criticism. It seemed obvious that the Bible is limited in various areas of science and history. The Bible is not a book of geology, geography, and biology; it is a book that contains divinely revealed precepts and principles especially important for salvation and ethical living. Christians should focus on the precepts and principles contained therein rather than become distracted with issues irrelevant to the preeminently spiritual message of the Bible.

A related view is known as *degrees of inspiration*, which says that the Bible contains teachings that reflect varying degrees of inspiration, trustworthiness, and authority. In practice, Christians function this way all the time. Usually the New Testament is considered more authoritative than the Old Testament; the words of Jesus are treasured more than the words of others (hence red-letter-edition Bibles); and some Bible passages are more popular, memorized, and hung on walls in Christians' homes. Sometimes people refer to this graded understanding of the Bible as representing a "canon within the canon." Parts of it are thought to contain more inspired, truthful, and hence authoritative texts than other parts. Although Christians may not be consciously aware of what they are doing in theory, in practice they consider there to be degrees within the quality of biblical revelation.

The difficulty with partial, limited, and degrees of inspiration theories is the difficulty of determining what parts of the Bible contain essential truths and what parts are historically, culturally, and scientifically limited. Who decides? To what authority do people appeal in order to make the determinations? In the nineteenth century, scholars believed that they were able to distill between the kernels and husks with historical-critical methods of interpretation. However, at the turn of the twentieth century, Albert Schweitzer challenged their optimism in his book *The Quest of the Historical Jesus*. Schweitzer argued that it was impossible, humanly speaking, to distill essential truths in the Bible from what is historically and scientifically relative. In fact, attempts to do so reveal more about the interpreters, who project their own assumptions and expectations on the biblical texts. Despite Schweitzer's challenge, biblical scholars still attempt to sift out the most historically reliable parts of the Bible; a present-day example is the Jesus Seminar, which gathered dozens of biblical scholars from around the world in order to evaluate the historicity of Jesus.

Despite difficulties in distilling the essential truths of the Bible, many Christians feel quite comfortable devotionally and theologically with a partial, limited, or degrees of divine inspiration theory of the Bible. After all, they would argue, Christians should not try to project onto the Bible what they hope to find but accept the Bible they actually have. If it contains incontrovertible errors in history and science—if nothing else—then Christians ought to deal with the Bible as it exists. They should not pander to a view of the Bible they can only hope for it to be. Advocates of this view of inspiration would argue that Christians ought to go beyond a naive, childlike view of the Bible, and not continue an unwillingness to accept realistically the Bible that God has given us. Just as God can use fallible preachers who preach less-than-perfect sermons, God can use a fallible Bible. God's work in the world has not been deterred by the nature of the Bible in the past, so there is no reason to suspect that a more realistic and mature understanding of it will prevent God's work from continuing in the future. According to this view of inspiration, as people read the Bible and become immersed in its teaching, even with its shortcomings and flaws, they may become more and more aware of God's revelation to them, as the Holy Spirit works in and through their lives.

Dialectical Theories

Dialectical theories of divine inspiration largely refer to the theological beliefs and values that go back to Karl Barth during the first half of the twentieth century. Sometimes dialectical theology is referred to as neoorthodox theology, which was the term given to Barth and others who followed in his theological tradition. A dialectical approach to theology does not rely on rational and empirical argumentation with regard to its affirmations; instead it relies on the present, personal work of God in the lives of people. With regard to the Bible and its inspiration, it is not the Bible that represents divine revelation, properly speaking. It is Jesus who represents the Word—the living Word of God. John 1:1 says, "In the beginning was the Word, and the Word was with God, and the Word was God." Although the Bible makes references to sacred writings as the "word of God," the Bible is only so in a conferred or derivative sense, since it is Jesus who is the true Word. Thus theology must be Christocentric, focusing on the person and work of Jesus today, since it is he who truly saves, leads, and guides us.

What, then, of the Bible? Barth thought that we cannot know the precise mechanism for how the Bible was inspired and how it can be thought of simultaneously to contain the words of God and the words of people. Christian attempts to discover the essential words of God in the Bible were theologically suspect; it represented human hubris with regard to knowing and relating fully with God. Both the Bible and interpreters' attempts to understand it are culturally bound by the limitations of human finitude and sin. Be that as it may, God endeavors to encounter people as they read the Bible. In fact, God has chosen to encounter people personally as they read the Bible or hear it proclaimed, since God uses such events as opportunities for personal self-revelation. The Bible may be understood in a secondary sense as the Word of God, but it is far more important to encounter the living Word—Jesus Christ—than anything written about him, regardless of the perfection or imperfection of the writing.

One of the difficulties in defining dialectical theology in general, and a dialectical theory of divine inspiration in particular, is confusion over the meaning of the term "dialectic." Historically, Plato wrote about Socrates's dialectical method of dialoguing with regard to philosophical issues until conclusions were reached, even if the conclusions were humbly considered tentative. During the nineteenth century, Georg Hegel talked about dialectic in terms of a progressive interaction between theses (theories), antitheses (counter theories), and subsequent syntheses (theoretical resolutions) that produced greater knowledge and understanding. He was confident that people were capable of finding, and obliged to find, truth, which is rationally and empirically attainable. In contrast to Hegel's intellectual optimism, Søren Kierkegaard agreed that people encountered theses and antitheses in life; however, not all dialectical issues can or should be resolved. Matters of living—of existence—supersede those of intellectuality, and people exist more authentically by living within the midst of those tensions than by trying to extricate themselves by rational and empirical means.

Barth's theology resembled the latter form of dialecticism, arguing more for a personalized than intellectual understanding of Christian beliefs and values, and focusing on faith more than reason and experience. For example, sin has to do with more than breaking the laws of God; it has to do with breaking relationship with God; and repentance has to do with more than confessing sin; it has to do with becoming reconciled with God. So, focusing on the revelatory nature of the Bible distracts people from the essence of Christianity—namely, people's relationship with God. A criticism of a dialectical theory of divine inspiration is that the Bible is viewed more as a human document than as something divinely inspired. Scripture may contain the word or words of God, but such a presence ought not to be people's focus. Historical and critical investigations of the Bible reveal interesting information that is informative and potentially helpful to readers as God encounters them through it. But the reliability of the Bible per se ought not to be the concern of Christians. Such views, expectedly, do not appeal to those who wish to affirm the divine inspiration so highly that the biblical text is considered entirely reliable, or at least, mostly reliable. According to Barth, the Bible may indeed be mostly reliable; however, that is not the point of its existence. The Bible is not there in order to serve as a resource book or encyclopedia that provides intellectual and factual information about the way things are. Instead it is there because God chooses to use it as a means to encounter people personally, which is the only means of eternal significance. As such, Christians may not find that they all interpret the Bible the same; since God encounters people individually, their theological and ethical understandings may differ.

Sometimes dialectical theology is referred to as fideism. Fideism asserts that faith and faith relationships with God are superior to reason, experience, and their theological constructs. Christians are to live by faith rather than by sight, regardless of whether it is rationally and empirically informed sight. Of course, dialectical and neoorthodox theologians may not generally call themselves fideists, but the term helps to emphasize how much they advocate Christianity based on faith, a personal relationship with God, and the need to rely on God's gracious care for them. As much as some Christians want to legitimate their beliefs and values on the indubitable foundation of the Bible as inspired and entirely reliable, dialectical theologians would say that their faith is misplaced on something created and should rather be on Someone uncreated—God.

Human Theories (Intuition, Illumination, Genius)

Theories of human inspiration of the Bible celebrate the human contribution to people's spirituality and religious nature. God may inspire people to write what becomes the Bible, but what is written reflects primarily their ideas rather than those of God. As such, God's involvement is more indirect and inspirational than directly inspiring. People shortchange themselves by attributing to God that which reflects their inner spirituality, understanding, and virtue.

Human-oriented theories of inspiration are not new or recent. Johann Herder, for example, wrote at the end of the eighteenth century about the poetic essence of the Bible. In *The Spirit of Hebrew Poetry*, Herder conceived of the Bible in both romantic and secular terms, arguing that it is best understood poetically and artistically. Thus, if people want to appropriate the Bible's depth of religious insight, it should be read as human poetry. This reading best enables people to glean the essence of what the Bible has to offer.

Some human-oriented views of the Bible hold that God inspires the authors, though not directly. Other views do not require belief in God per se. Most, however, believe that God inspires the Bible but does so indirectly. God may inspire biblical authors in the same way that a parent inspires a child or a teacher inspires a student. God may also inspire them to rely on their own intuition or innate spirituality, or illumine them in ways that bring out the best in people's human nature, reflecting the image of God, in which they were created. Deists, for example, believe that God created people with the mental and spiritual capabilities to understand and live out God's will for their lives without the direct involvement of God. In fact, in the writing of the Bible, some people may have exceeded their God-given gifts and talents, resulting in a kind of religious genius that produced its writing.

More traditionally oriented Christians may not find these theories of biblical inspiration all that persuasive. However, for those who tend toward a deistic understanding of God, the Bible becomes more understandable and persuasive in a rationally, scientifically, and technologically oriented world. They also do not have to deal with what seems to them to be an obviously fallible document, with improvable stories of healings, miracles, and angels.

Moreover, the Bible may thwart as much as help people to find the positive, transcendent aspects of their lives; but the Bible may still serve as an aid that encourages people to discover for themselves all that God wants for their lives—all that God has endowed them with since creation. Traditionally oriented Christians may not find these deistically oriented ideas all that persuasive in theory, but in practice they may have difficulty denying that they live like deists. After all, Christians do not always seem to live lives that exhibit the same manifestations of healings, miracles, and angels mentioned in the Bible. On the contrary, they live lives based on fulfilling their innate potential rather than meticulously following the Bible or in daily seeking God's plan for their lives. As such, a deistically oriented form of Christianity may represent a more realistic, perhaps pragmatic, approach to religion that cares less about establishing biblical foundations of truth than it cares for practically living day-to-day lives of common sense and peaceful spirituality.

■ Consensus and Divergence

Throughout church history, Christians have overwhelmingly affirmed that the Bible is divinely inspired. It is not a book like any other book; it is unique, one-of-a-kind, God-given. There is consensus among Christians, with little disagreement, that the Bible is indeed inspired, God-breathed. Thus the inspiration of the Bible represents one of the greater points of consensus among Christians, even though they may disagree on particular details about its inspiration.

Disagreements arise, certainly, with regard to the nature of the Bible's divine inspiration. As we have seen, numerous theories have arisen among Christians in church history. There is nothing close to consensus beyond the ancient affirmation in the Nicene Creed that God's Holy Spirit "spoke by the prophets."[7] Indeed, life might be less divisive if Christians were willing to agree on the Bible's divine inspiration without digressing into the particularities of what that means.

Because the concept of inspiration seems somewhat abstract—a notion not often expressed or widely discussed—Christians have been able to hold divergent theories of it without requiring undue rigor or shibboleths (religious tests) for their beliefs. However, people's beliefs carry implications. Usually it is not the issue of divine inspiration that causes angst and debate among Christians, but its implications—its consequences. In particular, questions

---

7. Nicene Creed, Creeds of Christendom, http://www.creeds.net/ancient/nicene.htm, accessed April 23, 2011.

related to the truthfulness or trustworthiness of the Bible have been especially divisive topics of discussion. How truthful is the Bible? How extensive is that truthfulness? Does it pertain only to matters of salvation, the Christian life, and the church? Does it include truth about history, science, and matters other than that of spirituality? These questions and others will be discussed in the following two chapters. But the starting point of Christians' beliefs usually relate, to one degree or another, to which theory of divine inspiration of the Bible they affirm.

8

The Bible, Truth, and Error

The book of Psalms contains some of the best-known, loved, and quoted portions of the Bible. It addresses many Christian beliefs, values, and practices—who God is, who we as people are, and how God wants to redeem and relate with people. It is not surprising that the Psalms say a great deal about Scripture as the Word of God. Psalm 119, for example, celebrates Scripture many ways. According to the psalmist, "Your word is a lamp to my feet and a light to my path" (Ps. 119:105), and "I treasure your word in my heart, so that I may not sin against you" (Ps. 119:11).

The book of Psalms also talks about the trustworthiness of God's Word. In Psalm 111, the psalmist writes a hymn of praise and thanksgiving for the wonderful works of God. Among the many works the psalmist mentions, the trustworthiness of God's "precepts"—God's Word, law, Scripture—are revered:

> Praise the LORD!
> I will give thanks to the LORD with my whole heart, in the company of the upright, in the congregation.
> Great are the works of the LORD, studied by all who delight in them.
> Full of honor and majesty is his work, and his righteousness endures forever.
> He has gained renown by his wonderful deeds; the LORD is gracious and merciful.
> He provides food for those who fear him; he is ever mindful of his covenant.

> He has shown his people the power of his works, in giving them the
> heritage of the nations.
> The works of his hands are faithful and just; all his precepts are
> trustworthy.
> They are established forever and ever, to be performed with faithfulness
> and uprightness.
> He sent redemption to his people; he has commanded his covenant for-
> ever. Holy and awesome is his name.
> The fear of the LORD is the beginning of wisdom; all those who prac-
> tice it have a good understanding. His praise endures forever.

Throughout the Bible, God's precepts are considered trustworthy, reliable, and true. Many similar attestations may be added to those from the Psalms. From appeals to fulfilled prophecy to Jesus's appeals to Scripture in facing temptation, the precepts of God represent sure guides as to how Christians should believe, value, and practice every aspect of their lives.

In ancient church history, there was no consensus with regard to the truth of Scripture, since a canon had not been established. Debates arose about which writings should and should not be included. Eventually the canon received conciliar approval, but still not everyone agreed. Although the canon of Scripture—what came to be known as the Bible—was thought to be trust-worthy, its establishment had required debate, persuasive argumentation, and compromise.

The various methods of biblical interpretation also served to deal with is-sues related to the trustworthiness, reliability, and truth of the Bible. Appeals to allegory, symbolism, and moral teaching, for example, exempted parts of the Bible from literal and historical scrutiny, which seemed inadequate to resolve perceived discrepancies and inconsistencies within the biblical texts.

When apparent discrepancies and inconsistencies could not be overlooked or when individual Christians, pastors, and scholars did not agree, the lead-ership of churches—the pope and magisterium in Western Christianity, for example—pronounced proper interpretations of the Bible. Ecclesiastical au-thority resolved questions of truth when the Bible alone was insufficient to resolve them.

When the Protestant Reformation occurred, questions raised had more to do with religious authority than with the trustworthiness of the Bible. The Roman Catholic Church maintained its right and responsibility to critique the growing individualistic tendencies of Protestants to interpret the Bible however each individual considered it right and proper. Such individualism was thought to fragment both biblical and historic Christianity, and who could predict how diversely Christianity in general, and the Bible in particular, might be understood? Yet, once Protestantism began, there was no way to stop a growing breadth of biblical interpretation, since no church leaders or magisterium had decisive authority to guide it.

Questions about the truth of the Bible arose with the rise of deism, especially in Great Britain, during the seventeenth century. Deists such as Lord Herbert of Cherbury and John Toland doubted the biblical stories about healings, miracles, and angels. Instead, they established Christianity as a religion based primarily on reason and nature. The mythological elements about supernatural phenomena were considered unnecessary, a distraction. God-given reason and common sense were sufficient for understanding and happy, successful living the way they thought God created the world and people.

The most influential and troublesome questioning of the truthfulness of the Bible arose during the nineteenth century with the rise of historical and critical methods of biblical interpretation. The methods in and of themselves were not problematic; however, the naturalistically oriented presuppositions brought to the biblical texts were. Previously such discrepancies had been overlooked out of reverence for the text or because of premodern assumptions that were not considered significant relative to the contributions of the Bible as a whole. Now the discrepancies and inconsistencies in the biblical text became a center-stage concern since biblical critics seemed to find less and less that was historically, scientifically, logically, and—to a certain extent—morally reliable.

Today Christians still find themselves embroiled in debate over the trustworthiness of the Bible. Is it reliable? Is it true? What is the nature of truth? What are ways in which it is understood? What are ways that it should be understood? How might differences in understanding truth affect Christians' view of the trustworthiness of the Bible? What of morally suspect actions of biblical heroes? Are biblical accounts about slavery, child sacrifice, war, genocide, women, and other issues culturally anachronistic or outright unjust?

In this chapter, we will talk about ways people—both Christians and non-Christians—understand truth and its relationship to the truth or trustworthiness of the Bible. We often use the words "truth" and "trustworthiness" together, though they are not identical. Some Christians place more emphasis on truth, including its precise definition and extent. However, others place more emphasis on the overall trustworthiness of the Bible, which may or may not pertain to exact standards of measurement from foundations of rationality and empirical verification. Of course, people trust the Bible because they believe it is inspired by God, who warrants their trust. Although trustworthiness will be used mostly to describe different views of the Bible, it is first necessary to talk about truth and the ways that people understand it.

■ What Is Truth?

It is difficult to begin a section on truth without recollecting Pontius Pilate's pitiable question to Jesus before Pilate condemned him to death. In trying to uncover why the Jewish leaders brought Jesus to him for trial, or perhaps out of genuine curiosity, Pilate asked: "What is truth?" (John 18:38). We may wish that Jesus had answered Pilate; however, almost immediately Pilate seems to have grasped truth at least enough to try to have Jesus released. Eventually Pilate caved to social and political pressures rather than to truth.

We do not intend to provide an extensive discussion of truth as it is understood today or how it has been understood throughout history. Such a discussion would take far too much time. So we will focus on issues of truth particularly related to questions germane to the trustworthiness of the Bible.

As John writes in his Gospel account, Jesus is famously quoted as saying, "I am the way, and the truth, and the life. No one comes to the Father except through me" (John 14:6). Jesus claims to represent "truth," according to John, but what is the nature of that truth? At the least, it has to do with becoming reconciled to God the Father; it also has to do with becoming Jesus's disciples. In John 8:31–32, Jesus says: "If you continue in my word, you are truly my disciples; and you will know the truth, and the truth will make you free." Again, the truth Jesus speaks of pertains primarily to being set free in order to become his disciples. Elsewhere, the word (or words) to which Jesus wants his followers to adhere includes Jesus's so-called great commission, which includes the following exhortation to his disciples: "teaching them to obey everything that I have commanded you" (Matt. 28:20). So adherence to the truth of Jesus includes no less than following him and abiding by all that he taught. But that truth does not necessarily extend beyond matters related to coming to God, following Jesus, and obeying his teachings. Or does it?

In the history of Western civilization that precedes the time of Jesus, two philosophical traditions—broadly speaking—arose with regard to how knowledge and truth are acquired. The tradition of rationalism is identified with the philosophy of Plato, and the tradition of empiricism is identified with the philosophy of Aristotle. Plato sought certain knowledge, which was not thought to be available in the finite world we live in. Knowledge that is of a universal, transcendent nature must consist of an immaterial reality not susceptible to the finite changeableness of the material world. Plato argued that people rationally apprehend unchanging forms (or ideas), of which our present world is a mere reflection or shadow. Yet through a rational process of "recollection," people become aware of universal truths that range from mathematics and geometry to philosophy and ethics. Reason and rational thinking are the key to attaining certain knowledge. So Plato's epistemology—the philosophy of how knowledge is attained—is known as rationalism.

In the ancient church, Christians were drawn to Platonism because it advocated an unchanging, immaterial realm that transcended the finite world we live in. Augustine, for example, considered people's rationality their highest quality endowed by God. Reason aided people not only in logical thinking but also in comprehending divine truths that transcend other human limitations. A philosophical development known as Neoplatonism, which emphasized a hierarchy in the created order, had special influence on Augustine. People represent God's highest creation just as rationality represents the highest human capacity; rationality is also inextricably bound up with people's spirituality. Although Augustine regarded rationality highly, it did not provide a sure foundation for all knowledge. People need to trust in God's revelation as found in the Bible, relying on its authority to guarantee the trustworthiness of God's revelation. The physical world, in and of itself, is inadequate to communicate all truths important for the happy, blessed lives God intends people to live. Fortunately, God aids people by illuminating their understanding of divine truths.

Aristotle represented a more empirical approach to how people acquire knowledge. Like Plato, Aristotle sought universal knowledge, but he thought that such knowledge was found in particular things in the world, which reflected their true essence. Whereas Plato relied more on deductive reasoning, Aristotle used both inductive and deductive reasoning. By inductively studying the natural world, crucial insight is gained in comprehending and understanding universal constants. In this regard, his understanding of epistemology is thought of more in terms of empiricism than rationalism, though later empiricists were not as convinced as Aristotle with regard to how certain our knowledge is of transcendent reality. For Aristotle, there was a kind of ascent from particular knowledge of the natural world to universal knowledge of its essence.

The philosophy of Aristotle was not well known by Christians during the time of the ancient church, but it became increasingly influential among Christians during the medieval era. In particular, Thomas Aquinas (or Thomas of Aquino) was greatly influenced by Aristotle's philosophy with regard to what Thomas referred to as natural revelation. Thomas thought that people's rational and empirical capabilities are able to discern many significant theological truths. The most famous, of course, was his five arguments for the existence of God, which included cosmological and teleological arguments. However, natural revelation had its limits, and at some point people need supernatural revelation, which requires faith. The Bible represents the primary supernatural revelation given by God, but such revelation is part of the greater tradition of the Roman Catholic Church, guaranteed both by the inspiration of the Holy

Spirit and through the enduring work of the Spirit in the church's popes and magisterium. So Thomas was confident in how much can be known by general human reason, but for the most crucial knowledge that we have about God, salvation, and the Christian life, special divine revelation is required.

This overview of epistemology brings us to one of the better-known theories of truth, known as the correspondence theory of truth. With regard to questions and concerns over the truthfulness of the Bible, it has played the major role in Christians' understanding. Keep in mind, however, that it is not the only theory of truth that will be discussed. As we will discover, the particular view of truth people hold influences the nature and extent to which they consider the Bible to be true.

People are not always consciously aware, of course, of thinking within the context of a particular theory of truth. In fact, they might even be offended that a particular theory is applied to beliefs, values, and practices that they consider Bible-based rather than having to do with philosophy. But everyone works with certain assumptions or presuppositions, which are intellectually identifiable, even if they are unaware of them. So, in order to gain a more critical understanding of people's view of the truth of the Bible, we must take time to study theories of truth that influence people, regardless of their awareness or willingness to be identified with them.

Correspondence Theory of Truth

The correspondence theory of truth affirms that truth correlates with something or someone when there is a one-to-one correspondence between what we rationally say and what we experience. Propositional statements that people make about the world and what they believe are thought to correspond to reality—the way things objectively are—that is, facts. Reality is thought to be objectively knowable, though reality consists of multiple dimensions that are more and less easily known. Physical realities (or objects), for example, may be more easily understood than psychological, social, and spiritual realities, but their truth ultimately corresponds to their being real, not imagined.

The aforementioned epistemologies of rationalism and empiricism are usually categorized with the correspondence theory of truth. Rational principles of mathematics and geometry, for example, are thought to correspond to the actual state of affairs in the world. So do our statements about psychological, sociological, and spiritual realities, though different means may be necessary for discovering and evaluating them. Thus, it is no wonder that when most people think about the trustworthiness or truth of the Bible, they do so with the correspondence theory of truth in mind.

With the rise of the Enlightenment, increased emphasis was placed on establishing reason and experience—rationalism and empiricism—as the foundations on which to establish truth. René Descartes and those who followed him wanted certainty that was rationally and empirically measureable, not subject to doubt, and that therefore resulted in indubitable truth. The affirmation of sure foundations of truth, sometimes known as "foundationalism," basically speaking, represents the view that there are epistemological starting points that produce knowledge that cannot be denied or refuted. Descartes and other Enlightenment thinkers looked to reason and/or empiricism on which to establish such irrefutable certainty.

The emphasis on foundationalism, however, veered away from the search for truth representative of previous philosophers and theologians, who were not so narrow with regard to what represented legitimate foundations of truth. Theologians such as Augustine and Thomas Aquinas, for example, had a lively understanding of the person and work of the Holy Spirit, who is not measureable rationally and empirically. Since they did not live in the context of the Enlightenment and modernist assumptions, it is anachronistic to claim them as Christian exemplars of what is known as foundationalist epistemology. They may have had great confidence with regard to the trustworthiness of the Bible, but they do not represent corroboration of modernist Christians who appeal to rational and empirical criteria in order to argue for the Bible as an equally sure foundation of truth.

Given the increased expectation for rational and empirical truth in general, it is no wonder that Christians expected the same degree of truth from the Bible. However, with the diminishing willingness of interpreters to give it a pass with regard to its factual and logically consistent exactitude, a growing crisis developed since the objectivism promoted by modernists exposed discrepancies and inconsistencies in the biblical text that previously had been disregarded. Historical and critical interpreters of the Bible, for example, in the nineteenth century became increasingly skeptical about the trustworthiness of the biblical texts. Thus they looked on the Bible as being more fallible than infallible, more a guide to truth than a foundation of it. The Bible may still be viewed as inspired, but inductive study of the biblical texts required greater nuance in conceptualizing divine inspiration due to textual problems that could no longer be ignored.

In response to growing skepticism, Christians responded over time in several ways. For example, advocates of inerrancy, dialectical theology, and postmodern Christianity, among others, responded to historical and critical interpreters of the Bible, most often identified with liberal Protestantism, in quite different ways. (Each of these views will be discussed in the next chapter.) Of course, questions about the truth of the Bible arose among non-Christians as well as Christians. So debate was not limited to within churches; it became apparent to everyone that the truth of the Bible faced mounting challenges.

One thing that is important to keep in mind as we study the various views of the truth of the Bible is that not every view accepts the correspondence theory of truth. Some of them will, but not all. So questions and concerns raised by the following views of the Bible's trustworthiness will appear quite different; some will consider the truth and error-free nature of it to be of superlative importance, while others will not. How can that be? It has to do, in part, with their theory of truth. Not all adopted the Enlightenment emphasis on the need for objective verification of truth—that is, of the need for rational and empirical legitimation of truth claims. So, before proceeding, we need to understand other theories of truth.

Coherence Theory of Truth

The coherence theory of truth places more emphasis on the degree to which people truthfully conceive of the world in a wholly coherent way, rather than in a way reducible to objective facts per se. This does not mean that facts are unimportant, but facts alone can be ambiguous and people interpret the same facts differently. People's knowledge is limited, and it is influenced by the particularities of the place and time in which their knowledge developed. This does not mean that people cannot discover truth, but truth is related more to the coherence of things understood together rather than separately. Values, virtue, and beauty, for example, are parts of life not altogether quantifiable by rational and empirical criteria. In addition, relationships and spirituality are not reducible to objective facts. The nature and extent of truth may transcend the mere study of observable evidence. So truth claims about particular parts or particular realities of the world are less important than mutually supportable inferences from multiple dimensions of existence, which cannot be reduced to objective verification.

Rather than go into a lengthy comparison of the correspondence and coherence theories of truth, let us discuss one theological truth that may help to clarify why a Christian might find the coherence theory more persuasive than the correspondence theory: faith. Throughout the Bible, people are exhorted to live "by faith, not by sight" (2 Cor. 5:7). The object of faith, after all, is God, who ultimately transcends human knowledge (Heb. 11:6). Faith has to do with what is unseen rather than what can be established by rationalism and empiricism (John 20:29). Indeed, much of what people believe in has to do with an unseen future that defies correspondence with currently available facts (Heb. 11:13–14). The faith the Bible calls people to has more to do with trust in God, dependent on a subjective relationship with God, than with objective criteria (Prov. 3:5–8; John 14:1). The subjectivity of relationships does not mean subjectivism and the rejection of objective criteria; but the truth of relationships is not wholly quantifiable objectively in the same way as, for example, scientific inquiries. In addition to faith, hope and love are also relationally oriented, since they are also based on a relationship with God, who is not thought to be reducible to rational and empirical data.

Since the time of medieval Christianity, faith was thought to consist of at least three characteristics:

1. *notitia* (Latin "knowledge");
2. *assensus* (Latin "assent"); and
3. *fiducia* (Latin "trust").

First, faith represents knowledge, since Christians believe in Jesus Christ, including facts about his life, death, and resurrection. Christians do not believe in any facts or religion; they believe in the Bible's gospel message. Second, it is not enough for people to know these facts; according to James, "even the demons believe—and shudder" (James 2:19). True faith must intellectually assent to the facts about Jesus, the gospel, and salvation. Third, people must entrust their lives to God as well as to the truth of the aforementioned facts for their salvation. This salvation was based on the life and ministry of Jesus, by the grace of God, through the person and work of the Holy Spirit. These latter aspects of faith—trust, grace, and salvation—do not lend themselves easily to rational and empirical legitimation. They are more spiritual truths than physical truths that are rationally established. During the Reformation, Protestants such as Luther emphasized faith as trust rather than as factual knowledge and intellectual assent, even if the latter unerringly corresponded with teachings of the church. Such trust requires confidence more than common sense or church affiliation, risk more than certainty, since God's guarantee of truth transcended human verification.

The coherence theory of truth becomes more understandable, in one sense, when considered in relationship to the growing emphasis on postmodernism. As already stated, postmodernism argues that human knowledge is contextual or "situated"; that is, people are finite, and their immediate context influences how they understand facts and values in the world. Some facts and values are less influenced by people's social, historical, and cultural contexts than others, but all people are influenced by the particular place and time they live in. Thus claims to having certain, unambiguous, and indubitable knowledge do not sync with how other people, in different places and times, claim to have knowledge that obviously disagrees with them. Postmodernism does not doubt that truth is knowable; certain truths are knowable (2+2=4, death, and taxes, to name a few). However, postmodernists doubt the indubitability (or the impossibility of doubt) of knowledge, especially the rational and empirical claims to a foundational legitimation for their propositional truth statements. Because of the limits of human finitude and, frankly, challenges to the extent of their knowledge due to sin, Christians should arguably be more open to how coherence represents a more adequate theory of truth than correspondence to facts alone. To be sure, postmodernism in general, and postmodern Christians in particular, may advocate views of knowledge and faith that challenge historic, biblical affirmations about God, truth, and salvation. But, they would argue, coherence comes far closer to the way life is lived than does a correspondence theory of truth.

Pragmatic Theory of Truth

The pragmatic theory of truth represents, in some respects, a distinctively American contribution to the discussion of truth. Pragmatists such as Charles Peirce, William James, and John Dewey argued that truth has to do with the practical outcome of affirmations of truth, beliefs, and values. Truth is tested by the outcomes produced. That is, truth pertains more to the practicality and productivity of people's beliefs and values than to idealistic criteria based on inconclusive debate over rational and empirical verifications. Absolute truth is not sought, but practical or pragmatic truth is. As such, knowledge is thought to be tentative, based on the outcome of the concepts we have. How effective are they? What do they produce? Pragmatists tend to be confident that greater truth is attainable, as truths, tentatively affirmed, are corrected through trial and error. Although truth claims are fallible, they lead people to increasingly greater probabilities of truth. Trial and error, rather than philosophical or theological evaluations, becomes the best test for truth.

From a Christian perspective, truth has more to do with how God intends to achieve certain ends than with stating facts, values, or principles per se. For example, it may be that God uses the Bible, preaching, and personal testimonies as ways to save people and aid them in Christian living, even though the mediums of the Bible, preaching, and personal testimonies fail tests of rational and empirical corroboration. But such fallibility is unimportant, relative to the way that God wants to work in and through the lives of people. Achieving God's end or goals for people is more important than how they are achieved.

Few Christians would describe themselves as adherents to a pragmatic theory of truth. Yet in practice it seems that Christians care less about affirming particular beliefs and values than about how successfully and happily they live their lives. If Christian beliefs and values benefit from what "works" for people, then people will continue to affirm them. However, if Christian beliefs and values cease to benefit people, then one, more, or all of them are discarded. In the United States, it seems as if pragmatism in general, and pragmatic Christianity in particular, is the religious "default setting" for the country. In fact, Christians sometimes join "God and country" into a kind of civil religion, which they affirm not so much because of a deep, heartfelt religiosity based on a biblical worldview but because it "works" for them. However, uncritical associations of Christianity with country (any country), political party (any political party), or any other part of culture seem to be based—consciously or unconsciously—on a pragmatic theory of truth rather than other theories of truth. Such cultural Christianity represents an accommodation to the world that displaces the Bible's truths.

Constructivist Theories of Truth

Constructivist theories of truth argue that personal, social, historical, cultural, and other factors influence the knowledge and truth that people have. So truth claims are historically and culturally situated, reflective of particular times and places. Because of the relative difficulty in discerning or implementing truth among people as a whole, claims to truth may become more influenced (and promoted) by historical and cultural factors than by rational or empirical factors. Thus truth claims may become influenced by exertions of personal or political power and ideology rather than by more objective facts, whether they are of an empirical or transcendent nature. Since those who claim truth of some sort cannot do so based on finite human criteria, they rely—consciously or unconsciously—on dogmatic methods in order to assert their understanding of truth. Such dogmatic methods may become coercive, oppressive, and even violent. Objective reality is not necessarily rejected. However, it is thought that people's construal of truth remains contingent, relative to their particular perceptions, social conventions, and interests. So how people—individually and collectively—construe reality may be based on coercive factors more than on free inquiry about the nature of things.

Early constructivists include Giambattista Vico and Karl Marx, but constructivist theories of truth became more common with the rise of postmodernism. Similar to what has already been said about postmodernism, truth claims made by people are thought to be historically and culturally relative. Thus it is doubted that there exists a sufficient rational and empirical foundation on which people in general, and Christians in particular, may make claims of absolute truth and morality. This includes truth claims about the Bible. From a constructivist approach, claims to propositional truth are thought to reflect wishful thinking more than arguable legitimation beyond a particular audience that shares the presuppositions of those making the universal truth claims. Such claims may indeed be made by people; however, appeals to an authoritative foundation represent a modernistic naïveté that ignores ideological power plays in arguing for indubitable truth. Indeed, Christians—past and present—are thought to succeed in promoting Christianity due to their effective enforcement of biblical theology (or ideology) rather than the rational and empirical force of their truth claims. The cultural and other forms of power exerted by Christians led to their dominance over competing theological and ideological worldviews. Thus Christianity's truth rests more on dogmatic, coercive means than on the persuasiveness of rational and empirical argumentation.

Constructivist theories of truth do not necessarily lead to relativism, skepticism, and nihilism. It is a caricature to draw these inferences in one's description of postmodernists. Christians influenced by postmodernism still make truth claims. But they make them with far more modesty and humility, acknowledging the contextuality of people's pronouncements of truth and of the prospect of the effects of sin on them. The effects of sin include how Christians and churches, both past and present, rely too much on coercive means of an ideological, cultural, political, or militaristic nature. Although they may claim to have the blessing of God, a more realistic self-assessment of Christianity might reveal a systemic use of sociocultural "power plays" that benefited churches rather than the "meek and mild" image sometimes attributed to Jesus and, theoretically, his followers.

Finally, if people encounter God and divinely inspired revelation, then they still must construct cognitively and verbally what they experienced. Even with regard to how "perfect" one considers the Bible, finite and sinful people still construct their interpretations of it. Certainly Christians believe that the Holy Spirit aids them in the interpretive process, but the variety of interpretations give evidence of the undeniable human components involved, even in the Bible.

Other Theories of Truth

Other theories of truth exist. They include arguments for truth based on consensus, speech act, redundancy, and so on. There are also pluralist theories of truth that argue that there may be more than one way for true statements to be made legitimately. However, for the sake of our present discussion, the aforementioned theories provide sufficient background for looking at ways Christians understand the truth of the Bible.

Most of the debate about the Bible's truth relates to the correspondence theory of truth. When people ask about the truth or trustworthiness of the Bible, they usually think in terms of its truthfulness or freedom from factual errors. So in the next section we will discuss what it is that people consider an error, discrepancy, or inconsistency. However, not all views that follow consider truth solely in terms of the correspondence theory of truth. In those instances, the significance of an alternative view of truth will be taken into consideration.

■ What Is an Error?

The discussion of what constitutes an error in the Bible could be very long. So, in order to simplify the discussion, we will draw on the definition of what may or may not constitute errors from the Chicago Statement on Biblical Inerrancy (1978).[1] The statement is heavily invested in arguing for the inerrancy of the Bible—that is, that the biblical texts contain no errors whatsoever. Clearly the statement works out of the context of a correspondence theory of truth. In the Chicago Statement, nineteen articles are related to the inerrancy of the Bible, which include both affirmations and denials. In each article of belief, a statement of affirmation is made, which is followed by a denial (see example below). The Chicago Statement represents one of the most widely regarded confessions about the trustworthiness of the Bible, and it has the added benefit of being brief.

We will focus particularly on the affirmations and denials that pertain to the nature of what may or may not constitute an error. Let us begin by looking at articles XII–XIV:

Article XII

We affirm that Scripture in its entirety is inerrant, being free from all falsehood, fraud, or deceit.

We deny that Biblical infallibility and inerrancy are limited to spiritual, religious, or redemptive themes, exclusive of assertions in the fields of history and science. We further deny that scientific hypotheses about earth history may properly be used to overturn the teaching of Scripture on creation and the flood.

---

1. "The Chicago Statement on Biblical Inerrancy," International Council on Biblical Inerrancy, Dallas Theological Seminary Website, DTS Mosher & Turpin Libraries, http://library .dts.edu/Pages/TL/Special/ICBI_1.pdf, accessed April 29, 2011. The original document is located in the Dallas Theological Seminary Mosher & Turpin Libraries.

Article XIII

We affirm the propriety of using inerrancy as a theological term with reference to the complete truthfulness of Scripture.

We deny that it is proper to evaluate Scripture according to standards of truth and error that are alien to its usage or purpose. We further deny that inerrancy is negated by Biblical phenomena such as a lack of modern technical precision, irregularities of grammar or spelling, observational descriptions of nature, the reporting of falsehoods, the use of hyperbole and round numbers, the topical arrangement of material, variant selections of material in parallel accounts, or the use of free citations.

Article XIV

We affirm the unity and internal consistency of Scripture.

We deny that alleged errors and discrepancies that have not yet been resolved vitiate the truth claims of the Bible.[2]

From the Chicago Statement, we hear several affirmations that the Bible is inerrant, trustworthy, and internally consistent. These affirmations suggest areas where debate exists concerning the degree to which the Bible is error free. The denials give specificity with regard to the nature of truth found in the biblical texts. In Article XII, the Chicago Statement denies that inerrancy is limited to spiritual, religious, or redemptive themes; its inerrancy extends to the fields of history and science as well. For example, the truth of the Bible trumps all scientific hypotheses of earth history. Thus it seems as if there is no limit to inerrant claims attributed to it.

In arguing for the complete truthfulness of the Bible in Article XIII, we find a glimpse of potential areas of debate about the biblical texts. The article again affirms inerrancy, but in its denial, the claim is that confusion may arise due to the evaluation of the Bible "according to standards of truth and error that are alien to its usage of purpose."[3] Presumably, there exist within the Bible qualifications as to what may or may not genuinely constitute an error. The qualifications include the following:

1. a lack of modern technical precision;
2. irregularities of grammar or spelling;

2. "The Chicago Statement on Biblical Inerrancy," articles XII–XIV.
3. "The Chicago Statement on Biblical Inerrancy," article XIII.

3. observational descriptions of nature;

4. the reporting of falsehoods;

5. the use of hyperbole;

6. the use of round numbers;

7. the topical arrangement of material;

8. variant selections of material in parallel accounts; and

9. the use of free citations.

Let us consider these qualifications. First, authors of the Chicago Statement argue that the Bible should not be evaluated using a kind of modern technical precision that had not developed during biblical times. This qualification seems reasonable, unless the authors also claim that in places the Bible does speak with modern technical precision. Then questions arise over when it does and does not speak accurately. It would be unpersuasive if people argued in one instance that the Bible speaks with modern technical precision but that in another instance it does not. Consistency in argumentation is crucial in discussing the nature and extent of the Bible's trustworthiness.

Second, irregularities of grammar or spelling occur in the biblical texts. Such irregularities should not count against the inerrancy of the Bible, according to the Chicago Statement. So free citations do not count as errors, if biblical authors quoted the Old Testament from memory or variant translations, rather than accessing a specific text. For example, Isaiah 6:9–13 is alluded to several times in the New Testament, but the meaning conveyed is quite different (compare Matt. 13:10–15; Mark 4:10–12; Luke 8:9–10; John 12:37–43; and Acts 28:25–27). Did people in the New Testament, including Jesus, actually misquote the Old Testament (for example, compare Ps. 8:2 and Matt. 21:16; and compare Prov. 24:17 and Matt. 5:43)? Were the restatements of the Old Testament actually inspired alterations of what had been said before? Were authors in the New Testament who quoted the Hebrew Bible aware of discrepancies between the Hebrew Masoretic Text of the Old Testament and its Greek translation, the Septuagint? Again, questions arise over when readers of the Bible can expect it to speak inerrantly and when its assertions need appropriate qualification.

Third, observational descriptions of nature should not be considered errors. Such descriptions include references to the "days" of creation before God created the earth, stars, and sun (Gen. 1:1–19); the "rising" of the sun (Ps. 50:1; Isa. 41:25); the "four corners of the earth" (Job 37:3; Isa. 11:12); and so on. But to what extent should readers of the Bible qualify its descriptions of nature? Does it include observational—but scientifically incorrect—descriptions of observing the sun rising, but not observational descriptions of the sun's creation in Genesis 1? Because of the observational and even poetic ways that the Bible sometimes describes nature, it makes sense to use caution in how such descriptions are interpreted. Consistency in how such passages are interpreted, however, raises questions about the appropriate interpretation of texts. Are interpreters consistent when they say the Bible is or is not scientifically accurate?

Fourth, the reporting of falsehood should not count against the inerrancy of the Bible. For example, if the Bible reports people's lies, then their lies should not count against its trustworthiness. However, it is not always clear if statements in the Bible are lies or if they are intended to be taken truthfully. Can a statement be considered a lie if the biblical texts do not clearly say that statements are lies? What of reports about events and dates in the Old Testament that were thought to be correct but were variously reported in the Bible (for example, compare dates in Gen. 15:13; Exod. 12:40–41; Acts 7:6; 13:20; Gal. 3:17)?

Fifth, the use of hyperbole (or exaggeration) and other literary devices designed to exaggerate in order to make a point is not considered an error. Let us consider, for example, Jesus's so-called Sermon on the Plain (Luke 6:17–49), which resembles the Sermon on the Mount (Matt. 5–7). In Luke 6:27–31, Jesus says:

> But I say to you that listen, Love your enemies, do good to those who hate you, bless those who curse you, pray for those who abuse you. If anyone strikes you on the cheek, offer the other also; and from anyone who takes away your coat do not withhold even your shirt. Give to everyone who begs from you; and if anyone takes away your goods, do not ask for them again. Do to others as you would have them do to you.

In theory, Christians may say that they obey the teachings of Jesus, but in practice they may "pick and choose" when they do so. In the aforementioned verses, Christians might say that we should pray for those who abuse us, but we might also say that it is unnecessary to turn the other cheek, donate to every beggar, or not press charges against a thief. Which passages should be interpreted literally and which should be interpreted as hyperbole that Jesus uses to make a point rather than be explicitly obeyed? Perhaps Luke 6:31 offers a way out, because Christians can argue that they are only following the principle of "doing to others what they would want others to do to them." However, does such argumentation lead to ethical subjectivism or relativism? How can Christians decide when and when not to obey literally the words of Jesus? Certainly, Christians debate over what parts of the Bible should or should not be interpreted hyperbolically.

Sixth, the use of round numbers does not constitute error; they were intended as approximations and not as exact calculations. For example, in the

Old Testament, references to population were estimations, often written in round numbers (for example, 50, 500, 5,000, etc.). But other instances are not as clear-cut. Numbers 1 and 26 talk about how more than 600,000 men plus women and children left Egypt in the exodus. Using round numbers is understandable, but did Moses lead more than one million people out of Egypt? Historical evidence suggests that the number of Israelites was probably smaller, perhaps fewer than 100,000 people. If so, then how accurate are other approximations in the Bible? Again, how do interpreters determine which biblical numbers ought to be interpreted as ballpark numbers and which ought to be interpreted with greater precision?

Seventh, the topical arrangement of material is not considered an error. The most notable example that comes to mind is the different chronologies of Jesus's life found in the Synoptic Gospels—Matthew, Mark, and Luke—and the Gospel of John. John's chronology is quite different, and so it is argued that John provided a topical, thematic, or theological arrangement of the events in Jesus's life. For example, there are hundreds of differences in words used, word orders, and other variations between the Gospels, but do such variations actually constitute errors? The fact that "harmonizations of the Gospels" have been written are testimony to the fact that some Christians do care about the differences. For some, the differences lead to the conclusion that errors exist; to others, the differences are harmonized—one way or another—proving that there are no errors. To still others, such differences are historically minor and thus irrelevant to the more significant theological teachings of the Bible. So when does one decide when a biblical account is topically arranged—when it conflicts with other biblical passages? Even if one accepts the topical arrangement of John's Gospel, there remain discrepancies among the Synoptic Gospels. The fact that such harmonizations continue to be written is a testimony to ongoing concern over the trustworthiness of the Bible. Of course, we have not begun to mention the number of discrepancies of a historical nature in harmonizing data between the New and Old Testaments, including genealogies, dates, locations, names, and so on. Such data may not seem essential to the salvific purpose of the Bible. However, for some, complete harmony between the Gospels and between the Gospels and other parts of the Bible is foundational to its truth.

Eighth, variant selections of material in parallel accounts are not considered errors. For example, in the Gospels, it may be that different authors chose to report on different aspects of the same events that occurred. The Gospel of John talks about Jesus ministering mostly in Judea, rather than Galilee, as reported in the Synoptic Gospels. In John, Jesus's ministry took place over three years, rather than one; and other events such as the cleansing of the temple occur at the outset of Jesus's ministry rather than at the end (John 2:13–25; contrast Matt. 21:12–17; Mark 11:15–19; and Luke 19:45–48). While the appeal to a topical arrangement may account for some of the discrepancies, they do not reconcile all differences, especially when they occur among all the Gospel accounts. As important as Jesus's birth, death, resurrection, and ascension narratives are to the Gospels and the book of Acts, clear differences occur in their chronological presentations.

Ninth, the use of free citations is not considered an error. Biblical authors did not always have sources readily available in quoting them, so it is inappropriate to expect exact quotations. What of New Testament citations of the Septuagint, which are themselves Greek translations of the Hebrew Bible? What of so-called red-letter editions of Jesus's words, when Jesus most likely spoke in Aramaic, yet the New Testament was written in Greek? English translations of Jesus's words thus represent words translated twice: first, from Aramaic to Greek, and second, from Greek to English. How precisely, then, can we claim to quote Jesus? In what sense does the Bible provide the *ipsissima verba* (Latin "the very words") of Jesus? Sometimes interpreters of the New Testament have claimed that allusions to the Old Testament and to the words of Jesus, which may not be exact quotations, are themselves inspired enhancements of what had previously been said. As such, the purported words of Jesus may be better understood as his *ipsissima vox* (Latin "the very voice"), which implies that the sense of Jesus's words is accurately reported, though the exact words he used are not. Such interpretive methods may be convincing to some, but if all the Bible is thought to be inspired and trustworthy, then one might expect greater knowledge of and fidelity to earlier statements.

Finally, Article XIV affirms the unity and internal consistency of the Bible, and it denies that alleged errors and discrepancies that have not yet been resolved discredit the truth claims of the Bible. Basically, the article admits that not all questions about the Bible have been resolved. It may be that they will be resolved in the future, perhaps with new archaeological discoveries, or that some apparent errors may not be resolved until God resolves them for us in eternity. In other words, no amount of questions, challenges, or controvertible evidence is sufficient to detract from the propositional statement that the Bible is inerrant.

Up to now, our discussion of what may or may not constitute an error has been somewhat general in orientation. We have refrained from giving too many examples but have preferred to speak about categories of issues related to the truthful, error-free nature of the Bible. To speak with greater particularity would take a long time. In fact, entire books have been written about uncovering errors in the Bible. Of course, challenges to the truth of it have been going on for centuries, especially after the rise of historical criticism. But more contemporary sources have gone into great detail highlighting the issues.[4] One could say that hundreds, if not thousands, of biblical statements have been investigated with regard to the degree to which they may or not constitute errors.

■ Inconvenient Truths

We speak ironically when talking about "inconvenient truths," but there are indeed more issues pertaining to the trustworthiness of the Bible than have been discussed. So far, we looked mostly at what the Chicago Statement refers to as standards of truth and error that are alien to the usage or purpose of the Bible. But there are other issues as well.

The Chicago Statement claims that, technically speaking, inerrancy applies only to the original writings, or autographs (Greek *autographa*, "self-writings") of the Bible. However, we do not have the autographs. So does the lack of originals make the discussion a moot point, irresolvable given the existing manuscripts of the Bible that we have? Inerrantists would say no because, due to the providence of God, the transcribed manuscripts and translations of manuscripts (Greek *apographa*, "from writings") that we have are sufficiently truthful to still be called inerrant.

Discussion of manuscripts leads to another issue of the transmission of those manuscripts over the centuries. How accurate are the manuscripts we have, given that they have been copied and recopied countless times? This might not be an issue, except for the fact that thousands of manuscripts exist, including partial manuscripts, and they do not consistently match one another. In fact, if you read the Bible in the original languages, such as those found in critical editions of the biblical texts, one of the first things you observe are the textual variants (or alternative wordings) listed at the bottom of the pages. Almost every page of the biblical texts has alternative wordings, word orders, and other variations. Heretofore, such textual variants were known mostly by those who studied the Bible in its original languages. But newer translations have become more up front about them, providing notations with regard to the more extensive variations. Although biblical texts agree more than disagree, the alternative readings represent a challenge to determining the meaning and truthfulness of the Bible.

One of the more notable debates over English translations of the Bible has to do with the King James Version. In 1611, the KJV was translated in England,

---

4. For example, see Dewey M. Beegle, *The Inspiration of Scripture* (Philadelphia: Westminster, 1963); and Beegle, *Scripture, Tradition, and Infallibility* (Grand Rapids: Eerdmans, 1973); and Thom Stark, *The Human Faces of God: What Scripture Reveals When It Gets God Wrong (and Why Inerrancy Tries to Hide It)* (Eugene, OR: Wipf & Stock, 2011).

based on the best available original-language manuscripts. The New Testament translation used the textus receptus, which the Dutch scholar Desiderius Erasmus had compiled from about a half dozen Greek manuscripts that came from the Greek-speaking Byzantine Empire. There were variants between the manuscripts, but they were the most reliable Greek sources available. With regard to the variants, Erasmus said:

> But one thing the facts cry out, and it can be clear, as they say, even to a blind man, that often through the translator's clumsiness or inattention the Greek has been wrongly rendered; often the true and genuine reading has been corrupted by ignorant scribes, which we see happen every day, or altered by scribes who are half-taught and half-asleep.[5]

Later textual scholars recognized additional problems with the textus receptus and the Hebrew sources used. Over time, an increasing number of biblical manuscripts was discovered. Some of the manuscripts, for example the *Codex Vaticanus* and *Codex Sinaiticus*, dated back to the fourth century and were thus hundreds of years older than the textus receptus and thus thought to be more reliable. After the late nineteenth century, most English Bible translations, such as the Revised Standard Version, New American Standard Bible, New International Version, and New Revised Standard Version, no longer used the textus receptus. Complicating matters, there are dozens of verses found in the KJV that do not appear in the later English translations because of their use of the older manuscripts. To advocates of the KJV, much of the Bible has been lost, and so translations other than the KJV (or the New King James Version) are rejected as illegitimate. However, adherents to the other English translations thought that the most likely explanation was that the textus receptus accrued editions and additions by transcribers not found in the earliest manuscripts (sometimes known as textual errors, copyists' errors, or errors in translation). Regardless of people's opinion about the causes, there were considerable differences between the manuscripts, and explanations given were equally problematic with regard to how they understand the trustworthiness of the Bible.

Moral Issues

What of those, including Christians, who read the Bible and think it contains not merely human elements but pervasive human elements? As such,

5. Desiderius Erasmus, "Epistle 337," in *Collected Works of Erasmus*, vol. 3, *Letters 298 to 445, 1514–1516*, trans. R. A. B. Mynors and D. F. S. Thomson; annotated by James K. McConica (Toronto: University of Toronto Press, 1976), 134, quoted in "Textus Receptus."

it is thoroughly fallible, containing not only errors of historic and scientific information but also moral failures. For example, slavery and its practices in the Bible have been extremely problematic in both church and world history. For centuries (if not millennia), the Bible was thought to condone the institution of slavery. Not only is slavery practiced widely throughout the Old Testament, but the New Testament also argues that slaves ought to remain as they are (for example, 1 Cor. 7:20–24; Eph. 6:5–8; Titus 2:9–10; 1 Pet. 2:18–21). In fact, slaves should be happy to remain as they are and serve their masters faithfully and without complaint. Of course, slave owners are to be good to their slaves, but there is no hint of the abolition of slavery. The one example of Paul arguing for the freeing of a slave, Onesimus, has more to do with a unique situation of a converted brother in Jesus Christ than with an act of advocacy on behalf of liberating slaves (Philem. 8–17).

Although some may argue that the Bible overall advocates "kinder and gentler" slaveholding practices than occurred in ancient or modern times, it still affirmed the institution of slavery. Yet over the past two hundred years, Christians changed their minds concerning what the Bible says about slaveholding. Despite seemingly clear-cut teachings about slavery, the majority view eventually said that the Bible does not promote the practice, even though nothing written about slavery in the Bible changed. So did Christians misinterpret the Bible for millennia, or did they prefer a novel interpretation of it in the nineteenth century, which advocated abolitionism? Regardless of one's opinion about what the Bible teaches about slavery, questions remain about the quality of moral teachings in the Bible.

Another issue of theological and moral perplexity in the Bible has to do with the tradition of polytheism in the Bible, exemplified by the very first of the Ten Commandments given to Moses and the Hebrew people: "You shall have no other gods before me" (Exod. 20:3). Consider also the apparent polytheistic practices of Jacob and his wives (Gen. 31:19; 35:2–4). This first commandment does not deny that there are other gods; it merely denies that the Hebrews should acknowledge any other god than Yahweh (Exod. 20:3). Not until the time of the divided kingdoms of Judah and Israel, hundreds of years after the time of Moses, did monotheism seem to become firmly established.

During this early period of religious development, practices of child sacrifice (Exod. 22:29, 34:20; Judg. 11:29–40; see also Gen. 22:2) and genocide (Num. 31:7–18; Deut. 7:1–6, 20:10–18) were not only practiced by the Hebrews but also seemed to be sanctioned by God. Although Christians have vigorously defended God and the Bible from promoting child sacrifice and genocide, the biblical evidence is disconcerting. Can every instance be justified, rationalized? Such practices were later condemned both in the Bible and by Christians, but even the condemnations of child sacrifice (Ezek. 20:18–26; Mic. 6:6–8) and genocide (Gen. 15:16; Lev. 26:27–29; 1 Sam. 15:2–3; Jer. 19:9; Ezek. 5:8–10) may not convincingly deny roots in the laws of Moses.

Even Jesus may be thought to have been wrong with regard to assertions that he would return publicly in glory after his death (Greek *parousia*, "coming," or "advent") and gather the elect within the lifetime of those present (for example, see Mark 9:1, and parallel accounts in Matt. 16:28; Luke 9:27; see also Mark 13:24–27, 30, and parallel accounts in Matt. 24:29–31, 34; Luke 21:25–28, 32). Even if Jesus can be exonerated of believing in the imminent end of the world, his followers did believe that the world's end would soon occur, especially as found in the writings of Paul (Rom. 8:18–19, 22–23; 1 Cor. 7:26, 29–31; 1 Thess. 4:15–17). To what degree did Jesus's expectation for the "end times" (Greek *eschaton*, "the last thing") affect his preaching, teaching, and ethics? To what degree did the disciples' expectation of Jesus's "second coming" affect their words and actions? To what degree were Paul and other first-century Christians affected? To this day, Christians still talk about the imminent return of Jesus, but what effect—positively or negatively—does such expectation have on both their Christian lifestyle and moral decision making? What are the liabilities of expecting too urgently Jesus's return, as well as the liabilities of being insufficiently expectant?

One does not have to agree or disagree with the aforementioned questions about the theological and moral perspicuity of the Bible. It is enough to recognize that the questions have been raised and that some people, at least, are not persuaded that either the form or the content of the Bible are without flaws, which make it look very human rather than divine. One way or another, Christians and churches have to decide what they believe about the trustworthiness of the Bible. Even if they are not persuaded by alternative views, it is incumbent on the leaders, if not other Christians, to give an explanation or defense of their views. First Peter 3:15 says: "Always be ready to make your defense to anyone who demands from you an accounting for the hope that is in you." While one's view of the Bible is not precisely the same as one's view of the "hope that is in you," they are close enough to encourage more honest reflection on the Bible and its trustworthiness.

Behavioral Scientific Issues

Additional questions arise about the trustworthiness of the Bible that extend beyond the particularities of content found in the texts. As already mentioned, there are sociological, psychological, and other behavioral scientific interpretations of the Bible that focus on complex human components not immediately noticed by readers. For example, to what degree was the writing of the Bible influenced by those who were educated, relatively secure financially, and predominantly male? If such factors influenced the writing of the Bible, then are certain deconstructive methods of biblical interpretation warranted for understanding both the benefits and liabilities of what the authors communicated? For example, what may we learn about the Bible by using a liberationist interpretation of the texts that focuses on issues of social, political, and economic power (and misuse of power) with regard to what the Bible says? Were polytheism, child sacrifice, and genocide due to barbaric practices of early Israel, which were reworked by later monarchs who sought to substantiate their "mon-archical" power by affirmation of "monotheism"? Are there additional human factors of a psychological, sociological, economic, political, or militaristic nature that crept into the biblical texts that resulted in the repressive treatment of the uneducated, the poor, and those who were enslaved?

Another approach to interpreting the Bible includes a Christian feminist approach. To what degree are the writings of the Bible influenced by male perspectives, male dominance, and possible mistreatment of women, children, and those who are not part of hierarchical male leadership? Of course, one may disregard such interpretive approaches to the Bible as being ideologically (or, at best, theologically) motivated and thus irrelevant and inappropriate for its interpretation. But not everyone will. Appeals to divine inspiration and even inerrancy will not prevent interpreters of the Bible from considering the possibility that subconscious, if not conscious, factors of human nature and enculturation influenced the formation of the Bible.

To these examples of biblical interpretation, others could be added. Their presence should be a reminder, especially to Christians, that truth in general, and truth of the Bible in particular, does not necessarily pertain to straightforward questions of truth, right and wrong, and so on. Answers to the questions people have about the Bible sometimes take hard work and frank openness to issues that arise. That does not mean that one's understanding of the trustworthiness of the Bible will necessarily change. But one should at least be aware of the breadth of issues related to its trustworthiness.

9

Views of the Bible's Trustworthiness

The trustworthiness of the Bible is for many Christians one of the most important issues to consider and get right. One's view on the matter ought not be that of indifference, especially as a Christian. On the contrary, it is a matter of life and death, or of eternal life and death. Debate about the trustworthiness of the Bible has been contentious throughout church history. It might seem that debate has increased rather than decreased over the past half century, but that is because people lack historical perspective. They too often think that debate is the worst *now*, or that Christians *today* have had to endure or defend challenges to the Bible more than anyone else. However, debate over the Bible has occurred throughout church history. From time to time, debate has heightened, including, for example, during the canonization of the Bible in the fourth century, and between Roman Catholics and Protestants during the Reformation in the sixteenth century. Debate over the Bible's reliability increased dramatically during the nineteenth-century rise of historical criticism. Certainly debate is not less volatile today than it was in times past, but the Bible, its trustworthiness, and its interpretation represent issues of longstanding dispute.

It should not be surprising that, over the span of church history, a variety of views about the trustworthiness of the Bible have arisen. Several categorizations will be used to talk about the Bible's trustworthiness, admittedly using relatively recent categories, such as inerrancy and infallibility. This is not because the substance of debate has changed all that drastically but because the terminology used to express them has. In fact, not all who hold the following views would recognize or accept the terms used, since they are written with specific meanings in mind—meanings that are not widely known or accepted, especially among those unschooled in biblical and theological studies. Some Christians actually reject outright any categorizations about their beliefs and values pertaining to the Bible. They say, for example, that they have no creed but Jesus Christ and no book but the Bible. This may be true, but their beliefs and values still fall within the categorization of terms listed below. They may not like being categorized, but they can be identified with one or more of the following views. They are terms commonly recognized today by Christians who talk about the trustworthiness of the Bible. We hope that our discussion of them will help to bring clarity and understanding to debates, which will in turn help readers decide for themselves their view of the Bible's trustworthiness.

■ Inerrancy

The first theory or doctrine of the trustworthiness of the Bible we will look at is inerrancy. However, just because people use inerrancy to describe their view of the Bible does not mean that you automatically know what they believe. It is a truism that whenever a term becomes especially important, controversial, or debated, there tend to arise competing definitions of the term. Such is the case with inerrancy.

We will present three views of inerrancy: absolute inerrancy, theological inerrancy, and inerrancy of purpose. Other terms are used to describe the doctrine of inerrancy; not every one of them will be discussed. But the following categories are broad enough to include most views of inerrancy. Because the views differ significantly, it is important to make sure of other people's understanding of the doctrine so that mutual understanding occurs. Again, just because people describe their view of the Bible as inerrant does not mean that you understand their theological point of view. You must first dialogue with people in order to make sure you share similar definitions of the term. When people cannot even agree on working definitions of key terms, more than misunderstanding may occur due to the volatile nature of debate pertaining to the trustworthiness of the Bible.

Absolute (or Full, Complete) Inerrancy

The belief that the Bible makes no errors with regard to anything said in it is called absolute inerrancy. Sometimes absolute inerrancy is known as full or complete inerrancy. The Chicago Statement on Biblical Inerrancy, discussed in the previous chapter, represents one of the best-known and most widely affirmed confessions of the doctrine. Absolute inerrancy affirms that the Bible, in its entirety, is free from all falsehood, fraud, or deceit. Its truth extends to matters of history and science; it supersedes scientific hypotheses about earth history thought to overturn biblical teachings, such as those regarding creation and the flood.

Absolute inerrantists are careful to explain what does and does not constitute an error. The nineteen articles of the Chicago Statement on Biblical Inerrancy, for example, state both what is affirmed about the Bible's trustworthiness and what is denied, thus guaranteeing its truth. In particular, it is argued that the Bible must be interpreted by its own criteria of truth, not by modern technical precision foreign to the biblical writers. Irregularities in grammar and spelling do not constitute errors, nor do observational descriptions of nature. The reporting of falsehoods do not constitute errors, nor do the use of hyperbole and round numbers. Finally, neither the topical arrangement of material, variant selections of material in parallel accounts, nor the use of free citations constitute errors.

Belief in absolute inerrancy does not negate the need to study the Bible's genre, historical context, and literary context. Indeed, such investigations help to discern important teachings in the Bible, which are thought to reinforce— rather than contradict—its truth.

In interpreting the Bible, absolute inerrantists refer to specific method-ological approaches to biblical interpretation in order to emphasize their particular theological concerns. For example, the Chicago Statement on Biblical Hermeneutics was written as a hermeneutical (or interpretive) complement to the Chicago Statement on Biblical Inerrancy. With regard to "interpreting the Bible according to its literal, or normal, sense," the Chicago Statement on Biblical Hermeneutics promotes a "grammatical-historical" approach to biblical interpretation because it is thought that grammatical consider-ations primarily, coupled with historical and literary considerations, best discern the meaning that the biblical authors expressed.[1] Sometimes the grammatical-historical method is referred to as grammatico-historical or historic-grammatical interpretation. Emphasis is placed on the grammar— that is, the very words of the Bible itself—rather than on historical-critical methods, which might distort the biblical authors' intended meaning. Let

---

1. "The Chicago Statement on Biblical Hermeneutics," Articles of Affirmation and Denial (Topic No. 2), 1978, International Council on Biblical Inerrancy (ICBI), Dallas Theological Seminary Archives, Repository of ICBI Archives, http://www.churchcouncil.org/iccp_org/Docu ments_ICCP/English/02_Biblical_Hermeneutics_A&D.pdf, July 8, 2003 (accessed August 20, 2011), article XV.

the Bible speak for itself, advocates of inerrancy would say. So, listen to the words of the Bible themselves rather than wonder about historical and critical questions that may distract from the plain and obvious meaning of the biblical texts.

Belief in absolute inerrancy draws on a correspondence theory of truth that insists on a one-to-one correspondence between what the Bible says and the facts. The facts include faith-based statements about God and creation, sin and salvation, history and science. The truths of the Bible can be stated propositionally, and their indubitability is legitimated by rational and empirical means. Affirmation of the Bible's propositional truths is thought to be a guarantor of the doctrine of inerrancy. A great deal of scholarship is directed toward apologetics and the defense of its truth, despite the challenges of historical and critical methods of biblical interpretation, alternative theories of truth, and postmodern deconstructions of the Bible. But absolute inerrantists are confident that the trustworthiness of the Bible will be more and more persuasive as Christians rightly interpret it. According to absolute inerrantists, both truth and time are on their side, and the more time people study the Bible, the more true it will be proven to be by historiography, archaeology, or the unfolding of world events.

Theological (or Limited) Inerrancy

The belief that the Bible is true with regard to what it says about theological matters related to God, creation, humanity, sin, salvation, Christian living, resurrection, and eternal life is called theological inerrancy. As such, the Bible is limited, more or less, to spiritual, religious, and redemptive themes. For this reason, theological inerrancy may also be called limited inerrancy because the Bible is not thought to address every conceivable matter past, present, and future.

A commonly expressed version of theological inerrancy is that the Bible is not necessarily inerrant about matters of history and science, which are not directly relevant to the theological truths it states. That does not mean that the Bible is not historical or scientific; it has much to say about historical events and the nature of the world. But historical and scientific information not related to the theological truths of the Bible, pertaining to salvation and the Christian life, should not be evaluated with the same expectations of rational and empirical verification. Discrepancies and inconsistencies in historical statements, for example, do not detract from the overall trustworthiness of God's revelation about spiritual matters. Likewise, the Bible was not intended to function as a science textbook, so the prescientific worldview of biblical authors does not count against the divine inspiration of their theological statements about God and salvation.

Whenever limits are introduced to the discussion of any issue, questions arise with regard to the degree of the limitations. How far is the Bible limited? How does one decide with certainty about its limits? If even one error is found in the Bible—however one might define an error—then what is to prevent "slippery-slope argumentation," endangering the trustworthiness of the whole of the Bible? With regard to slippery-slope argumentation, we already discussed how its logic is not necessary, and that the argument can be used (misleadingly) against most views of the Bible. For example, most absolute inerrantists do not subscribe to the dictation theory of inspiration. Advocates of dictation theory say that any theory other than theirs falls prey to slippery-slope argumentation. Yet absolute inerrantists do not think that other views of divine inspiration face a slope that is all that slippery, or all that steep, to prevent them from rejecting dictation theory while at the same time affirming absolute inerrancy. In other words, from the perspective of theological inerrancy, there is no necessary reason to suspect that prescientific observations of the universe invalidate the Bible's revelation about God and spiritual matters. Theological inerrantists do not think that too much is risked, with regard to the Bible, to think of inerrancy primarily in terms of its spiritual, religious, and redemptive themes. Thus they gladly refer to their view of the Bible as inerrant, but their beliefs differ from those who affirm absolute inerrancy, since insignificant flaws may exist regarding historical and scientific matters.

Most theological inerrantists would probably resonate most with the correspondence theory of truth, since they still think that the Bible syncs with theological facts, though not necessarily with all historical and scientific ones. However, some theological inerrantists might be drawn to the coherence theory of truth because the theory helps to illustrate that some people's concept of truth does not need to apply to every dimension of life—past, present, and future—in order to affirm the trustworthiness of the Bible. Why not accept the Bible for what it is—a book about God and matters related to God—rather than expect from it exhaustive, minutiae-oriented statements about every imagined issue? Moreover, historical and critical investigations of the Bible reveal that not all chronological and scientific discrepancies can be resolved, and the hope of future resolution—in the present life or in the life hereafter—distracts people from the essence of the Bible's teachings. However, since the Bible inerrantly speaks to us about God, salvation, and the Christian life, we should celebrate and live in accordance with the divine revelation given to us, since it represents inerrant truth about spiritual matters.

Inerrancy of Purpose

Inerrancy of purpose refers to the belief that the primary purpose of the Bible is soteriological (from Greek *sōtēria*, "salvation"); that is, it has to do with revealing God to people to save them, reconciling people to God in this life and for eternal life. The Bible is God's divine revelation, and it does not err in fulfilling its salvific purpose. In this regard, the Bible is inerrant because it provides truth about God, salvation, and the subsequent Christian life. It does not err or fail to serve as God's means to redeem people and become reconciled with them. Thus advocates of inerrancy of purpose still want to describe the Bible as inerrant.

Although the Bible does not err in bringing people to salvation, it does not mean that the Bible may not err in other ways. Advocates of inerrancy of purpose consider salvation to be of preeminent importance. Other issues are secondary, at best, including matters of inconsequential relevance to people's salvation. People are not saved by propositional statements of truth, even those pertaining to God. They are important, but it is God who saves and not a set of propositions that must be avowed about the Bible. People are saved by faith through God's grace, not by rational and empirical disputation pertaining to every "jot and tittle" about the Bible (see Matt. 5:18 KJV, NKJV).

The Bible may indeed contain errors, and they ought not to be made light of or dismissed, even if they "die the death of a thousand qualifications." Preoccupation with errors may distract people from the salvific purpose of the Bible, thinking instead that apologetics or other theological disputations are what God wants and that apologetics saves people. The presence of errors no more prevents people from being saved than fallible, error-filled sermons preached by imperfect, sin-tainted ministers. Yet God's Holy Spirit may work through such ministers, just as God works through the Bible we have, rather than the Bible for which we might hope.

There is no necessary reason to identify a particular theory of truth with the inerrancy of purpose, since most Christians who advocate this view would probably want to argue that they present a biblical rather than philosophical position. However, inerrancy of purpose resembles a pragmatic theory of truth, since its concern is for the purpose or "work" for which God inspired the Bible—namely, to redeem people. It is not that questions of truth and error, right and wrong, are unimportant. But they are not the primary purpose for which God, through the presence and work of the Holy Spirit, uses the Bible. Again, such issues are important, but it is far more important that God saves people, and God has chosen to save people as they read or hear the gospel proclaimed.

■ Infallibility

Christians have long used the word "infallibility," which conveys the meaning of not misleading or failing those who read the Bible. The term "infallibility" goes back at least as far as Roman Catholic beliefs about papal infallibility at Vatican I during the nineteenth century. In the twentieth century, infallibility was increasingly used alongside inerrancy to describe the Bible, implying that it neither misleads nor errs. However, as the doctrine of inerrancy not only came under greater scrutiny but also became a point of division among Christians, the word "infallibility" was chosen more and more to describe Christians' understanding of the Bible.

The meaning of "not misleading" is not as clear-cut as other descriptions of the Bible because it is difficult to quantify what is and is not misleading. Robert Johnston, for example, distinguishes between "complete infallibility" and "partial infallibility."[2] This distinction, representative of technical qualifications not immediately relevant to our discussion, reflects the varied meanings of the term. "Complete infallibility," on the one hand, may not actually differ all that much from inerrantist views but avoids liabilities associated with the doctrine of inerrancy. Such infallible views argue that the biblical texts are authoritative, inspired, and trustworthy because their cultural limitations insufficiently detract from the truth they convey. Thus use of the term "infallibility," it is argued, allows for more liberty in studying the Bible, understanding it, and applying it to life.

"Partial infallibility," on the other hand, considers inerrancy a liability and wants nothing to do with the term, since it does not acceptably describe the Bible. The biblical texts are thought to contain irresolvable errors and contradictory statements in both historical and scientific matters, and so infallibility—rather than any version of inerrancy—best describes the Bible. Despite acknowledging that errors exist, they are considered to be of minor import, inconsequential to the overall trustworthiness of the Bible, and the purposes for which God inspired it. Substantively, partial infallibility may not represent a view different from either theological inerrancy or inerrancy of purpose, depending on one's particular definition of terms. But use of the term "inerrancy" per se is too great a liability for various reasons—its lack of precise biblical precedent, lack of ancient historical reference, continuing intellectual quagmires, tendency for divisiveness among Christians over the term, and so on. Thus "infallibility" communicates high regard for biblical authority, inspiration, and trustworthiness, but without the conceptual and evidential liabilities of inerrancy.

2. Robert K. Johnston, *Evangelicals at an Impasse: Biblical Authority in Practice* (Atlanta: John Knox, 1979), 15–47.

Depending on the particular view of infallibility people affirm, they may hold to different theories of truth. A correspondence theory of truth may be held; it is just that the errors that occur are inconsequential relative to the other contributions of the Bible. Likewise, a theory of truth oriented more toward the coherence theory may be held, arguing that the Bible is true enough and that errors in the biblical text do not prevent God from working however God wants in inspired and authoritative ways. With regard to the authority of the Bible, I. Howard Marshall says the following about infallibility:

> It may be objected that to put the matter this way is to make the teaching of Scripture a relative rather than an absolute standard. This is simply not so. The authority of Scripture remains absolute. Any element of relativism comes in at the stage of interpreting what Scripture says, since its meaning is not always crystal clear, and here the inerrantist is as much in difficulty as anybody else, since (as we have seen) he still has to interpret Scripture to find out what its inerrant message is.[3]

In 1942, the National Association of Evangelicals formed as an ecumenical Christian organization that wanted to unite Christians who disagreed theologically with the mainline-oriented National Council of Churches, on the one hand, and the fundamentalist-oriented Federal Council of Churches, on the other hand.[4] In the statement of faith, many of the churches disliked the controversies and debate about inerrancy because it did not reflect their theological traditions, which talked about the Bible in different theological ways. For example, they used biblically oriented terms such as "authoritative" and "inspired," or they drew on the wording of Protestant confessions that describe the sufficiency of the Bible. Although such churches had what they considered to be high views of the Bible, they wanted to avoid unnecessary and unproductive debates that occurred outside their theological traditions, too often associated with Christian fundamentalism. "Infallibility" was chosen as a compromise term that affirmed a high view of the Bible without the intellectually and ecclesiastically divisive liabilities of inerrancy.

Immediately after the formation of the National Association of Evangelicals, other evangelically oriented groups demanded inerrancy as a necessary belief. For example, the Evangelical Theological Society, established in 1948, made belief in the doctrine of inerrancy the only requirement for its founding

---

3. I. Howard Marshall, *Biblical Inspiration* (Grand Rapids: Eerdmans, 1982), 72.

4. Technically, the National Council of Churches did not organize until 1950, but its organization united the Federal Council of Churches (1908) and other ecumenical organizations such as the International Council of Religious Education, which predated the National Association of Evangelicals. The Federal Council of Churches was established in 1941.

membership. Other evangelically oriented churches and parachurch groups likewise demanded inerrancy as a requirement for membership. But when groups thereafter tried to bring about ecumenical cooperation among churches and parachurch organizations (for example, the World Evangelical Fellowship in 1951[5] and the Lausanne Movement in 1974), infallibility was chosen rather than inerrancy. Advocates of inerrancy, however, considered its advocacy a "battle" within Christendom, typified by Harold Lindsell's 1978 book *The Battle for the Bible*.[6] For Lindsell, affirmation of inerrancy represented one of the theological lines that must be drawn that no Christian of evangelical note should step over.

■ Sufficiency

Some Christians do not articulate a particular opinion or theology concerning the trustworthiness of the Bible as specified in the doctrines of inerrancy and infallibility. Instead they prefer to read, study, and apply the Bible for what it is, without naming a particular term or doctrine to define the nature of truth in the Bible. It is not because they do not believe in the trustworthiness of the Bible; it is because they consider such views to be a theological (or ideological) intrusion on the reading, interpretation, and application of the Bible. Is it not enough, after all, to talk about the authority and inspiration of the Bible, which are words or descriptions found in the Bible itself? Can we not read the Bible on its own terms rather than for what we hope it to be? To say more about the nature and extent of the Bible's trustworthiness unnecessarily complicates honest, studious interpretation of it. The attempt to articulate a particular opinion or theology about the Bible may promote extrabiblical factors that influence the interpretation of it, conceding too much to modern or postmodern concerns that alter what the Bible says. Let the Bible speak for itself, rather than encumber it with ideas—even those motivated by pious Christian beliefs and values—that may thwart investigation into its truth.

There is no recognized way to describe this view of the trustworthiness of the Bible, especially since it generally tries to avoid the specification of a formalized opinion or theology about the topic. So, at the risk of doing an injustice to historic Christian descriptions of the "sufficiency" of the Bible, we chose the term in order to help us distinguish between those who want to articulate a particular doctrine of the trustworthiness of the Bible (inerrancy

5. The World Evangelical Fellowship represents a worldwide reorganization of the World Evangelical Alliance, established in England in 1846. In 1982, the ecumenical organization renamed itself the World Evangelical Alliance.

6. Harold Lindsell, *The Battle for the Bible* (Grand Rapids: Zondervan, 1978).

or infallibility, for example), on the one hand, and those who do not, who consider such opinions unhelpful or irrelevant. Christians have described the sufficiency of the Bible in a number of ways, though not usually with regard to its trustworthiness. Yet it communicates meaning from the Bible as well as from church history. Historic references to the Bible as sufficient represent more humble claims for it than previous claims to its trustworthiness. It could be argued that the word "sufficiency" better embodies the claims for the Bible in 2 Timothy 3:16: "All scripture is inspired by God and is useful for teaching, for reproof, for correction, and for training in righteousness." In other translations, the Greek word ōphelimos is variously translated as "useful" (NRSV, NIV) and "profitable" (KJV, NASB). These terms seem more modest in description of the Bible than "inerrancy" and "infallibility"; perhaps sufficiency better captures the meaning of the text. In fact, the previous terms seem more influenced by modernist assumptions than by those resembling biblical assumptions, since they seek and debate over rational and empirical legitimation for biblical propositions. So, let us explore further why sufficiency may be thought to be an apt description of the Bible's trustworthiness.

First, it has precedence in the Bible. In 2 Corinthians 12:9, for example, Paul says: "But [God] said to me, 'My grace is sufficient for you, for power is made perfect in weakness.' So, I will boast all the more gladly of my weaknesses, so that the power of Christ may dwell in me." This statement is made in the context of Paul praying for healing from some impediment—a "thorn" in the flesh (2 Cor. 12:7). Paul does not explain what the thorn was, but prayed three times that God would remove it. God did not remove it, yet Paul realized that—by God's grace—no impediments prevented God from working in and through the apostle. Likewise, no impediments in the Bible prevent God from working in and through it.

Second, during the Reformation, the Protestants affirmed the sufficiency of the Bible, but they did so in rejection of the Roman Catholic understanding of the term. Roman Catholics distinguished between the "material" and "formal" sufficiency of the Bible. Material sufficiency has to do with how the Bible contains the information (or material) necessary for people's salvation and living the Christian life; formal sufficiency has to do with how church tradition, including popes and the magisterium, are needed in order to understand truly the entirety of the Bible. In contrast, Protestants believed that the Bible contains the necessary information and that no additional help is needed by either church tradition or ecclesiastical pronouncements by church leaders. As such, the Bible only (sola Scriptura) is needed by individuals, due to its "perspicuity"—that is, its containment of information that is both understandable and efficacious, by the grace of God, for anyone who reads the

Bible. Thus the Bible represents the only sufficient rule for Christian beliefs, values, and practices. Later some Protestants called it the norm, or "norming norm," of Christianity, but the meaning is essentially the same.

Historically speaking, both Roman Catholics and Protestants have referred to the sufficiency of the Bible, though their understandings of it differ. Later Christians identified the Bible's sufficiency with almost every belief about the Bible imaginable, including those of inerrancy and infallibility. So caution must be used in citing the term, since there is no standardized definition for it. This is because sufficiency is thought to describe aptly the view of the Bible's trustworthiness, since it conveys a more humble, indeterminate view of trustworthiness than in previous views described. Sufficiency does not reject the trustworthiness of the Bible, nor does it require it. Rather, sufficiency suggests that God's grace is at work through the Bible and that impediments need not thwart the fulfillment of God's purposes for it.

Describing the Bible as sufficient suggests that it contains all that is necessary to know about God, people, reconciliation between God and people, and the attendant Christian life. Sufficiency also suggests the Bible's trustworthiness without specifying the particularities of what that means. For some people, this usage of sufficiency falls woefully short of their understanding of the term biblically, historically, or theologically. This is understandable, again, since there is no consistent historic precedent for its usage. However, the fact that there is longstanding use of the term "sufficiency" to describe the Bible makes it appealing as a descriptor in contrast to "inerrancy" and "infallibility." Describing the Bible as sufficient and trustworthy, without predetermining a particular view of its truth, permits people greater liberty to read and study the Bible inductively and apply the biblical texts as they encounter them.

How can the Bible be considered trustworthy if people acknowledge moral, historical, and scientific failures, as mentioned above? Trustworthiness is not always measured in terms of perfection, and the revelatory nature of the Bible may even include flawed information. After all, God used imperfect people throughout biblical history in order to fulfill God's plans for Israel, the early church, and the world. Roman Catholics came to accept flawed clergy and laity in the church after the Donatist controversy, when God's grace and work in the world were considered more important in fulfilling the reign of God than perfect church members. Likewise, Protestants emphasized the importance of preaching in addition to the Bible, but they did not think that pastors had to be perfect or that their preaching had to be perfect in order for God's words to be proclaimed efficaciously. If, indeed, the Bible is flawed, then it will take more work to interpret and apply it truthfully, but it may still be accepted as both authoritative and inspired to those who believe.

This view of the trustworthiness of the Bible would accept the correspondence theory of truth. However, instead of appealing to propositional statements that affirm the truth of the Bible, it would appeal to them in order to affirm that errors and possibly immoralities exist in it. So when Christian apologists appeal to the correspondence theory of truth vis-à-vis other theories, they may actually be setting themselves up for rebuttal. Indeed, the trajectory of biblical scholarship over the past two centuries has poignantly challenged Christian apologetes, harmonizations, and other strategies to preserve the truth of the Bible. While inerrantists, for example, may dismiss critics of the Bible for inappropriate assumptions about its humanness, the critics may in turn respond with their own criticism about the inappropriate modernist assumptions by inerrantists about the divineness of the Bible, exempting it from honest inductive investigation.

From the perspective of the Bible as sufficient, apologetic attempts to argue for its absolute, indubitable truth may actually misunderstand and misrepresent God's purposes for the Bible in the lives of people. Inerrantist apologetics are thought to focus too much on preserving an idealized understanding of the Bible and not enough on truth, even when it does not look as perfect and controversy-free as one might wish. Moreover, too little emphasis may be placed on who God is and how God's works are graciously fulfilled through Jesus and the Holy Spirit as well as the Bible. Again, it is God who saves us, not the Bible. It is not through Christians' theologizing and apologetics on behalf of the Bible that God's reign is fulfilled, but through their faithful study and proclamation of it in word and deed, trusting in God to bring the spiritual increase.

■ Indefectibility of the Church

This view of the Bible, similar to the aforementioned view, thinks that people are looking in the wrong place when it comes to the truth of God's revelation. In the sufficient view, the statements or propositions of the Bible may become a distraction from encountering God. With regard to the indefectibility of the church, this view argues that the truth of God's revelation in the world should be identified with the church rather than the Bible. After all, Jesus came to save people, who make up the church. It is the people of God, not the Bible, who represent those for whom God is primarily concerned and who consequently represent the greatest witness to the truth of God.

The church—the community of believers in Jesus Christ—represents the true followers of God, those for whom Jesus gave his life in atonement of sin and the ones in whom the Holy Spirit dwells and works in the world today.

The church's witness represents the primary recipients of God's blessings, and Christians—not the Bible per se—are the ambassadors of God's way, truth, and life. The Bible aids people so that they may believe and join the fellowship of believers in the church. If the Bible was to fail or disappear for any reason, the church would not cease to exist. However, if the church were to fail or disappear for any reason, then what purpose would the Bible have? It is the church, rather than anything else, that gives evidence of the reality of God, God's truth, and God's reign in the world.

The word "defect" has to do with flaws, inadequacies, or imperfections. No one would claim that the church is indefectible; most people are well aware of its defects, fallibility, and susceptibility to err. Be that as it may, the church will not cease to believe and proclaim God, and God will not depart from those who believe. God has made the church—made up of true believers—holy through the righteousness of Jesus and the atonement, and he continues to work in and through it. As Jesus said, he will build the church, "and the gates of Hades will not prevail against it" (Matt. 16:18). Because of this indefectibility, the church represents the greatest testimony to God and everything God stands for.

The Bible may remain the church's primary authority in matters of Christian beliefs, values, and practices. But its authority and trustworthiness are based not on the Bible's historical, scientific, and other matters evaluated by rational and empirical criteria. Instead, the trustworthiness of the Bible is guaranteed by the reality of the church, the greatest testimony to the power and authority of God. From this perspective, the appeal to inerrancy or infallibility as ways to defend Christianity failed due to the increased scrutiny of the Bible, which led to its failure to provide an indubitable foundation of truth. But the church has never ceased to believe and proclaim God, due to the presence and work of the Holy Spirit. The reality of God's work in the lives of Christians and the church should be the focus of defending Christianity, not something other than the goal of God's work in the world, which is the salvation of people, who are the church.

Advocates of the indefectibility of the church share similarities with Roman Catholicism to the degree that Catholics believe that the teaching leadership of the church—the popes and magisterium—along with the Bible and church tradition are needed to represent appropriately God and God's truth in the world. However, Catholics do not officially challenge the rational and empirical truth of the Bible, whereas Protestants who advocate the indefectibility of the church do challenge it. Such Protestants would consider it wrongheaded to try to preserve a view of the truth of the Bible no longer defensible in a post-historical-critical approach to the Bible. Of course, they also would resist the Catholics' understanding of the authority of the church, especially of that of the pope. But such differences would not prevent them from siding with the church rather than the Bible as the place to focus Christians' assurance regarding the truth of God and God's work in the world. Thus, despite the Bible's excellences with regard to religious authority and divine inspiration, the truth of God's work in and through the world appears more through the reality of the church—of true believers—than through the Bible, which is more a means of God's workings than an end in itself.

■ Nonpropositional View

A nonpropositional view of divine revelation emphasizes that, properly speaking, Jesus Christ represents the true "Word" of God (John 1:1). It is not propositions about Jesus that are important; it is our encounter with him, who is a person. People are not saved by the Bible; they are saved by Jesus, who is God. This view is not so much concerned about the factuality of statements or claims to possess propositional truth; it is concerned about whether people encounter the Word of God—Jesus—as they read the Bible or hear it proclaimed. The Bible bears witness to Jesus, and in one sense it becomes the Word of God or is indeed the Word of God as God chooses to bear witness to God's self to particular readers or hearers of the Bible.

Certainly we speak with propositions, and so does the Bible. However, people should not confuse propositional statements about Jesus with Jesus himself. The Bible bears witness to Jesus, and that witness is important in telling us about him, about salvation, and about the Christian life. Christians proclaim Jesus to others, for example through preaching, and proclamation is itself an important witness to Jesus. But people should not become focused on the witness, but instead on the person of Jesus. Barth, for example, warned people about focusing so much on the Bible that it becomes bibliolatry or Bible-idolatry. Rather than promoting the truth of the Bible or of its proclamation, Christians should promote the truth of Jesus, who is indeed "the way, and the truth, and the life" (John 14:6). People ought not worship creation (or parts of the creation) but the creator. Likewise, they ought not settle for words, propositions, and apologetics—as important as they may be—and neglect Jesus.

Advocates of a nonpropositional view, such as Barth, did not consider it important to defend the truthfulness of the Bible, since it—like proclamation—was more a witness to the Word of God rather than being the Word of God. The Bible and its proclamation may be considered the Word of God in a secondary, derivative sense, as attested in the Bible (Dan. 9:2; Rom. 3:2). However, the Bible and its proclamation are fallible due to their obvious human characteristics. It is naive, at best, and suppressive at worst, to deny the fallibilities of the Bible. Thus the Bible should be subject to historical and critical interpretations since they are useful in learning about the history and nature of the Bible. But the importance of the Bible is not whether it contains perfect, error-free accounts of Jesus and other records of God's self-revelation in encountering people. It is the encounter or event of meeting God that is as important today as it was in biblical times.

Critics of a nonpropositional view fear that it is too subjective. It is thought to rely too much on a fideist or relational understanding of truth rather than on an understanding of truth that can be corroborated through factual data and propositional argumentation. Fideism argues that authentic Christianity is based on faith or a faith relationship with God rather than on reason or experience, rationality or evidence. A relational understanding of truth may give a logical sense of coherence, but it fails to satisfy the expectation that all truth is God's truth. But advocates of a nonpropositional view would not care about lacking rational and empirical verifications since they have encountered the God of creation, of all things. If God chooses to be revealed through fallible means, then so be it, since God is God and cannot be grasped or controlled by people's reasoning and empirical investigations.

Because of the need to rely personally on God, it is difficult to predict precisely how advocates of a nonpropositional view might interpret the Bible in any given instance. This unpredictability increases the questions and concerns of those who criticize it. Yet Jesus seemed to explain this relational view of truth when he said that it was more important to follow him than the Scriptures, though the Scriptures witness or testify to him. Jesus said, "You search the scriptures because you think that in them you have eternal life; and it is they that testify on my behalf. Yet you refuse to come to me to have life" (John 5:39–40). God has chosen to be revealed through the Bible, and Jesus too is revealed in it. Throughout church history, Christians have testified to God's self-revelation to people in the Bible. Such testimonies are used by God to serve as the opportunity or event in which God encounters people today, and it is that encounter that is important, saves people, and leads them in authentic Christian living.

Sometimes *Heilsgeschichte* is identified with a nonpropositional view of the Bible. *Heilsgeschichte* (German "holy history") represents the belief that God does not so much reveal truth as much as God reveals God's own self in the midst of human history. The biblical accounts of God's encounters with people represent a "holy history" or "salvation history," which serves as a means or medium by which others may encounter the living God. Again, the focus is not on historical or scientific propositions but on events that reveal how God encounters people and how people today may encounter God themselves.

■ Deciding for Oneself

Having studied views of the Bible's trustworthiness, readers may have one of two responses. On the one hand, they may see obvious differences between the views, and one view clearly seems right. On the other hand, readers may see nominal differences between some of the views and wonder how they really vary from one another. To those for whom the differences are unmistakable, the discussion should help them to solidify their beliefs and values about the Bible. To those for whom the differences are indistinct, it may be because the terms are sometimes used interchangeably. For example, people might affirm inerrancy but function more with an infallibilist view. Others might not see a difference between an infallibilist view and those of the sufficiency view or of the indefectibility of the church. Indeed, it is important to remember that categories and labels are helpful in *beginning* to investigate topics, but in-depth studies usually require greater scrutiny and nuance in their evaluation. As such, the views mentioned above represent more of a starting point rather than the ending point for considering the trustworthiness of the Bible. Even those who are certain about their view ought to be at least cognizant of the fact that not everyone shares their conviction about the specific views, much less their identification with one of them.

Even if readers think that they understand conceptually the various views and their implications, they still may not be sure of what they believe about the Bible's trustworthiness. In such instances, we sometimes encourage people to ask of themselves not what they believe in *theory* but how they *practice*. What does their practice or use of the Bible tell people about what they really believe? Here are other questions: When they read the Bible, what do they expect? Do they expect truth about God and salvation? Do they expect truth about ethical living? Do they expect truth about the Bible's history and scientific matters? Is the truth obvious, or does it require critical study? Do people expect the Bible to be an answer book, or do they expect answers only after they prayerfully as well as thoughtfully consider what it says? When they read the Bible, do they expect to encounter God? Even in historical and critical studies of the text, do they expect to grow in intimacy with God? If they authentically encounter God, does it matter what they believe about the Bible and its trustworthiness?

Certainly people's beliefs about the Bible's trustworthiness are inextricably bound up with how they understand and apply it in life. So we encourage people to decide, rather than remain undecided about, what they believe, how they value the Bible, and how they live in accordance with it. Sometimes there is virtue in suspending judgment, but we tend to think that in the long run people hurt themselves spiritually and in other ways by not making a decision. Indecision wreaks havoc on biblical interpretation; the same is true for applying it to life. Although views of the Bible's trustworthiness may be tentatively held, they can help people to be more intentional about their studies and open to how God wants to use the Bible in and through their lives. It is our hope that people become more confident and competent in their knowledge, interpretation, and application of the Bible.

CONCLUSION

10

What Then Should We Do?

According to the Gospel of Luke, John the Baptist had an effective ministry in Judea prior to the launch of Jesus's ministry. John called people to repentance for the forgiveness of sins and to be baptized. People responded positively to his ministry, and John further challenged them: "Bear fruits worthy of repentance" (Luke 3:8). Again, people responded positively, saying: "What then should we do?" (Luke 3:10). John exhorted them, based on their particular life situations:

> In reply he said to them, "Whoever has two coats must share with anyone who has none; and whoever has food must do likewise." Even tax collectors came to be baptized, and they asked him, "Teacher, what should we do?" He said to them, "Collect no more than the amount prescribed for you." Soldiers also asked him, "And we, what should we do?" He said to them, "Do not extort money from anyone by threats or false accusation, and be satisfied with your wages."
>
> Luke 3:11–14

John did not think that it was enough to hear the truth—to hear the Word of God. He also challenged people to put into practice what they had heard. They were not only to repent and be baptized, but John also exhorted them to live in accordance with all his teachings. It was not enough to hear the Word of God or even to read and study it; people were expected to live new lives, with new beliefs and values, based on what they had learned.

Similar exhortations occur in the book of James. In chapter 1, James says: "But be doers of the word, and not merely hearers who deceive themselves" (James 1:22). As much as we encourage people in general, and students in particular, to read and study the Bible and to develop their own theological beliefs about it, such studies are pointless without the openness and commit-ment to putting them into practice. Biblical and theological studies can be immensely interesting, but we encourage students to undertake them with the eventual goal of applying what they have learned to their lives and their relationships with God and God's creation, especially with people—those who are our neighbors, according to Jesus (Matt. 19:19; 22:39; Mark 12:31).

■ From Sacred Scripture to Text and Back

Some Christians talk about the importance of moving from the study of the Bible as "text" to its study as "sacred Scripture." The former textual study of the Bible is important because it helps to uncover insights that surpass what people can imagine they may learn from it. In this book, we mostly focus on biblical and theological studies because we think that too few undertake the kind of critical, historical, and theological study of the Bible that is invaluable for their Christian understanding and life. Yet people should not be content with studying the Bible only; they need to go back to reading the Bible as "sacred text," lest they forget that God wants people to be doers of the word as well as hearers of it.

We think that critical studies of the Bible help people in general, and Chris-tians in particular, to grow—like Jesus—"in wisdom and in years, and in divine and human favor" (Luke 2:52). No one need question the value of biblical and theological study, logical thinking, familiarity with church history, and consideration of relevant experience when studying the Bible. The benefits of such studies far outweigh their potential liabilities, given suitable intellectual and prayerful precautions in undertaking them. We think that Christianity affects every dimension of life, and so we strongly recommend that people develop more integrative approaches to the study of the Bible and to its practi-cal application to Christian faith and living.

At the heart of Christianity lies a vital spirituality that includes personal relationship with God. Critical studies need not hinder but can help Chris-tian spirituality, though sometimes damages have occurred to people's faith development and to their Christian understanding. After all, good things—if used inappropriately—can become more of a curse than a blessing. Especially when used by those for whom Christianity is unimportant, historical and critical methods of interpretation can be employed to undercut or dismiss the cruciality of the Bible. Such studies may also have a negative effect upon those intellectually or spiritually unprepared for the theological gravity of questions raised. So we do not want to minimize real-life dangers involved with progressing in academically informed studies of the Bible.

But we think that such dangers have more to do with people's failure to recognize the interconnectedness between values too often separated and put at odds with one another: faith and reason, trust and critical thinking, testimony and historical evidence, confession and science, sacred Scripture and text. All in all, every study of the Bible—whether it be done critically or devotionally—provides opportunity to experience the fullness of what God offers people through the person and work of Jesus Christ and the presence and power of the Holy Spirit.

■ The Bible and Christian Spirituality

It would take far too long to present the many ways that the Bible serves as a means of grace by which God works in and through the lives of those who read it, regularly hear it proclaimed, and earnestly study it with heart, soul, mind, and strength. Throughout church history, study has functioned as a spiritual discipline that aids people in their faith development. Study often focuses on the Bible. Such studies may be undertaken devotionally, for example, through meditative practices such as *lectio divina* (Latin "divine reading"), when people meditate on the words of the Bible. Spiritual disciplines are thought to be ways appointed by God, described in the teachings of the Bible, and confirmed by the testimonies of Christians throughout church history, by which people are nurtured spiritually and grow in intimacy in their relationship with God.

Although the devotional reading of the Bible has historically been valued most for faith development, we think that biblical and theological studies undertaken critically also serve as means of grace by which people grow intellectually, personally, spiritually, and in other ways. Critical studies need not be an impediment to faith development but can be an invaluable aid to it. Learning about the various genres and historical and literary contexts of the Bible may be as essential to Christian understanding and living as any other spiritual discipline.

Likewise, theological studies of the Bible and other beliefs about God and salvation provide a holistic Christian perspective crucial for spiritual maturity. So, by investigating what Christians believe about the Bible, it is our hope and prayer that students of the Bible excel—by the grace of God—in all aspects of their interpretation, understanding, and application of it. Although this book is a concise guide for students of the Bible, we hope it will be valuable for their spiritual and intellectual formation as well, which are equally important in studying the Bible as God revealed it.

Appendix 1

Books of the Hebrew Bible

- **The Law**

  Genesis, Exodus, Leviticus, Numbers, Deuteronomy

- **The Prophets**

  Former Prophets: Joshua, Judges, Samuel (1 and 2), Kings (1 and 2)

  Latter Prophets: Isaiah, Jeremiah, Ezekiel, and the Twelve (Hosea, Joel, Amos, Obadiah, Jonah, Micah, Nahum, Habakkuk, Zephaniah, Haggai, Zechariah, Malachi)

- **The Writings**

  Psalms, Proverbs, Job, Song of Solomon, Ruth, Lamentations, Ecclesiastes, Esther, Daniel, Ezra-Nehemiah, Chronicles (1 and 2)

Appendix 2

Books of the Protestant Old Testament

- **The Pentateuch**

  Genesis, Exodus, Leviticus, Numbers, Deuteronomy

- **The Historical Books**

  Joshua, Judges, Ruth, 1 Samuel, 2 Samuel, 1 Kings, 2 Kings, 1 Chronicles, 2 Chronicles, Ezra, Nehemiah, Esther

- **The Poetical and Wisdom Books**

  Job, Psalms, Proverbs, Ecclesiastes, Song of Solomon

- **The Prophetic Books**

  Isaiah, Jeremiah, Lamentations, Ezekiel, Daniel, Hosea, Joel, Amos, Obadiah, Jonah, Micah, Nahum, Habakkuk, Zephaniah, Haggai, Zechariah, Malachi

Appendix 3

Books of the Apocryphal/ Deuterocanonical Writings

- **Books included by the Roman Catholic, Greek Orthodox, and Russian Orthodox Churches, and Protestant Apocrypha**

  Tobit, Judith, Additions to Esther, Wisdom of Solomon, Ecclesiasticus, Baruch, Additions to Daniel, 1 Maccabees, 2 Maccabees

- **Books included by the Greek Orthodox and Russian Orthodox Churches, Protestant Apocrypha, and Appendix of the Latin Vulgate**

  1 Esdras and the Prayer of Manasseh

- **Books included by the Greek and Russian Orthodox Churches**

  Psalm 151 and 3 Maccabees

- **Books included by the Greek and Russian Orthodox Churches and Protestant Apocrypha**

  3 Esdras

Appendix 4

Books of the
New Testament

- **Gospels**

  Matthew, Mark, Luke, John

- **The Acts of the Apostles**

- **The Letters of Paul**

  Romans, 1 Corinthians, 2 Corinthians, Galatians, Ephesians, Philippians, Colossians, 1 Thessalonians, 2 Thessalonians, 1 Timothy, 2 Timothy, Titus, Philemon

- **The General Letters**

  Hebrews, James, 1 Peter, 2 Peter, 1 John, 2 John, 3 John, Jude

- **Revelation**

Select Bibliography

Adam, A. K. M., ed. *Handbook of Postmodern Biblical Interpretation*. St. Louis: Chalice, 2000.

Adam, A. K. M., Stephen E. Fowl, Kevin J. Vanhoozer, and Francis Watson. *Reading Scripture with the Church: Toward a Hermeneutic for Theological Interpretation*. Grand Rapids: Baker Academic, 2006.

Bailey, Randall C., ed. *Yet with a Steady Beat: Contemporary U.S. Afrocentric Biblical Interpretation*. Atlanta: Society of Biblical Literature, 2003.

Bartholomew, Craig G., Colin Greene, and Karl Möller, eds. *After Pentecost: Language and Biblical Interpretation*. Scripture and Hermeneutics Series. Vol. 2. Grand Rapids: Zondervan, 2001.

Bartholomew, Craig G., C. Stephen Evans, Mary Healy, and Murray Rae, eds. *"Behind" the Text: History and Biblical Interpretation*. Scripture and Hermeneutics Series. Vol. 4. Grand Rapids: Zondervan, 2003.

Bartholomew, Craig G., Robin Parry, and Scott Hahn, eds. *Canon and Biblical Interpretation*. Scripture and Hermeneutics Series. Vol. 7. Grand Rapids: Zondervan, 2006.

Bartlett, John R., ed. *Archaeology and Biblical Interpretation*. London: Routledge, 1997.

Bauer, David R., and Robert A. Traina. *Inductive Bible Study: A Comprehensive Guide to the Practice of Hermeneutics*. Grand Rapids: Baker Academic, 2011.

Bielo, James S. *Words upon the Word: An Ethnography of Evangelical Group Bible Study*. New York: New York University Press, 2009.

Billings, J. Todd. *The Word of God for the People of God: An Entryway to the Theological Interpretation of Scripture*. Grand Rapids: Eerdmans, 2010.

Bockmuehl, Markus, and Alan J. Torrance, eds. *Scripture's Doctrine and Theology's Bible: How the New Testament Shapes Christian Dogmatics*. Grand Rapids: Baker Academic, 2008.

Bray, Gerald L. *Biblical Interpretation: Past and Present*. Downers Grove, IL: InterVarsity, 1996.

Brown, Jeannine K. *Scripture as Communication: Introducing Biblical Hermeneutics*. Grand Rapids: Baker Academic, 2007.

Brown, Michael Joseph. *What They Don't Tell You: A Survivor's Guide to Biblical Studies*. Louisville: Westminster John Knox, 2000.

Brown, William P., ed. *Character and Scripture: Moral Formation, Community, and Biblical Interpretation.* Grand Rapids: Eerdmans, 2002.

Coggins, R. J., and J. L. Houlden, eds. *A Dictionary of Biblical Interpretation.* Philadelphia: Trinity Press International, 1990.

Corley, Bruce, Steve Lemke, and Grant Lovejoy, eds. *Biblical Hermeneutics: A Comprehensive Introduction to Interpreting Scripture.* Nashville: Broadman & Holman, 2002.

Court, John M., ed. *Biblical Interpretation: The Meanings of Scripture—Past and Present.* New York: T&T Clark, 2003.

Croy, N. Clayton. *Prima Scriptura: An Introduction to New Testament Interpretation.* Grand Rapids: Baker Academic, 2011.

Danker, Frederick W. *Multipurpose Tools for Bible Study.* Minneapolis: Fortress, 1993.

Day, Linda, and Carolyn Pressler, eds. *Engaging the Bible in a Gendered World: An Introduction to Feminist Biblical Interpretation in Honor of Katharine Doob Sakenfeld.* Louisville: Westminster John Knox, 2006.

Dockery, David S. *Biblical Interpretation Then and Now: Contemporary Hermeneutics in the Light of the Early Church.* Grand Rapids: Baker, 1992.

Dockery, David S., Kenneth A. Mathews, and Robert B. Sloan, eds. *Foundations for Biblical Interpretation: A Complete Library of Tools and Resources.* Nashville: Broadman & Holman, 1994.

Dyck, Elmer, ed. *The Act of Bible Reading: A Multidisciplinary Approach to Biblical Interpretation.* Downers Grove, IL: InterVarsity, 1996.

Efird, James M. *How to Interpret the Bible.* Eugene, OR: Wipf & Stock, 2000.

Farkasfalvy, Denis M. *Inspiration and Interpretation: A Theological Introduction to Sacred Scripture.* Washington, DC: Catholic University of America Press, 2010.

Fee, Gordon D. *Gospel and Spirit: Issues in New Testament Hermeneutics.* Grand Rapids: Baker, 1991.

Fee, Gordon, and Douglas Stuart. *How to Read the Bible for All Its Worth.* 3rd ed. Grand Rapids: Zondervan, 2003.

Felder, Cain Hope, ed. *Stony the Road We Trod: African American Biblical Interpretation.* Minneapolis: Fortress, 1991.

Firth, David G., and Jamie A. Grant, eds. *Words and the Word: Explorations in Biblical Interpretation & Literary Theory.* Downers Grove, IL: IVP Academic, 2008.

Fitzmyer, Joseph A. *The Interpretation of Scripture: In Defense of the Historical-Critical Method.* New York: Paulist Press, 2008.

Foskett, Mary F., and Jeffrey Kah-Jin Kuan, eds. *Ways of Being, Ways of Reading: Asian American Biblical Interpretation.* St. Louis: Chalice, 2006.

Goldingay, John. *Key Questions about Biblical Interpretation: Old Testament Answers.* Grand Rapids: Baker Academic, 2011.

Goldsworthy, Graeme. *Gospel-Centered Hermeneutics: Foundations and Principles of Evangelical Biblical Interpretation.* Downers Grove, IL: IVP Academic, 2006.

González, Justo L. *Santa Biblia: The Bible through Hispanic Eyes.* Nashville: Abingdon, 1996.

Gorman, Michael J., ed. *Scripture: An Ecumenical Introduction to the Bible and Its Interpretation.* Peabody, MA: Hendrickson, 2005.

Grahmann, Bob. *Transforming Bible Study: Understanding Scripture Like You've Never Read It Before.* Downers Grove, IL: InterVarsity, 2003.

Green, Joel B. *Practicing Theological Interpretation: Engaging Biblical Texts for Faith and Formation*. Theological Explorations for the Church Catholic. Grand Rapids: Baker Academic, 2012.

———. *Seized by the Truth: Reading the Bible as Scripture*. Nashville: Abingdon, 2007.

Grudem, Wayne, Leland Ryken, C. John Collins, Vern S. Poythress, and Bruce Winter. *Translating Truth: The Case for Essentially Literal Bible Translation*. Wheaton: Crossway, 2005.

Gruenler, Royce Gordon. *Meaning and Understanding: The Philosophical Framework for Biblical Interpretation*. Grand Rapids: Zondervan, 1991.

Hauser, Alan J., and Duane F. Watson, eds. *A History of Biblical Interpretation*. Vol. 1, *The Ancient Period*. Grand Rapids: Eerdmans, 2003.

———. *A History of Biblical Interpretation*. Vol. 2, *The Medieval through the Reformation Periods*. Grand Rapids: Eerdmans, 2009.

Hayes, John H., ed. *Dictionary of Biblical Interpretation*. Nashville: Abingdon, 1999.

Helmer, Christine, and Taylor G. Petrey, eds. *Biblical Interpretation: History, Context, and Reality*. Atlanta: Society of Biblical Literature, 2005.

Henrichsen, Walter A., and Gayle Jackson. *Studying, Interpreting, and Applying the Bible*. Grand Rapids: Zondervan, 1990.

Kaiser, Walter C., Jr., and Moisés Silva. *Introduction to Biblical Hermeneutics: The Search for Meaning*. Rev. ed. Grand Rapids: Zondervan, 2007.

Kitzberger, Ingrid Rosa, ed. *The Personal Voice in Biblical Interpretation*. New York: Routledge, 1999.

Klein, William W., Craig L. Blomberg, and Robert L. Hubbard Jr. *Introduction to Biblical Interpretation*. Rev. ed. Nashville: Thomas Nelson, 2004.

Legaspi, Michael C. *The Death of Scripture and the Rise of Biblical Studies*. New York: Oxford University Press, 2010.

Levering, Matthew. *Participatory Biblical Exegesis: A Theology of Biblical Interpretation*. Notre Dame, IN: University of Notre Dame Press, 2008.

Mabee, Charles. *Reading Sacred Texts through American Eyes: Biblical Interpretation as Cultural Critique*. Macon, GA: Mercer, 1991.

Marshall, I. Howard. *Beyond the Bible: Moving from Scripture to Theology*. Grand Rapids: Baker Academic, 2004.

Martin, Dale B. *Sex and the Single Savior: Gender and Sexuality in Biblical Interpretation*. Louisville: Westminster John Knox, 2006.

Muller, Richard A. *The Study of Theology: From Biblical Interpretation to Contemporary Formulation*. Grand Rapids: Zondervan, 1991.

Nichols, Stephen J., and Eric T. Brandt. *Ancient Word, Changing Worlds: The Doctrine of Scripture in a Modern Age*. Wheaton: Crossway, 2009.

Osborne, Grant R. *The Hermeneutical Spiral: A Comprehensive Introduction to Biblical Interpretation*. Downers Grove, IL: InterVarsity, 2006.

Sandys-Wunsch, John. *What Have They Done to the Bible? A History of Modern Biblical Interpretation*. Collegeville, MN: Liturgical Press, 2005.

Schüssler Fiorenza, Elisabeth. *Sharing Her Word: Feminist Biblical Interpretation in Context*. Boston: Beacon, 1998.

———. *Wisdom Ways: Introducing Feminist Biblical Interpretation*. Maryknoll, NY: Orbis, 2001.

Segovia, Fernando F., ed. *Interpreting Beyond Borders*. Sheffield, UK: Sheffield Academic, 2000.

Silva, Moisés, ed. *Foundations of Contemporary Interpretation*. Grand Rapids: Zondervan, 1996.

Smith, James K. A., and Henry Isaac Venema, eds. *The Hermeneutics of Charity: Interpretation, Selfhood, and Postmodern Faith*. Grand Rapids: Brazos, 2004.

Soulen, Richard N. *Sacred Scripture: A Short History of Interpretation*. Louisville: Westminster John Knox, 2009.

Sparks, Kenton L. *God's Word in Human Words: An Evangelical Appropriation of Critical Biblical Scholarship*. Grand Rapids: Baker Academic, 2008.

Stott, John R. W. *Understanding the Bible*. Grand Rapids: Zondervan, 1999.

Sugirtharajah, R. S. *Postcolonial Criticism and Biblical Interpretation*. New York: Oxford University Press, 2002.

———. *Postcolonial Reconfigurations: An Alternative Way of Reading the Bible and Doing Theology*. St. Louis: Chalice, 2003.

Tate, W. Randolph. *Biblical Interpretation: An Integrated Approach*. Peabody, MA: Hendrickson, 2008.

Thompson, David L. *Bible Study that Works*. Nappanee, IN: Evangel, 1994.

Tiffany, Frederick C., and Sharon H. Ringe. *Biblical Interpretation: A Roadmap*. Nashville: Abingdon, 1996.

Vanhoozer, Kevin J., ed. *Dictionary for Theological Interpretation of the Bible*. Grand Rapids: Baker Academic, 2005.

Vanhoozer, Kevin J., Charles A. Anderson, and Michael J. Sleasman, eds. *Everyday Theology: How to Read Cultural Texts and Interpret Trends*. Cultural Exegesis. Grand Rapids: Baker Academic, 2007.

Virkler, Henry A., and Karelynne Gerber Ayayo. *Hermeneutics: Principles and Processes of Biblical Interpretation*. Grand Rapids: Baker Academic, 2007.

Voelz, James W. *What Does This Mean? Principles of Biblical Interpretation in the Post-Modern World*. St. Louis: Concordia, 1997.

Volf, Miroslav. *Captive to the Word of God: Engaging the Scriptures for Contemporary Theological Reflection*. Grand Rapids: Eerdmans, 2010.

Walsh, Richard G. *Mapping Myths of Biblical Interpretation*. Sheffield, UK: Sheffield Academic, 2001.

Watson, Francis. *Text, Church, and World: Biblical Interpretation in Theological Perspective*. Grand Rapids: Eerdmans, 1994.

Westphal, Merold. *Whose Community? Which Interpretation? Philosophical Hermeneutics for the Church*. The Church and Postmodern Culture Series. Grand Rapids: Baker Academic, 2009.

White, J. Benton. *Taking the Bible Seriously: Honest Differences about Biblical Interpretation*. Louisville: Westminster John Knox, 1993.

Wink, Walter. *Transforming Bible Study*. Nashville: Abingdon, 1989.

Yarchin, William. *History of Biblical Interpretation: A Reader*. Peabody, MA: Hendrickson, 2004.

Subject Index

Scripture Index

New Testament